China's economy is transforming. Some aspects of that transformation, such as the rise of the Chinese consumer, are well known. But how many of us understand how China is building an innovation economy? This book plugs an important gap in our knowledge. And, importantly, it is co-authored by a man at the heart of China's economic policy making, Ding Xuedong, Chairman of China's sovereign wealth fund.

Lord James Sassoon, *Chairman of China British Business Council (CBBC), UK*

This book gives a comprehensive and insightful account of Chinese theory, experiments and practices of building an innovative country and is an important piece of work that will help the outside world to understand the independent innovation policies in China. From my point of view, by improving the innovative capabilities of the whole society, China aims to adjust economic structure, transform development pattern, and build an innovation-based nation. In so doing, China's exploration, practices and experiences have facilitated opening up and cooperation, and hopefully our endeavor can contribute to the sustainable development of the world.

Professor Wan Gang, *Vice Chairman of the 11th Chinese People's Political Consultative Conference (CPPCC), and Minister of Science and Technology, China*

China's economic growth has been impressive and innovation will be one of the key drivers for its future development. China has created an enabling environment for growth by encouraging public and private sector enterprises to improve competitiveness, quality and productivity by using world class technology, research and development, global standards and best practices. The authors Chairman Ding and Dr. Jun Li have effectively covered China's pursuit of a national innovation agenda, China's current and planned innovation incentive structure and a road map for the future. China's peaceful rise will be strengthened by strong and equitable economic growth which will be reinforced with strong structural reforms, promoting science and technology and continuous innovation. The book highlights China's policies to promote innovation and is relevant for all emerging economies.

Shaukat Azia, *Prime Minister of Pakistan (2004–2007)*

Ding Xuedong and Jun Li's book is a refreshing comprehensive but also a deep and clear analysis of the innovation process in China. For the first time the theoretical background and the real achievements of the innovation process are analyzed both at the national, regional and sectorial level. It is an excellent instrument in order to move brain and action. A must for scholars and policy makers. Not only in China but at a global level.

Professor Romano Prodi, *Prime Minister of Italy (1996–1998 and 2006–2008), Tenth President of the European Commission (1999–2004)*

An essential text for anyone interested in innovation and China. The authors – an academic and experienced government policy maker – have delivered insights that go beyond mere statistics. The range of sources, examples of policy impact and critical conclusions are impressive. In short, the best institutional perspective on innovation available.

Professor David Brown, *Director of Lancaster China Management Centre, Lancaster University, UK*

T0304021

Incentives for Innovation in China

There is concern in China that the strategy which has delivered massive economic growth is unsustainable in the long run, that China's economy is too dependent on low value added manufacturing and not enough based on high value technological innovation. This book assesses the policies implemented in recent years to address this, policies which include increasing the pool of human capital, especially by training very large numbers of graduate engineers, investing massively in improved infrastructure such as institutions of higher education, telecommunications and transport, and providing financial incentives – both direct government funding for private sector innovation activities and fiscal incentives which encourage innovation by reducing the tax burden on innovators. The book examines the impact of these policies, providing detailed studies of firms' innovation activities both in particular sectors and in particular regions. Throughout, the book discusses how effective China's innovation policies are and how innovation in China is likely to develop in future.

Xuedong Ding is Chairman and CEO of China Investment Corporation (CIC), Beijing, China.

Jun Li is a Senior Lecturer at Essex Business School, University of Essex, UK, and a Visiting Professor at the Business School of Jianghan University, Wuhan, China.

Routledge contemporary China series

Incentives for Innovation in China

Building an innovative economy

Xuedong Ding and Jun Li

Routledge
Taylor & Francis Group

LONDON AND NEW YORK

First published 2015 by Routledge

2 Park Square, Milton Park, Abingdon, Oxon OX14 4RN
711 Third Avenue, New York, NY 10017, USA

Routledge is an imprint of the Taylor & Francis Group, an informa business

First issued in paperback 2017

British Library Cataloguing in Publication Data
A catalogue record for this book is available from the British Library

Library of Congress Cataloging in Publication Data
Ding, Xuedong.
Incentives for innovation in China: building an innovative economy /
Xuedong Ding and Jun Li.
   pages cm. – (Routledge contemporary china series; 124)
   Includes bibliographical references and index.
   1. Technological innovations–Economic aspects–China. 2. Industrial
policy–China. 3. Industrial promotion–China. 4. China–Economic
policy. I. Li, Jun (Senior lecturer) II. Title.
   HC430.T4D563 2015
   338′.0640951–dc23   2014034926

ISBN: 978-0-415-60394-2 (hbk)
ISBN: 978-1-138-10204-0 (pbk)

Typeset in Times New Roman
by Wearset Ltd, Boldon, Tyne and Wear

Contents

Figures

Tables

Abbreviations

xx   Abbreviations

MOCI
MOE   Ministry of Coal Industry
MPCC   Ministry of Science and Technology
              multiparty cooperation committee
              parties
              National Bureau of Statistics
              National Defense Science, Technology and Industry Commission
              national innovation system
              New Industry Venture Capital Programme

ADBC   Agricultural Development Bank of China
CAE   Chinese Academy of Engineering
CAS   Chinese Academy of Sciences
CASS   Chinese Academy of Social Sciences
CBD   China Development Bank
CBRC   China Banking Regulatory Commission
CIRC   China Insurance Regulatory Commission
CNCC   China National Coal Corporation
CNNC   China National Nuclear Corporation
CNPC   China National Petroleum Corporation
CNTVC   China New Technology Venture Capital Corporation
CPC   Communist Party of China
CPCC   Communist Party Central Committee
CSRC   China Securities Regulatory Commission
EI   Engineering Index
EximBank   Export-Import Bank of China
FDI   foreign direct investment
GCI   Global Competitiveness Index
GDP   gross domestic output
GEM   Growth Enterprise Market
GERD   gross R&D expenditure
GII   Global Innovation Index
HEIs   higher education institutions
HNTEs   high and new technology enterprises
ICBC   Industrial and Commercial Bank of China
IEA   International Energy Agency
InnoFund   Innovation Fund for Small Technology-based Firms
IPO   initial public offering
LMEs   large and medium-sized enterprises
LSGs   Leading Small Groups
M&A   merger and acquisition
MLNP   Outline of Medium and Long-term National Plan for Science and
              Technology Development

MOCI	Ministry of Coal Industry
MOE	Ministry of Education
MOEPI	Ministry of Electric Power Industry
MOFI	Ministry of Fuel Industries
MOPI	Ministry of Petroleum Industry
MOST	Ministry of Science and Technology
MPCC	ministry-province cooperation committee
Mt	million tonnes
NBS	National Bureau of Statistics
NDSTWC	National Defence Science and Technology Working Committee
NIS	national innovation system
NIVCP	New Industry Venture Capital Programme
NPC	National People's Congress
NSFC	Natural Science Foundation of China
NSTC	National Science and Technology Commission
OECD	Organisation for Economic Co-operation and Development
PBOC	People's Bank of China
PPC	Productivity Promotion Center
PRI	public research institution
RD&D	research development and demonstration
RMB	renminbi
SASTIND	State Administration for Science, Technology and Industry for National Defence
SCI	Science Citation Index
SCLAO	State Council Legislative Affairs Office
SDRC	State Development and Reform Commission
SEA	State Energy Administration
SERC	State Electricity Regulatory Commission
SETC	State Economic and Trade Commission
SEZs	special economic zones
SINOSURE	China Export and Credit Insurance Corporation
SIPO	State Intellectual Property Office
SME	small and medium-sized enterprise
SOEs	state-owned enterprises
S&T	science & technology
STI	science, technology and innovation
SZSE	Shenzhen Stock Exchange
Tce	tons of coal equivalent
TFP	total factor productivity
VAT	value added tax
VCGF	Venture Capital Guiding Fund
WEF	World Economic Forum
WHO	World Health Organization
WIPO	World Intellectual Property Organization
WTO	World Trade Organization
YRD	Yangtze River Delta

Preface

China has been pursuing an ambitious national innovation agenda in earnest since 2006 and the whole world is watching and debating on China's prospect of success in innovation with great interest. Typical questions in the debate are: Is China the next hub for innovation? Is China a breeding ground for innovation? Is China a global innovation powerhouse? Can China eclipse the USA on innovation? These questions are so relevant to the outlook of global competition that the underlying question is in fact this: What will happen to technological leaders and both developed and developing countries if China successfully develops cutting-edge technological capabilities on top of its already world-class low-cost production (Altenburg et al., 2008; Kaplinsky and Messner, 2008)? There are two camps in the debate with utterly dividing viewpoints.[1] Who will win the debate? Only time will tell!

We are motivated to write this book by three reasons. First, we are fascinated by the dramatic changes China has undergone with great effect over the last three decades in its effort to fulfil what the current Chinese President Xi Jinping referred to as the "Chinese dream of national rejuvenation" in his president's inaugural speech on 18 May 2013.[2] China's dream of prosperity and peaceful rise is particularly manifested in the 'Outline of Medium and Long-term National Plan for Science and Technology Development' (MLNP) released in 2006. The master plan set out an overarching goal of making China an "innovation-oriented" economy by 2020 and a "world-leading science power" by 2050. The vision of nation-building and national innovation strategy in China, if successful, will completely overhaul the country's growth model, enhance the well-being of Chinese people, and contribute significantly to the world's social and economic development. In view of the dazzling pace of changes resulting from China's determination to transform the country into an innovative economy, we deem it necessary to document the trajectory of development, to record experiments of incentive policies, and to assess the impacts of China's policy for promoting science, technology and innovation (STI).

Second, China is an open economy and is part of the big family of emerging economies. Many of the emerging economies share with China both the same aspirations of, and similar obstacles to, innovation. We have been blessed with opportunities to visit many emerging economies due to our job and research commitments. The interactions we have had with policy-makers and business leaders in these countries, together with our first-hand observations of national developments there, reinforce strongly a view that the lessons of China's ongoing experiment in innovation-oriented transformation are of great relevance to many of the emerging economies.

Third, we are nonetheless puzzled by the lack of thorough documentation and in-depth assessment of China's incentive policy for innovation in the literature so far. Since China launched its MLNP and subsequently released a wide range of policy initiatives, there exists a fast growing interest in China's innovation programme from business leaders, policy-makers and the academic community all over the world. A few major studies of Chinese innovation have done us an excellent service. One of these works is a book entitled *Innovation with Chinese Characteristics: High-Tech Research in China* published in 2007 by Palgrave in collaboration with SITRA, the Finnish Innovation Fund. The research project was led by Linda Jakobson, a researcher at the Finnish Institute of International Affairs (FIIA), to examine a big question: Is innovative high-tech research expected to emerge from China in the coming ten years? The excellent book has four objectives: to comprehend the objectives of China's national innovation strategy; to examine the government policies, policy-making bodies and funding mechanisms; to take an overview of China's R&D and innovation in four priority areas; and to assess China's prospect for fulfilling its grand strategic goals. These objectives are pursued in five well-researched chapters that offer an overview of the national innovation system and an analysis of four selected sectors in information and communications technology, nanotechnology, energy technology and biotechnology. Owing probably to its research plan to produce a 'small book', the topic of incentive policy for innovation has received scant attention.

Another major work was an 18-month study of science and innovation in Asia conducted by James Wilson and Names Keeley of DEMOS, an influential think tank in the UK. The research was published in 2007 in a pamphlet entitled 'China: The Next Science Superpower?' Billing China's MLNP as the most ambitious programme of research investment since John F. Kennedy embarked on the race to the moon, the DEMOS research project was to capture the raw power of the changes that are under way, to explore the potential for Chinese science and innovation to head in new and surprising directions, and to identify opportunities for collaboration for the UK and Europe. Once again, the pamphlet has only a fleeting mention of incentive policy for innovation in China.

By far, the OECD's review of innovation policy in China (OECD, 2008) was, and still is, the most comprehensive study of China's innovation system and policies. With a total of 646 pages, the bulky book examines the main features and performance of the Chinese innovation system, and the role of policy and government in innovation in great detail. The six annexes in Part Three of the book supplement the main text with statistics, case studies and highlights of policies for encouraging the indigenous innovation of enterprises. The book assesses in detail the strengths and weaknesses of the main policy instruments which the Chinese government used for promoting science, technology and innovation

(STI). Surprisingly, it offers far too little about China's fiscal and financial incentive policies which are the core of the innovation programme in China. Hence, it is our intention to produce a book to fill this unmistaken gap.

China's aspiration to innovate is grounded on certain national strengths. China already boasts a pool of 2.6 million engineers and each year the country adds 700,000 engineering graduates to fill the tanks of its innovation engine. Also, China has greatly improved its innovation infrastructure through massive investment in higher education institutions, telecommunication systems, transportation, etc. In addition, as a latecomer, China can learn from the examples of countries that went before it. Still, after monumental efforts to develop human capital and innovation capacity, China is facing serious challenges in incentivizing innovators to make innovations to flourish. If China can get the incentive policies right, these policies can serve to increase the overall level of R&D spending throughout the economy, to affect the distribution of R&D among sectors so as to favour the more promising sectors and loosen constraints, such as the supply of S&T workers, to directly support certain technology development in activities assumed to have high long-term social returns through direct budgetary grants and subsidies, to encourage capital investment in imported plant and equipment in part to promote technology absorption, and to draw foreign direct investment (FDI) into selected industries to serve as a conduit for new technologies and possibly also as the axes for cluster development in technology zones (Bleda and del Río, 2013; Falk, 2007).

Incentivizing innovation can take a variety of forms: (1) Governments as lead users.[3] Through this approach, governments can use public procurement to encourage innovation by providing a 'lead market' for new technologies. In other words, governments provide the missing link between private sector R&D investment and the public sector by acting as the 'first buyer' of new technologies, thereby sharing risks and benefits of high-tech R&D procurements with future suppliers, and bundling of demand to reduce market fragmentation. Over the last few years, public procurement has become an integral part of China's national innovation policies. (2) Improvement of the intellectual property regime. An intellectual property regime is of critical importance as it defines a whole set of detailed provisions: what can be patented (or copyrighted), the standards of novelty, the life of the patent, the breadth of the patent, the process by which patents are granted and challenged, and the enforcement mechanism (Stiglitz, 2008). An improved intellectual property regime will give inventors and innovators the incentive to be innovative. In this respect, China has made a great deal of effort to shore up its intellectual property system.[4] (3) Financial incentives. Measures of this kind are to direct government funding to private sector innovation activities through grants, loans, subsidies, etc. (4) Fiscal incentives. These are tax relief measures which encourage firms to carry out innovation activities by reducing their cost. In this book, we keep our focus mainly on the financial and fiscal incentives simply because they are the least researched aspects of all four forms of incentive for innovation in China.

In pursuit of the objective of building an innovative economy, China has proved to be open and flexible. International good practices were adopted and assimilated; new approaches spontaneously sprang locally and were later absorbed into national initiatives and disseminated. This sense of pragmatism is once again a further manifestation of the guiding philosophy of Chinese economic reforms – 'crossing the river by touching the stone', and has given China's innovation system a range of intriguing characteristics. Some important questions emerge. What is China's evolving system of innovation? How does China incentivize innovators? What are institutional innovations in policy-making and implementation? Can China's policies and practices in support of innovation withstand the test of time? Additionally, China's quest for innovation echoes a very similar need of many other emerging countries. Policy-makers in these countries will be looking at China and wondering: Does China's bold experiment offer a fresh line of thinking and an alternative option? What lessons can be learned from Chinese practices? Business leaders will be following China's reforms of innovation system and contemplate: What opportunities do China's efforts to build an innovation country offer to business development and collaboration? To all these important questions, we have not found a comprehensive study that offers badly needed answers. This is simply because the topic is hugely under-researched. Nevertheless, an understanding of Chinese innovation strategy and its supporting mechanisms in a globalized environment is of crucial importance for keeping abreast with the development of the Chinese innovation system. It will also open new perspectives for academic inquiry, policy development and transnational cooperation.

Accordingly, the objectives of this book are:

- to fill in a clear gap in our knowledge of innovation management in China from an innovation incentive perspective;
- to comprehend Chinese institutional innovations designed to create an incentive structure for stimulating innovations;
- to examine the extent to which Chinese experiences are transferable to other emerging economies.

The book consists of nine chapters in four parts. The first part contains the first two chapters that lay down the context of China's efforts to pursue a national innovation agenda, including an overview of China's innovation programme, the evolution of the national innovation system, and innovation characteristics of firms. The second part focuses specifically on the development of Chinese innovation incentive structure and support mechanisms. There are three chapters in this part which examines in detail the fiscal incentives, financial incentives, and the development of government-led venture capital funds. The third part investigates innovation incentives and impacts in respective sectoral and regional settings. The two chapters in this part examine ways of incentivizing innovation in the energy sector and the Yangtze River Delta. The final part assesses the effectiveness of innovation policies in China. The first chapter in this part assesses the impact of incentives on innovation from a national innovation system lens. This is followed by the last chapter that evaluates Chinese experiences and examines lessons other emerging economies might learn from China.

In conducting research for, and writing up of, this book, we have benefited from the incredible assistance of many people, to whom we express our gratitude. In particular, we would like to thank Wang Linjiang and Yuan Weigang, Chairman and CEO of Heaven-Sent Capital Management Group respectively, for sharing with us in a number of interviews their profound insights into the operations of China's Venture Capital Guiding Funds (VCGFs). We also thank the Administrative Committee of Zhongguancun Science Park for sharing with us their experiences in managing VCGFs. We particularly appreciate Ms Wang Jia and Ms Liu Fan for their excellent research assistance with preparation of a number of draft chapters, compiling of most economic data and translation of a few draft chapters from Chinese into English. Without their unbelievable help, this book would not have been possible.

We must also thank our editor Peter Sowden at Routledge for his patience and understanding when we had to miss deadlines time and again due to need for more research on many more issues in order to keep pace with changes and developments of policy initiatives in China.

Finally, we are profoundly grateful to our family members who cared about what we were doing and offered us moral support throughout.

Notes

1 A good reference to the debate is an online one: 'China innovation: Is China a global innovation powerhouse?' *The Economist*, available at www.economist.com/debate/days/view/1041 (accessed 10 January 2014).
2 See '"Chinese dream" is Xi's vision', *China Daily*, 18 May 2013, available at www.chinadaily.com.cn/china/2013npc/2013-03/18/content_16315025.htm (accessed 10 January 2014).
3 For an excellent discussion on the topic, see Edler and Georghiou (2007) and OECD (2008).
4 Wechsler (2011) provides a critical analysis of the evolution and present state of Chinese intellectual property policy.

1 Aspire to innovate

Building an innovative economy

More than three decades of economic reforms in China are full of eye-opening, jaw-dropping and history-deciding dramatic events but three watershed years have stood out above all others as the highlights of this period of Chinese contemporary history. The first is undoubtedly the year 1978 which heralds a new era in reforms and developments and will be remembered forever as one when a new leaf of history was turned and the stage for the unfolding of all the dramas of economic reforms was set. The second is the year 1992 which witnesses the famous tour of southern China by Deng Xiaoping that reignited the momentum of actions and sped up economic reforms. The third is 2006 which marks another turning point when China pronounced the building of an innovative economy as its new national strategy and placed independent innovation with Chinese characteristics at the heart of the strategy. In the landmark document of the strategy, the Outlines of Medium and Long-term National Plan for Science and Technology Development (2006–2020) (MLNP), independent innovation is defined to include three types of innovation, namely original innovation, integrated innovation, and re-innovation based on assimilation and absorption of imported technologies.[1] The formulation and implementation of the MLNP can be seen as a crucial step towards ensuring China will be on course in its pursuit of prosperity for the next few decades. It is also a decisive measure to ensure China will not fall into the so-called 'Middle Income Trap', commonly referred to as the stagnation of economic growth as the supply of both surplus low-cost labour and international advanced technology has dried up (Woo, 2012). Moving up the industrial value chain is not easy to achieve as the experiences of Southern Asian countries have demonstrated. Firms in these countries moved from simple assembly in the 1960s and 1970s to process improvements and development by the early 1990s very quickly, but further achievements in climbing up the value chain since then have been rather disappointing (De Meyer and Garg, 2005). Limited knowledge transfers from foreign multinational companies to local firms were to blame despite the inflow of heavy FDI (ibid.). Hence, the Chinese government rightly states that the pursuit of an innovation-oriented strategic goal of nation-building should aspire to innovate independently with due consideration of Chinese contexts and that efforts to improve independent innovation capability should be integrated with all aspects of the country's modernization drive. Apparently, building an innovative economy is the biggest project China has ever undertaken.

The concept of an innovation-oriented economy and its basic characteristics

In retrospect, China's innovation drive was inspired by the success of many innovation-oriented countries and the powerful idea of national competitiveness-building. In 1990, the American scholar Michael E. Porter published a landmark book, entitled *The Competitive Advantage of Nations*, and proposed a theory of national comparative advantage. In explaining the competitive advantages of nations, he suggests four distinct stages of national competitive development, i.e. factor-driven, investment-driven, innovation-driven and wealth-driven stages, and stresses that the first three stages represent successive upgrading of a nation's competitive advantage while the fourth stage illustrates a drift and decline. He also asserts that the competitive advantage of nations is determined by four intertwined groups of factors in a metaphor of 'diamond', i.e. key industries' factor conditions and demand conditions, firm strategy, structure and rivalry, and related and supporting industries. Porter's influential theory has spurted a worldwide interest in the concept of innovation-oriented economy among policy-makers and academics alike.

Advance in the understanding of what constitutes an innovation-oriented economy has given China plenty of food for thought. As concerns about innovation moved up the country's policy agenda, China started drawing lessons from the histories of economic development in advanced countries and their experiences of policy-making and implementation. For more than 50 years after the Second World War, many countries strove to explore ways of industrialization and modernization from their respective initial conditions. In view of resource endowment, development strategy and technology policy, countries in the world can generally be categorized into three groups: resource-based economies, dependent economies and innovation-based economies. Specifically, China saw resource-based economies as those whose economic development is reliant on the richness of natural resource endowment for the creation of national wealth, such as the oil-exporting countries in the Middle East; dependent economies are those whose development is dependent on capital, markets and technologies of advanced countries, e.g. some Latin American countries. In contrast, innovation-oriented economies are those whose national competitiveness is primarily built upon the deployment of science, technology and innovation (STI) as their fundamental strategy and the enhancement of innovation capability, such as the USA, Japan and Finland. Experiences of development from different types of economies show to China that an innovative economy is essentially underpinned by the development of knowledge and technologies, originated significantly from within the national innovation system and that the building of independent innovation capability should underpin China's socio-economic development.

The consensus on the importance of innovation in national development led to the search for an understanding of the key features of an innovation-oriented economy. It was held that the metrics for identifying these features should include both quantitative and qualitative changes. Quantitatively, an innovation-oriented economy can be characterized by: (1) high investment in innovation. R&D expenses, for example, are found to normally exceed 2 per cent of GDP in major innovation-oriented countries; (2) high innovation impact. For instance, an innovative economy generally sees technological progress contribute to over 70 per cent of total factor productivity (TFP); (3) strong independent innovation capability. Dependency on foreign technology in these countries is often below 30 per cent; (4) high knowledge and innovation output. Worldwide, 99 per cent of invention patents are owned by the major innovation-oriented countries, while patents granted by the USA, Europe and Japan together account for 97 per cent of the world total. It was estimated that 86 per cent of global R&D investment is sourced from advanced countries such as the US, EU and Japan, while 98 per cent of incomes generated from technology transfer and licensing worldwide are earned by high-income countries in the field of international technology trade.[2]

Qualitatively, an innovation-oriented economy can be seen as one where innovation has become a key driver of development and that, through institutional, organizational and cultural innovation, builds a high performing national innovation system (NIS) with fitting national characteristics to maximize the impact of innovation-based activities on the national economy.

China identified the United States, the United Kingdom, France, Germany, Japan, Denmark, Finland, Sweden, Ireland, Israel, South Korea and Singapore as countries of excellence in innovation investment, knowledge generation, innovation output and self-contained innovation capability, and has aspired to emulate the success of these countries in the development of an innovative economy.

Building an innovative economy in China: four considerations

A necessity for China's choice of prosperity

China's surging modernization drive started from the late 1970s. The Communist Party of China (CPC), in its 12th National Congress held in September 1982, set out the target of national development as quadrupling annual output value of industry and agriculture in 20 years, that is, an increase from RMB0.71 trillion in 1981 to RMB2.8 trillion in 2000.[3] At the heart of the modernization programme was the ultimate goal of socio-economic development to improve people's livelihood and the country's prosperity. At the turn of new millennium, this choice of prosperity was deliberated as two newly defined objectives of economic development. The first objective was to build China into a relatively affluent country, officially coined as "a moderately prosperous society in all aspects", announced in the annual Plenum of CPC in 2002. The policy objective was underscored by two key indicators: (1) to quadruple the country's gross domestic output (GDP) to RMB36 trillion (more than US$4 trillion) by 2020 from the base level of 2000, and (2) to increase per capita GDP to US$3,000 by 2020 from US$1,000 in 2000. The aspiration was to become a member of the middle-income country family in 20 years' time. The second objective was to establish a harmonious society. Hu Jintao, then Chinese President, defined a harmonious society as one that features democracy, rule of law, equity, justice, sincerity, amity and vitality in his speech delivered in June 2005 at the opening ceremony of a training course to a new cohort of major provincial- and ministerial-level leaders at the Party School of the CPC Central Committee.[4] From this perspective, building a society of moderate prosperity for the entire Chinese population can also be understood to feature accelerated economic development, enhanced democracy, advanced science and education, prosperous culture, harmonious society, higher living standard, and more efficient use of resources and eco-friendly environment.[5] Undoubtedly, the transformation of a country in a size like China with one-fifth of the world's population into a society of relative prosperity and harmony is the most magnificent, hugely challenging process of social progress the world has ever seen. To achieve both goals, first and foremost, China needs to change its course of development. This is because the existing growth model has inflicted the country with problems of "unstable, unbalanced, uncoordinated, and unsustainable development" as described by Wen Jiabao, the former Premier, in his speech at the 18th National Congress of CPC on 12 November 2012.[6] The recent global economic crisis starting in 2008 reinforces the view that the days of massive Chinese export to the West are over and that the current growth model can neither be replaced by one with unbridled and wasteful investment spending, particularly in real estate, nor by one with GDP-centric growth. Both approaches would place considerable strains on China's resources and environment, drive up inflation and threaten social stability.

Michael Porter makes two powerful points in his theory of comparative advantage of nations in that prosperity should be driven by competitiveness and that competitiveness is ultimately underlined by productivity (Porter, 1990). The pursuit of building a moderately prosperous society means that China will move into the stage of development where per capita GDP increases from US$1,000 to US$3,000. International experiences suggest that a low-income country will usually experience dramatic changes in economic and social structure during its transition to a middle-income country (US$800–3,000) (Chenery *et al.*, 1986). In this critical period of industrialization, rebalancing China's unsustainable growth model with a particular emphasis on productivity and competitiveness is key, and innovation has become a focal point of such rebalancing efforts. In recognition of the rebalancing act as both a long-term and the most pressing short-term task, the Chinese government has carefully engineered a shift of policy focus to sustainable growth from the undesirable mode of high growth and has consciously reset its annual growth target at 7 per cent until 2020.[7]

Providing that China were not to fundamentally improve its innovation capability and that the contribution of its technical progress to economic growth were to remain at the level of 39 per cent, China's goal of quadrupling GDP between 2000 and 2020 could only be possible if it maintained a virtually impossible high investment rate of 52 per cent. Additionally, supposing China were capable of maintaining investment at 40 per cent of GDP as seen in recent years, it would still have to raise the contribution of technical progress to TFP to 60 per cent, a rise of 20 percentage points from the level in 2000, in order to achieve the economic growth objective of building a moderately prosperous society. Inevitably, the conclusion is that the country's pursuit of prosperity will have to be driven by a significant increase in productivity powered by innovation.

Nevertheless, China's productivity growth has shown sign of slowdown since 2000. The Organisation for Economic Co-operation and Development (OECD) estimated that annual TFP growth in China averaged 3.7 per cent during 1978–2003, but slowed to 2.8 per cent by the end of that period (*The Economist*, 2005). Zheng *et al*. (2009) also found that against an average rate of 3.3 per cent during 1978–1995, TFP growth slowed down to 1.9 per cent during 1995–2005. Clearly, without a significant improvement of productivity, China's comparative advantage will be undermined and China's ambition to build a society of prosperity and harmony will be compromised.

An inevitable change in the mode of economic growth

China has achieved remarkable economic growth over the past 30 years. From 1978 to 2007, annual GDP grew at an average of 9.67 per cent. For a long time, however, in order to speed up economic development and industrialization from a humble technological and economic base, China followed the mode of growth which features high input and high accumulation of production factors such as labour, natural resources and capital. This was particularly made possible by the existence of a large pool of surplus labour, particularly in rural China, from which the country has drawn its main source of comparative advantage upon the supply of relatively cheap labour and has undertaken a labour-intensive industrialization strategy led by the export sector. The approach was a great success. However, growing evidence has suggested that the demographic dividend, known as the positive effect of a large working-age population on productivity and economic growth (Bloom *et al*., 2003), is about to come to an end after driving growth in China for many years (e.g. Cai, 2010). Statistics released by China's National Bureau of Statistics (NBS) show that China's working-age population shrank for the first time in recent history in 2012. By the end of December 2012 the population of Chinese citizens aged between 15 and 59 decreased by 3.45 million from the same time a year earlier.[8] NBS acknowledged that this was only the beginning of a long-term trend that would persist between now and at least 2030. Accordingly, China may have reached the Lewis turning point where economic growth can no longer rely on the absorption of absolute surplus labour with a constant wage (Cai, 2010; Wang and Weaver, 2013). Despite the ongoing debate on whether or not China has reached a Lewis turning point, there are growing reports of labour shortage in key manufacturing hubs in coastal cities, reinforcing an increasing sense that labour in China is not as cheap as it used to be. The British publication *The Economist* even claimed the end of cheap China in an article that focused on the implications of soaring Chinese wages for global manufacturing.[9] Apparently, if China is reaching a new period of labour shortage, China will have no choice but to switch to a new growth model that can provide a new source of comparative advantage.

China needs to change its growth model also because the strategy of 'exchanging market for technology' has seemingly not delivered what the policy-makers had wished for. Under its 'market for technology' policy, China has become the second largest recipient of FDI just after the USA over the past decades. It is noted that China's opening to foreign investment was not motivated by a shortfall of domestic savings; rather, through the policy of a 'market for technology', FDI, foreign trade and technology transfer were expected to contribute to the modernization of the national economy (OECD, 2008). While FDI has led to knowledge spillover, it has not appeared to generate much needed technology transfers. In their assessment of the effectiveness of the strategy of 'exchanging market for technology', Zhang, Wu and Ai (2009) found that China may benefit from the strategy at the early stage and that firms will cease to learn from FDI once a threshold level is reached. Evidence from China's telecommunication equipment industry suggests that innovation capability and self-developed technologies have been the key to leading domestic firms' catching up with multinational corporations (Fan, 2006).

A need for a balanced, environmentally friendly development

China's large population, shortage of resources, and fragile ecological environment have put unprecedented pressure on the realization of balanced, sustainable socio-economic development in all respects. China's per capita possession of resources is rather low. In the Chinese government's white paper, entitled 'China's Energy Conditions and Policies', released in December 2007, for example, it was estimated that average per capita possession of many crucial resources such as energy, water resources, lands, mineral resources in China was only half or less than half of the world average level. In 2005, the total per capita possession of freshwater resources in China was 2,145 cubic meters, a quarter of the world's per capita consumption; per capita possession of oil and natural gas was about one-fifteenth of the world average; and per capita possession of major mineral resources was only 58 per cent of the world average, which ranked 52nd in the world.[10] While China's per capita possession of resources is far below the world average level, the country's resource consumption per unit output is far higher than the world average level. Comparing China's energy utilization efficiency with that of developed countries, there is a glaring gap. In a report entitled 'China's Resource Possession and Consumption' published in November 2011, the Ministry of Housing and Urban-Rural Construction estimated that if Japan's energy utilization efficiency is used as a benchmark, the energy utilization efficiency in China would be 11.5, while Italy is 1.33, France 1.5, Germany

1.5, the United Kingdom 2.17, US 2.67, Canada 3.5. Moreover, China's output per ton standard coal was estimated to be equivalent to 29.6 per cent of that of the United States, 16.8 per cent of that of the European Union, 10.3 per cent of that of Japan.[11] The combination of insatiable needs for resources as a result of GDP-centric growth and low resource utilization efficiency has inevitably placed considerable strains on China's resources and environment.

Mounting evidence has shown that China's high growth rate has been achieved largely by high inputs and high consumption of resources, whose negative effects and adverse impacts have now been widely felt. In terms of ecological environment, the overall function of various types of ecosystems is in decline and the range of environmental deterioration is expanding, which has severely damaged the environment. The areas with native forest depletion, grassland degradation, shrinkage of wetlands, desertification and soil erosion were estimated to have reached 3.56 million square kilometers.[12] Environmental pollution is becoming increasingly serious, spreading from lands to offshore waters, from surface water to groundwater, and from general pollutants to toxic and harmful pollutants. Environmental pollution has also shown a tendency of a coexistence of single-source pollution with multiple-source pollution, an overlapping of living pollution with industrial emissions, and a combination of various old and new pollutions with secondary pollutants. In China's first ever green national accounting report compiled by the Chinese Administration of Environmental Protection and National Bureau of Statistics in 2006, annual economic losses caused by environmental pollution were estimated to be equivalent to 3 per cent of GDP.[13]

Therefore, energy, resources and environmental constraints have become the most pressing issue in China's future development. Compared with other concerns, these constraints will be more severe due to the scarcity of primary source of energy and other important natural resources and the irreversibility of large-scale environmental destruction. The GDP-centric economic growth has intensified the tension between man and nature, and poses a big challenge for building a harmonious society. To meet the challenges, China clearly needs to place technological development as a top priority in order to overcome energy, resources and environmental constraints, to achieve a transition from a resource-hungry economy to a resource-saving one, and from an environment-neglecting growth pattern to an environment-friendly one, and to ultimately achieve balanced and sustainable economic and social developments.

China's basic national conditions such as a supersize population, low per capita resource endowment, and fragile environment determine that China can no longer simply maintain GDP-centric, rapid economic growth at the expense of environmental sustainability. A recent study suggests that if China were to achieve its economic and social development goals by 2020, it would have to (1) reduce per unit GDP of energy consumption by 50–60 per cent, (2) reduce per unit GDP of water consumption by 80 per cent, with a reduction of agricultural water consumption by an annual average of one percentage point and recycling of industrial water as much as over 85 per cent, and (3) increase recycling of waste, for example, an increase in utilization of steel scrap, by more than 50 per cent and recycling of common non-ferrous metal as much as 50 per cent.[14]

In September 2004, the then Chinese President Hu Jintao remarked that "If we do not fundamentally transform economic growth pattern, energy will be no longer sustainable, and the ecological environment will be unable to shoulder the burden."[15] More recently, at the opening session of the annual meeting of parliament on 5 March 2014, Premier Li Keqiang declared 'war' on pollution and unveiled detailed measures to tackle what has become the country's hot-button social issue.[16] Clearly, China ought to tap into science and technology advancement alongside accelerated restructuring of economic and industrial structures and enhanced capacity of independent innovation in order to fundamentally transform its mode of economic growth.

A need for enhancing core competitiveness of enterprises

After 30 years' reform and opening up, Chinese enterprises have succeeded to some extent in building competitive advantage, exemplified by the success of a growing number of indigenous enterprises in the international market and the growth of China's international trade surplus. It can be argued, however, that Chinese enterprises have built global comparative advantage primarily on low labour costs and synergies of domestic and international markets. The contribution of STI to the international competitiveness of Chinese enterprises remains low. At present, the low capability of Chinese enterprises to develop key technologies independently results in their dependence on foreign technologies. According to the statistics compiled by the State Administration of Foreign Exchange, China's net payment of patent royalties and licensing fees to foreign intellectual property (IP) owners amounted to US$16.7 billion in 2012, an almost four-fold increase from US$4.3 billion in 2004. Moreover, in equipment investment that made up 40 per cent of new fixed capital in China, 60 per cent was spent on imported equipment.[17] Although China's number of invention patents ranked eighth in the world, it only accounted for 1.8 per cent of the world total. China's granted invention patents only accounted for 0.2 per cent of the authorized non-Americans' total in the United States.

Due to the lack of home-grown core technologies and brands, Chinese firms are primarily limited to compete in the low end of the global value chain in many areas of manufacturing. For example, although China has already been the world's top manufacturing hub in computers, mobile phones, colour TV sets, DVDs and motorcycles, it simply is an assembly workshop of foreign companies, importing most key components from overseas and capturing a very small proportion of added value. American scholars estimated that Chinese manufacturers only captured 1.8 per cent of the value created in the iPhone and 2 per cent in the iPad as compared with 58.5 per cent and 30 per cent of respective values accrued to Apple.[18] Similarly, the average profit margin of a TV set made by a Chinese enterprise was estimated to be less than RMB10, and the gross profit of a China-made computer accruing to the Chinese manufacturer was only 5 per cent of its value.[19]

Due to the weak independent innovation capability and low level of technology, a great deal of technical equipment for industrial production, especially those for high-end products, is mainly dependent on imports. For example, imports made up more than 70 per cent of China's advanced textile machinery, 80 per cent of manufacturing equipment for integrated circuit, and almost all fibre optic equipment.[20] In this sense, China is still a 'manufacturing country' rather than a 'creative country'. To promote the core competitiveness of Chinese enterprises, China is striving to build itself into an innovative economy by increasing R&D investment, and Chinese enterprises are encouraged to be the key players of technological innovation and to develop a batch of home-grown brands and products with independent intellectual property rights, core technology and innovation capacity.

Building an innovative economy: objectives and strategy

China's objectives of building an innovative economy

In 2005, the Chinese government issued the MLNP which heralds a new era in S&T development for the next 15 years. The MLNP serves as a blueprint for the S&T development of China in the new era.

As specified in the MLNP, the ultimate goal of building an innovative economy in China is to significantly enhance China's capacity in independent innovation in order to promote socio-economic development and safeguard the national security. It is also aimed to enhance the country's comprehensive strength in basic research and frontier technology research and in generating S&T achievements of global impacts. As a result, innovation can transform the country to become one of the world's leading innovative economies and can provide strong support for building a moderately prosperous society by 2020.

Specifically, the MLNP set out eight objectives of S&T development:

1   To acquire a series of core technologies in the equipment manufacturing and information industries that are closely related to the national competitiveness, and to develop technologies of international excellence in the general manufacturing and information industries.
2   To advance overall agricultural S&T capability to the level of international excellence, increase overall agricultural productivity, and promote national food security.
3   To achieve breakthroughs in technologies of energy generation, energy conservation and clean energy, optimize energy structure, and move energy consumption indicators of per-unit major industrial products to or close to international advanced standards.
4   To build a technical development mode of circular economy in key industries and key cities, and provide S&T support for building a resource-saving and environment-friendly society.

5   To significantly enhance capacity in major diseases prevention and control, contain spread of major diseases including AIDS and hepatitis, achieve R&D breakthroughs in new drug and key medical device development, and equip industrial development with technological capacity.
6   To enable the defence-related S&T to meet the needs of independent and information-based development for modern weapons and equipment, and help safeguard national security.
7   To establish a number of world class research scientists and research teams, generate a series of innovative achievements of significant impacts in the mainstream of research fields, and reach international excellence in frontier technologies in information, biology, material and aerospace fields.
8   To build a number of centres of international excellence in scientific research institutions and universities, and a number of enterprise R&D institutes with international competitiveness, and create a relatively sound national innovation system (NIS) with Chinese characteristics.

China also set the four key metrics of an innovation-oriented economy by 2020 as follows:

1   Gross R&D expenditure (GERD) as a share of GDP exceeds 2.5 per cent.
2   The contribution of progress in S&T to economic growth[21] accounts for more than 60 per cent.
3   Dependency on foreign technology[22] falls to below 30 per cent.
4   Both the number of granted invention patents per capita and international citations of Chinese scientific papers are ranked among the top five in the world.

The key targets set forth in the MLNP have since been deliberated and modified in the successive 11th and 12th national five-year plans as can be seen in Table 1.1. In the 12th national five-year plan, three metrics (contribution of progress in S&T to economic growth, dependence on foreign technology, and international ranking for per capita patents granted to Chinese nationals) have been dropped and are replaced with six new metrics.

China's strategy of building an innovative economy

The principles and overall arrangement for independent innovation

The MLNP lays out four principles for S&T development in China as 'independent innovation, leapfrogging in key areas, S&T supporting economic and social development, and S&T leading the future'. Independent innovation is elaborated as the strengthening of original innovation, integrated innovation, and re-innovation based on introduction, assimilation and absorption with a view to enhancing national innovation capability. Leapfrogging in key areas means that China should only select those key areas of innovation where the country has

Table 1.1 The national targets of building an innovative economy

	11th FYP	12th FYP	MLNP
	Targets set for 2010	Targets set for 2015	Targets set for 2020
R&D expenditures as % of GDP	2.0	2.2	2.5
Contribution of progress in S&T to economic growth (%)	>45		>60
Dependence on foreign technology (%)	<40		<30
International ranking for per capita patents granted to Chinese nationals	10th	5th	5th
International ranking for number of citations of scientific papers by Chinese scientists	14		5th
R&D personnel in 10,000 working population (person-year)		43	
Number of patents granted in 10,000 residents		3.3	
Patent application of R&D workforce (per hundred person-year)		12	
Technology market transaction nationwide (RMB billion)		800	
High-tech value-added as % of manufacturing as a whole	18	18	
Citizens with basic science qualification (%)	3.27	5	
International ranking for patents granted to Chinese nationals	15th		
Human resources in S&T (million)	50		
Personnel engaged in S&T activities (million)	7		
R&D workforce, full-time equivalent (million person-year)	1.3		

Sources: the 11th National Five-Year Plan; the 12th National Five-Year Plan; and the MLNP.

already built a foundation or has had strengths and where they are of critical importance to the national economy and people's livelihood. After identifying these strategic areas of innovation, China should then concentrate all its efforts to achieve major breakthroughs and to leapfrog the world's technology leaders in technological development. S&T supporting economic and social development is taken to mean that China should aim to make breakthroughs in key and general technologies to match the country's pressing needs, and to support sustainable socio-economic development. S&T leading the future means that China should proactively set its agenda for frontier technological research and basic research from a long-term development perspective, whilst China should nurture new market demands and foster the development of emerging industries to define the country's future socio-economic development.

The MLNP offers a roadmap for S&T development in China, including: (1) to define some key areas, and make breakthroughs in a series of major and key technologies to fully enhance China's capacity in providing S&T support. MLNP specifies 11 key areas in national economic and social development, from which, 68 projects with clearly defined tasks and a high possibility of technological breakthrough in the near future are prioritized; (2) to implement key and special programmes according to the national needs, for achieving leapfrogging development and filling gaps in research fields; and (3) to roadmap and conduct frontier technological research and basic research, improve the capacity of ongoing innovation and lead the sustainable socio-economic development. Twenty-seven frontier technologies in eight technological fields, as well as 18 areas of basic research, were prioritized, and four key scientific research programmes were implemented.

Emphasis on enhancing China's independent innovation capability

As the core of China's national competitiveness, independent innovation capacity is considered crucial for China to address future challenges. It serves both as a major strategy to lead the future S&T development in China and as a fundamental approach to achieving its objective of building an innovative economy. Good practices of S&T development worldwide indicate that only a country with strong independent innovation capacity can win in the fierce international competition. China's over-dependence on foreign core and key technologies suggests that these technologies cannot be acquired from external sources and that they have to be developed through independent innovation. This is particularly true in key areas concerning national economic lifeline and national security.

In the process of building an innovative economy, China has given top priority to the enhancement of independent innovation capacity. As will be seen in the chapters that follow, measures have been taken to accelerate the implementation of major national S&T programmes, to increase investment in capacity-building of independent innovation, and to incentivize innovation in the public and private sectors. Emphasis has been placed on a shift from imitating innovation of other countries to enhancing independent innovation, in order to acquire more indigenous scientific discoveries and technical inventions for strengthening domestic enterprises in international S&T competition. Policies have gradually been in place to push through actions in these areas: (1) shift from focusing on R&D of single technology to integrated innovation that targets key strategic products and emerging industries, to develop key and strategic products that are of strong technical relevance and can drive the development of other industries, and to achieve key technological breakthrough and integrated innovation on this basis; (2) shift from focusing on the piecemeal reform of scientific research institutions to the comprehensive institutional reform in the S&T sector, to establish an innovation system in which enterprises play a leading role while the market plays a decisive role and enterprises, universities and research institutions collaborate closely, and to promote the overall development of the national innovation system (NIS); (3) shift from focusing on serving economic growth to serving broader sustainable socio-economic development; and (4) shift from general S&T exchange to proactively leveraging global S&T resources, to undertake international S&T cooperation and exchange at broader and deeper scales, and to facilitate independent innovation to move up the STI value chain.

S&T institutional reform

The enduring legacy of the pre-reform planning system means that institutional innovation is urgently needed in China to promote S&T progress and to enhance independent innovation capacity. To build an innovative economy, it is important to deepen S&T institutional reform, further optimize its S&T structural layout, increase participation of the whole society in innovation, and accelerate the transformation of S&T achievements into real productive force. Greater efforts have been made to further overhaul the NIS aimed at fully leveraging the government's steering role in setting innovation agenda and roadmap, markets' decisive role in S&T resource allocation, enterprises' role in undertaking technological innovation, and national research institutions and universities' key role in new scientific discoveries. By and large, institutional innovation concerning all stakeholders in the NIS is to integrate all forces of the innovation system so as to provide favourable institutional supports for China to build an innovative economy.

The deepening S&T institutional reform and the development of a NIS with Chinese characteristics have focused on the following aspects:

1   Establish a technological innovation system that is enterprise-centred and in which there is interactive learning between enterprises, universities and research institutions. While greater emphasis is on enhancing enterprises' own innovation capacity, actions have been taken to encourage enterprises, research institutes and universities to cooperate with each other in order to meet the innovation needs of enterprises.
2   Develop a knowledge innovation system that enhances scientific research capacity in higher education institutions. In an attempt to build an innovation

system that is open, flexible, competitive and cooperative, China has promoted cooperation and resource integration between research institutes and universities. Efforts have also been made to enhance the development of an S&T system for public welfares, to develop research-oriented universities, and to establish a series of research centres that are state-of-the-art and can share resources on basic research and frontier technologies.

3   Build a national defence S&T innovation system that integrates military mission-led innovation with civilian purposes and combines military efforts with civilian support. China has taken action to build closer ties between military and civilian S&T in terms of macro management, development strategy and planning, R&D activities and S&T industrialization, to strengthen the development of technologies that can be used for both military and civilian purposes, and to develop a preferable system in which the outstanding national S&T teams serve national defence S&T innovation and the national defence S&T achievements can be readily transformed into civilian use.

4   Create regional innovation systems with their own characteristics and advantages. Efforts are being made to fully leverage the characteristics and advantages of regional socio-economic development, to integrate the development of regional innovation system and innovation capacity, to deepen local S&T system reform, to promote the integration of central and local S&T capabilities, and to leverage the key roles of universities, research institutions and national high-and-new-tech industrial development areas in regional innovation systems. China has also provided stronger support to S&T innovation in driving regional socio-economic development, enhancing S&T capacity-building in central and western regions, and strengthening the development of S&T system at regional (municipal) levels.

5   Develop a social and network-based S&T intermediary service system. To address the key problems such as small-scale, single function and poor service of the S&T intermediary service sector in China, policies have been developed to foster and develop various types of S&T intermediary service institutions, to fully leverage the key roles of universities, research institutions and civil groups in offering S&T intermediary services, and to steer service organizations to grow along the path of professional, standardized and scale-based development.

Cultivation of talent for innovation

Talented personnel play a vital important role in science, technology and innovation. Distinguished scientists and outstanding teams in S&T are a decisive factor in the development of national science and technology. At present, competition for talent has become a focus of international competition. No matter whether they are developed or developing countries, all regard human resources in science, technology and innovation as a strategic resource and a core factor of enhancing the country's competitiveness, and thus vigorously strengthen capacity-building for trained personnel in science, technology and innovation. Continuous training of a large number of high-quality S&T personnel with innovation aspirations is directly related to the future of China's S&T development.

In order to promote the development of talent, the Chinese government has maintained that trained personnel are the country's primary resources, and take the identifying, training, employing and attracting outstanding talented personnel as an important task in the development of science, technology and innovation, and establish a sound incentive mechanism which is conducive to the training and employment of trained personnel. The government has continued to create conditions conducive to innovation and tolerance of failure for better growth of talented personnel and build scientific innovation platforms and provide opportunities for all kinds of personnel with the potential in S&T to fulfil their potential of talents. Major S&T research and infrastructure projects, key disciplines and scientific research bases and international academic exchanges and cooperation projects have been treated as the core and efforts have been made to train academic leaders and build innovation teams. The government has strengthened the integration of technological innovation with personnel training, has encouraged the cooperation of research institutes with universities to together train research personnel, supported postgraduates to undertake or participate in research projects, inspired undergraduates to participate in scientific research and cultivate their exploration interests and scientific aspirations in the practice of innovation. Enterprises have been encouraged to employ high-level S&T personnel and cultivate outstanding technological personnel.

Innovation culture and innovation spirit with Chinese characteristics

China's new innovation strategy places the development of an innovation culture as one of the critical measures in recognition of the close relationship between a nation's culture and its technological innovation performance. Creativity and innovation are facilitated by an innovation-conducive culture, which is in turn reinforced by the thriving of innovative activities. Building an innovative economy underpinned by an innovation culture with Chinese characteristics means preserving good traditions of Chinese culture while enhancing the sense of self-reliance and self-esteem and strengthening creativity of the whole society. The essence of this innovation culture is to advocate rational critique, to respect individualism, and to tolerate failure. It is also imperative that academic freedom and democracy are promoted, that exploration and individual ambition and initiatives are encouraged, and that new ideas and new perspectives are given space to develop and contend. All this will need the development of a policy framework that stimulates innovative thinking, nurtures academic critique, and develops a relaxed, harmonious, healthy and progressive culture of innovation. Measures have been taken to strengthen research ethics and curb the impetuous and unhealthy academic atmosphere in S&T research. Efforts have also been made to provide more opportunities and bigger stages for young talents to shine, and to create an environment conducive to innovation and entrepreneurship in the whole society.

Notes

1 See the document in its Chinese version at www.gov.cn/jrzg/2006-02/09/content_183787.htm (assessed 12 February 2009).
2 See Li Yuanyuan '国家创新系统的发展过程和创新型国家的基本特征' (The development of national innovation systems and the characteristics of innovative nations), available at www.china.com.cn/xxsb/txt/2006-11/06/content_7324209.htm (accessed 28 October 2013).
3 See 胡耀邦在中国共产党第十二次全国代表大会上的报告 (Hu Yaoban's speech in the Twelfth National Congress of the Chinese Communist Party), available at http://cpc.people.com.cn/GB/64162/64168/64565/65448/4526430.html (assessed 6 January 2012).
4 See 'Building harmonious society crucial for China's progress: Hu', *China Daily*, 27 June 2005, available at http://english.peopledaily.com.cn/200506/27/eng20050627_192495.html (accessed 6 January 2012).
5 See Xu Xianchun's presentation, entitled 'The System of Xiaokang Indicators: A Framework to Measure China's Progress', at The 3rd OECD World Forum on 'Statistics, Knowledge and Policy': *Charting Progress, Building Visions, Improving Life*, Busan, Korea, 27–30 October 2009, available at www.oecd.org/site/progresskorea/44120516.pdf (accessed 2 February 2011).
6 See 'Wen pinpoints key tasks facing China in five years', available at www.china.org.cn/china/18th_cpc_congress/2012-11/10/content_27067312.htm (accessed 15 December 2012).
7 Wen Jiabao, then Chinese premier, remarked at the annual opening ceremony of the parliament. See 'China ditches double-digit Growth', *Financial Times*, 5 March 2012, available at www.ft.com/cms/s/0/4a67e58e-668b-11e1-863c-00144feabdc0.html (accessed 6 March 2012).
8 See 'Chinese labour pool begins to drain', *Financial Times*, 18 January 2013, available at www.ft.com/cms/s/0/ad1e00e6-6149-11e2-957e-00144feab49a.html (accessed 18 January 2013).
9 See 'The end of cheap China: what do soaring Chinese wages mean for global manufacturing', *The Economist*, 10 March 2012.
10 See 中国的能源状况与政策 (China's energy conditions and policies), available at www.gov.cn/zwgk/2007-12/26/content_844159.htm (accessed 15 June 2011).
11 See 我国资源拥有与消耗状况 (China's resource possession and consumption), available at www.mohurd.gov.cn/xytj/tjzldtyxx/dfjsxzzgbmxx/200804/t20080423_160556.html (accessed 28 October 2013).
12 See 全国生态保护"十一五"规划 (Eleventh five-year planning of national ecological protection), available at http://sts.mep.gov.cn/stbh/js/200610/t20061018_94783.htm (accessed 15 June 2011).
13 See 两部门发《中国绿色国民经济核算研究报告2004》 (Two ministries released China Green National Accounting Report 2004), available at www.gov.cn/gzdt/2006-09/07/content_381190.htm (accessed 15 June 2011).
14 See '走中国特色自主创新之路，建设创新型国家' (Follow the path of independent innovation with Chinese characteristics, build an innovative country), available at http://news.xinhuanet.com/politics/2008-01/31/content_7533162_3.htm (accessed 20 September 2010).
15 See 'CPC plenum adopt decision on ruling capabilities', *People's Daily* online, 20 September 2009, available at http://english.peopledaily.com.cn/200409/20/print20040920_157561.html (accessed 6 January 2012).
16 See 'China to declare war on pollution: Premier Li' in *China Daily* online, 5 March 2014, available on www.chinadailyasia.com/news/2014-03/05/content_15122685.html (accessed 6 March 2014).

17 From remarks of Deng Nan, Vice Chairman of China Association of Science and Technology in her speech on the Forum of Chinese Prosperity in All Aspects on 8 December 2005, available at http://news.xinhuanet.com/fortune/2005-12/09/content_3896987.htm (accessed 15 June 2011).
18 Information from a presentation 'Who profits from innovation in global value chains? iPhones and windmills' by Jason Dedrick, School of Information Studies, Syracuse University, available at www.wita.org/attachments/calendarevents/1294/Value%20 (accessed 6 January 2012).
19 See '经济日报：激活企业创新之源' (Economic Daily: revitalizing the sources of firm innovation), available at http://news.xinhuanet.com/politics/2005-11/03/content_3723316.htm (accessed 20 July 2011).
20 See '郭铁成：我国科技发展的突出问题和转型升级战略' (Guo Tiecheng: The main problems of our country's technological development and strategies of restructuring and upgrading), available at www.cas.cn/xw/zjsd/200811/t20081107_1685907.shtml (accessed 20 July 2011).
21 According to the State Statistics Bureau, contribution of progress in S&T to economic growth is calculated as follows: $S\&T = ((Y - \alpha K - \beta L)/Y) \times 100\%$, where Y, K and L represent the average growth rate of output, capital and labour, and α and β represent the elasticity of K and L respectively.
22 The metric of dependence on foreign technology (DFT) in China's S&T planning is calculated as follows: DFT = spending on imported technology/(spending on R&D + spending on imported technology − earnings from exported technology). See Gao Chanlin, 'How to understand the measurement of the indicator of dependence on foreign technology', available at www.sts.org.cn/fxyj/zbtx/documents/2008/08041606.htm#_ftn1 (accessed 25 September 2013).

2 China's national innovation system

China's innovation aspirations could be supported or thwarted by the strength of its national innovation system (NIS) as the overall innovation performance of China depends on how its system of innovation is capable of generating and exploiting new knowledge. In his influential work, Freeman (1987) defines a national innovation system as "the network of institutions in the public and private sectors whose activities and interactions initiate, import, modify and diffuse new technologies" (p. 1). The term 'system' refers to the set of institutions whose actions and interactions have a bearing on the innovative performance of organizations in the nation. A NIS integrates innovation actors, innovation environment and innovation mechanism to facilitate efficient allocation of innovation resources and to increase innovation performance at the national and regional level through its support to interactive learning and collaboration between innovation players for the fulfilment of strategic objectives of national innovation. Seeing the innovation process as a system underscores the appreciation that innovations no longer depend on one organization's own effort, that successful innovations result from interaction and collaboration between organizations, and that a nation's success in innovation relies on the strength of its system that is capable of generating and exploiting new knowledge. Over the past 60 years, China has gradually developed and overhauled its NIS in the hope that it will spur the country to become an innovation-driven economy in the twenty-first century.

The evolution of the national innovation system

The embryonic form of national innovation system in China can be traced back to the early 1950s when the new government embarked on the development of a modern economy under a planned economic system. Technological innovation was seen as an integral part of the modernization drive at the time. Yet, the system thinking of innovation was not featured in practice, mainly due to the inherent conflict between the planned economic system and the system thinking of innovation. It was not until after 1978 when China launched unprecedented economic reforms to embrace the market-oriented economic system and globalization that the development of the NIS took a significant turn. The year 2006 served as a watershed when China set the transformation of itself into an innovative economy as an overarching aim of national development strategy. The development of the NIS has since gained momentum. Broadly speaking, the evolution of China's NIS can be divided into three periods.

The government-led formative period: 1949–1977

The Communist Party of China (CPC) came into power and formed a new government in 1949 after the end of the civil war. The new government inherited an economy characterized with a war-savaged industrial system, a massively underdeveloped education system, and weak technological capabilities. To rectify these problems in order to lay down the foundation of a modern industrial system, the government set out, among other measures, to construct 156 large-scale turnkey projects in its first five-year plan which covered the period 1953-1957, relying on technology transfer almost exclusively from the former Soviet Union and Eastern European countries. These projects mainly concentrated in heavy industry, including power generation, mining, smelting and chemical manufacturing.[1] In parallel with industrial development, the higher education sector and the science and technology (S&T) system were quickly placed as the priority of development and they were cast in the same mould of the former Soviet Union's system. Policies and their implementations in this period laid down an early industrial and technological foundation for further development in many years to come.

In 1956 the Chinese government launched a campaign of 'advancing science' through the launch of the country's first ever long-term technology development plan – 'The Long-term National Plan for Science and Technology Development 1956–1967' (thereafter the 12-year plan). The 12-year plan set out a number of key objectives of S&T development in attempts to nurture developments in emerging S&T domains. New institutions were created to support the implementation of the 12-year plan, notably the establishment of the National Science and Technology Commission (NSTC) in 1956 and the National Defence Science and Technology Working Committee (NDSTWC) in 1958 for oversight of science and technology policies at the national level, and the repositioning of the Chinese Academy of Sciences (CAS), which was established in 1949, as a leading institution of knowledge production for the undertaking of key research projects as identified in the 12-year plan. This heralded the formation of a top-down, mission-oriented institutional set-up in the national S&T system, comprising CAS, high education institutions (HEIs), industrial ministry-affiliated research institutes, and regional academies of sciences under the oversight and coordination of the NSTC, Ministry of Education (MOE) and the NDSTWC. By 1966 prior to the Cultural Revolution, the number of scientific research institutions in China totalled 1,700, with 120,000 active scientific researchers.

Scientific research and technological innovation during the period 1949–1977 was predominantly government-led. The central government used a five-year framework as a planning tool to set innovation priorities and used administrative directives as mechanisms for allocating resources to innovation projects. Three distinct features of the innovation system in this period can be identified. First, the government was the primary source of investment in innovation, and its allocation of resources was in strict alignment with the pre-set tasks in national five-year plans and annual action plans. Second, innovation was primarily mission-oriented and was motivated by the perceived needs of the country's economic growth, social development and national security. Priorities of innovations were given to the heavy industry and military industry but innovation activities in the military and civilian sectors were highly segregated. Skewed and disjointed efforts led to a concentration of disproportionate resources on military-oriented high-tech fields as opposed to a lack of resources and innovation in consumer goods that the country badly needed. Third, innovators primarily undertook innovation tasks as assigned by the government. The performance of their innovation undertakings neither had direct link with rewards nor was associated with risks and losses incurred by failed innovation projects.

During this period, enterprises, mainly state-owned enterprises (SOEs), were designated primarily as production units without any obligation of undertaking independent R&D. Few had R&D facility either. R&D was primarily conducted in public research institutions (PRIs), and R&D outputs were transferred to the recipients in accordance with the predetermined plan of the state. Universities were generally responsible for education and learning, research tended to be pure science-oriented, and only a few research outputs were actually transferred to enterprises. This model appeared to have aligned well with the planned economic system as it exhibited an incredible ability to mobilize the whole nation's strength of research to achieve national goals of mission-oriented innovation. The highlights of this early system of national innovation were the success of such mission-oriented programmes as developments of atomic bomb, hydrogen bomb and artificial satellite.

This model, however, had inherent drawbacks in that scientific knowledge production and industrial application was not connected, leading to a lack of feedback of market needs into the knowledge production system, low commercialization of R&D, and a lack of incentive for technological innovation. The case of Jiefang, a well-known national brand for the home-made truck, illustrates the typical failure of this innovation system. Forty years after the first trucks were made by adopting technologies from the USSR, the core technologies had rarely been upgraded and the design was never changed, despite its dominance in the domestic truck market.

The market-oriented transition period: 1978–2005

The Third Plenary Session of the 11th Central Committee of the CPC held in 1978 endorsed China's radical change in the direction of economic development by launching the programme of reform and opening up to the outside world. This marked the beginning of China's prolonged transition from a planned economy to a market-oriented economy and a new era in the development of the NIS. In the National Science Conference held in Beijing in the same year, Deng Xiaoping proclaimed that science and technology are primary productive forces. The ideological change gave rise to a new guiding principle that would position science and technology as a critical source of growth in the country's modernization endeavour. The embeddedness of the new ideology in the reform and opening up programme ushered science and technology innovation into a new spring. Four significant changes can be identified in this market-oriented transition period of NIS.

The first change was China's deliberate choice for a policy of offering foreign companies market access in exchange for technology transfer (often dubbed 'market for technology') in order to ditch China's science and technology backwardness and to catch up with the advanced world at a greater speed. A radical measure in the establishment of four special economic zones (SEZs) in the south of China[2] was taken early on to pilot this new strategy of attracting FDI. The model of SEZ was later rolled out to the whole coastal area and selected cities in the inland area. In the meantime, economic and technological development zones and high-tech parks were set up across the country for similar purposes. In the implementation of the market for technology policy, there emerged all sorts of foreign-invested enterprises, hundreds of thousands of large complete sets of imported equipment for fertilizer, chemical fibre and other products as well as various automobile production lines with different brands introduced from different foreign countries.

The second considerable change was the shake-up of the country's S&T system. This became inevitable as the system constructed under the planned economic regime was at odds with the emerging market-oriented economic system and the country's demand for closer alignment in production/innovation/knowledge systems in the light of the fast pace of global technological innovation. This change started when the Chinese government issued 'Decisions on the Reform of Science and Technology System' in 1985, a landmark document to guide the significant overhaul of the S&T system. The rationale of the reform was underlined by the principle as spelled out in the document – 'economic construction must rely on the development of science and technology, and the development of science and technology must serve economic construction'.[3] In 1996, the Chinese government issued another landmark document, entitled 'Decisions on Deepening Reform of the Science and Technology System during the Ninth Five-Year Plan Period', and laid out a tentative system of innovation that was more compatible with the mode of socialist market economy and norms of science and technology development. This new innovation system was underpinned by (1) a technology development system led by enterprises and supported by industry-university-research institution collaboration, (2) a scientific research system underlined by research institutes and HEIs, and (3) an open, market-based S&T service system.

Correspondingly, reforms of the S&T system over this period were undertaken at three different levels.

At the operational level, the focus was on redressing a fundamental problem found in the S&T system of excessive government control and inflexible S&T planning. Actions were first taken to transform over 2,000 applied research and technology development-oriented PRIs affiliated to governments of all levels into market-oriented research institutes. In the meantime, the traditional S&T appropriation system was replaced with one where S&T activities would be funded by three separate sources, i.e. S&T fund, technology development contracts and fixed contract of funding. Furthermore, the technology market was developed for market-oriented research institutes to explore opportunities of technology transfer and commercialization. Correspondingly, Chinese governments in succession launched three major projects in the 1990s. The Project 211 starting from 1993 was the government endeavour to develop about a hundred Chinese universities into research-intensive, world-class centres of learning.[4] The Technology Innovation Project launched in 1996 aimed to support enterprises to become key players of indigenous innovation. The Knowledge Innovation Project in 1998 aimed to transform the Chinese Academy of Sciences into research centres of international excellence. These three projects have since formed the backbone of the NIS.

At the organizational level, measures were taken to remove the separation of research institutions from enterprises, isolation of production from research, design and education, separation of military technology from civilian technology, and regional separation in scientific research. Reforms also emphasized strengthening enterprises' technology absorption capacity, enhancing links between S&T and production, and promoting collaboration among industries, universities and research institutions.

At the S&T personnel management level, actions were taken to reform the S&T personnel management system in an attempt to encourage mobility of talents and to create a favourable environment for S&T personal development.

The third change was the push for a new institutional set-up in order to implement the proposed reforms as mentioned above. For example, the need for facilitating the university-PRI-industry link led to the enactment in succession of the Patent Law in 1984, Law on Technology Contracts in 1987 and Law on Promoting the Transformation of Science and Technology Achievements in 1996 as well as a series of preferential policies concerning promotion of technology transactions, which accelerated the commercialization and industrialization of scientific research achievements. In order to optimize allocation of S&T resources, China also established the National Natural Science Foundation (NSFC) in 1986 to create an essential source of funding to support basic research.

The fourth change in the NIS during this period was the launch of a series of national innovation programmes targeting the country's key areas of innovation as seen in Table 2.1. These programmes constituted the backbone of China's innovation programmes and have continued to this day.

At the same time, there gradually emerged a tendency of joined-up management of major S&T programmes by S&T-related government bodies at the central and local levels.

During this period, the administration of S&T innovation was transformed first from use of government directive or mandatory plan to use of government indicative or guiding plan, and later to one that is 'market-oriented and government-coordinated'. The latter system of innovation administration displayed three distinct features: (1) funding of innovation was broadened to include enterprise investment and financing from financial institutions in addition to government appropriation; (2) technological innovation was market-oriented and was dominated by acquisition and absorption of imported technologies; (3) enterprises, universities, research institutions and S&T intermediaries gradually became the mainstay of innovation, and cooperation between innovation subjects was increasingly strengthened.

Under this system, China's overall S&T strength was considerably enhanced. In 2005, R&D investment as a share of GDP reached 1.3 per cent; the personnel (Full-time Equivalent, FTE) engaging in R&D was up to 1.2 million man/year; the number of published scientific papers ranked fifth in the world; the number of domestic invention patent applications amounted to 93,000 while the number of patents granted reached 21,000.

The Chinese government employed various tax incentives and preferential land policies to attract foreign investments, which made China one of the largest foreign investment recipients in the world. Coupled with the advantage of low labour cost, international transfer of technologies, equipment and management know-how contributed to the miracle of 'Made in China'.

The construction of the NIS has also started to bear fruit. Jefferson *et al.*'s (2003) analysis of innovation in China's large and medium-sized enterprises show that R&D activity, measured by both inputs and outputs, in the 1995–1999 period became more intensive, that most of the increase arose from a relatively few number of enterprises, and that patent application intensity nearly doubled over the same period. They conclude that rapid increases in R&D and new product intensity among high-end performers and the emergence of high-frequency patentees may harbinger an emerging core of high-end R&D performers. Nevertheless, their research also found that a broad-based takeoff of R&D activity was not yet observed.

Moreover, R&D undertakings by most organizations were concentrated on those projects that either involved simple adoption and minor modification of externally developed technology with an opportunity to make a razor-thin profit or were at the end of the technology life cycle. This was illustrated by the R&D input in 2005: the proportion of expenditure in trial and development increased to 76.95 per cent of China's overall R&D expenditure, much higher than in basic research and applied research. Correspondingly, technological innovation activities were mainly imitative and incremental in nature, and were based on technology imports with very few ingredients of indigenous innovation and radical innovation. An overdependence on foreign technologies resulted in a significant lack of motivation and capability to innovate on the part of enterprises.

Table 2.1 China's STI programmes, 1981–2005

Programme	Starting year	Objective
6th Five-Year Plan (1981–1985)		
National Key Technology R&D Programme	1984	Foster key technologies to upgrade traditional industries and create new ones
State Key Laboratory Proramme	1984	Support selected laboratories in universities, PRIs and firms
7th Five-Year Plan (1986–1990)		
National High-technology R&D Programme (863 Programme)	1986	Foster China's overall innovation capacity in high-tech sectors and enhance its international competitiveness
Spark Programme	1986	Support technology transfer to rural area and promote development of agriculture based on S&T achievements
Touch Programme	1988	Support development of high-tech sectors by setting up S&T industrial parks and incubators
State Key and New Product Programme	1988	Support new high-tech products for key industries
Technology Achievements Diffusion Programme	1990	Diffuse technologies to upgrade traditional industry and develop high-tech industry
8th Five-Year Plan (1991–1995)		
The Climbing Programme	1991	
The Project 211	1993	Support 100 Chinese universities to develop into research-intensive, world-class centres of learning

The Independent innovation-oriented development period, 2006 onward

9th Five-Year Plan (1996–2000)		
Technological Innovation Project	1996	Support domestic enterprises to become key players of independent innovation
National Programme on Key Basic Research Projects (973 Programme)	1997	Support basic research
Knowledge Innovation Project	1998	Support the CAS to transform into research centres of international excellence
Innovation Fund for Technology-based SMEs	1999	Support innovative activity of high-tech SMEs
Special Technology Development Project for Research Institutes	1999	Support central government-related technology development research institutes
Action Plan for Thriving Trade by Science and Technology	2000	Facilitate exports of high-tech products with high value added and foster international competitiveness
10th Five-Year Plan (2001–2005)		
Agricultural S&T Transfer Fund	2001	Foster the development of S&T achievements in agriculture and the diffusion of agricultural technologies

Source: adapted from OECD (2008).

The independent innovation-oriented development period: 2006 onward

After nearly 30 years in implementation, the policy of 'market for technology' faced predicaments: policy effectiveness diminished, impacts on the national economy waned, but damages to the environment and resources mounted. Technology imports undoubtedly helped China improve manufacturing capability; enterprises, however, neither had access to nor had actually acquired advanced technological capability that were deemed to be essential to China's technological upgrading. This explained why China was unable to develop product innovations embodied with home-developed intellectual property and hence faced constraint on the development of industries imposed by developed countries. At the same time, the breadth and depth of S&T integration in economic development remained insufficient, even though the market mechanism was playing a greater role in the allocation of S&T resources and research institutions and S&T personnel had greater motivation and capability to innovate in response to market needs.

As a result, from the early twenty-first century the Chinese government proposed to strengthen core competitiveness and to explore a new way of innovation with Chinese characteristics. At the National Science and Technology Awards Conference held in 2005, Premier Wen Jiabao proclaimed:

> Independent innovation is the underpinning of the rise of a country. While we need to import and assimilate advanced achievements from the rest of the world, more importantly, we need to innovate independently because core technology cannot be bought with money.[5]

It is against this background that in 2006 the Chinese government issued the 'Outline of Medium and Long-term National Plan for Science and Technology Development (2006–2020)' (MLNP), which set out the development strategy expressed as: 'independent innovation, leapfrogging in key areas, S&T supporting economic and social development, and S&T leading the future'. In addition to defining key areas and priorities of innovation, the Plan charted a clear path of reform of the S&T system and building of the NIS. This mainly included: (1) supporting and encouraging enterprises to become key innovation players; (2) deepening reforms of PRIs and establishing a modern research institution system; (3) promoting reforms of S&T management system; and (4) comprehensively promoting the construction of the NIS with Chinese characteristics. At the same time, the MLNP also listed a number of important policies and measures in nine dimensions, covering various aspects of innovation systems including finance and taxation, government procurement, financing, industries and regions. The purpose was to strengthen intellectual property strategy and technology standard strategy, and encourage enterprises to explore ways of re-innovation and independent innovation through technology acquisition and absorption.

There have been four major changes in the NIS since 2006. First, national S&T programmes have been restructured and differentiated into two distinct streams: major special programmes and basic programmes. The major special programmes are deemed as the most essential programmes of all and aimed at achieving breakthroughs in developments of strategic products, industrial generic technologies and major S&T projects. The central government set forth five criteria for selection of projects in the programme: (1) projects should address the country's strategic need and should be able to produce core technologies with home-grown intellectual property that support the development of new strategic industries; (2) projects should focus on critical generic technologies that can have far-reaching impacts on industrial competitiveness; (3) projects should aim at the critical bottlenecks that have constrained China's social and economic development; (4) projects should be of strategic importance in military and civic applications; (5) projects should deploy resources that are affordable within the country's financial means. An example of major special programmes is the big plane project which received the State Council's approval in 2007.[6] The 12th five-year planning listed 11 areas where support to major special programmes would be prioritized.

The basic programmes refer to those programmes as listed in Figure 2.1 and are regarded as the basic form of government support for S&T. They are made up of three components. The first component is the major programmes that are mainly concerned with major basic and applied research. The second component is the policy guidance programmes that aim at using policies to creating an innovation-friendly environment conducive to enterprise-led innovation. The third component is a range of programmes aiming at meeting the specific needs of technological innovation.

Second, major effort was made to implement the 'technological innovation guiding project', which aimed to use policy instruments as a lever to make enterprises the mainstay of innovation activities. Two specific efforts in this respect included the launch of the innovative enterprise pilot scheme in 2008 and the formation of four industry-specific strategic innovation alliances facilitated by the central government.

Third, experiments on financing of innovation shifted to focus on the development of innovation-oriented financial instruments, including the establishment of the SME Innovation Fund (InnoFund).

Fourth, 'cross-ministerial department meetings' at the central level and 'ministerial and provincial meetings' across central and regional level were set up as a new mechanism for approval of S&T projects and coordination of project implementation.

It is not only essential but also feasible for China to implement the above-mentioned S&T development strategy. After over 30 years of reform and opening up, the national conditions to support independent innovation are gradually falling into place. For example, 95 Chinese enterprises entered the ranks of the global top 500 in 2013[7] and a number of home-grown innovative enterprises like Haier and Huawei have emerged. China is now a leader in superconductor, large-scale water-turbine generator set manufacturing and aerospace. The higher education sector has transformed from elite education to mass education (the

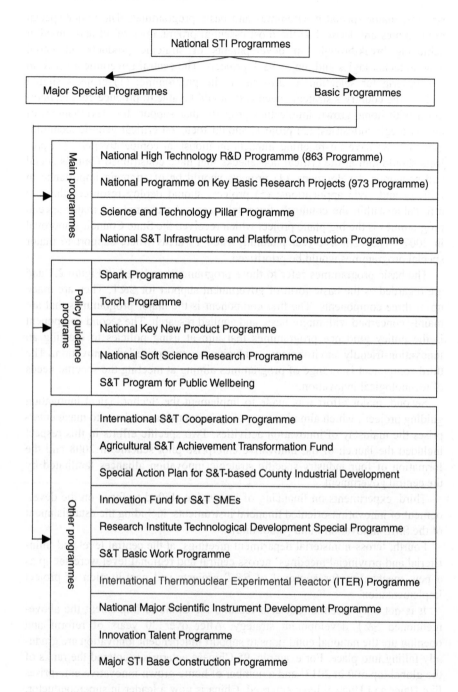

Figure 2.1 China's STI programmes at a glance.

enrolment rate has reached over 21 per cent). China now has a large pool of talent from graduates of domestic HEIs and returnees from abroad. The number of research institutions, colleges and universities with considerable S&T strength are growing, and a number of national science programmes and foundations have been launched.

Nevertheless, it should also be noted that the current push for independent innovation is fundamentally different from the policy of independent development and self-reliance adopted in the 1960s and 1970s. The current pursuit of independent innovation is firmly built on the idea of learning from all possible sources and absorption of overseas advanced technology in the light of global economic integration and opening to the outside world. It is not a return to the dated closed-door policy and is not aimed at reinventing the wheel.

Since 2007, China has placed strengthening of independent innovation capability and building of an innovative economy as a core of the national development strategy and the key to enhancing the overall national strength. Up to now, China has established a relatively comprehensive system of modern S&T and generated a large pool of scientists and engineers. As will be seen in Chapter 8, China's overall level of S&T development lies at the forefront of developing countries, and scientific research in some fields has already reached the level of international excellence. S&T achievements are producing greater impacts on the society.

Currently, the Chinese government is focusing its effort on advancing national technological innovation projects and pushing enterprises to become genuine actors of technological innovation through measures such as formation of industry-specific strategic innovation alliances, the development of industry-focused innovation service platforms, and the development of 500 top innovation-based enterprises. The overarching aim is to increase the impact of S&T on the economy.

National innovation system: components and governance

The components of the national innovation system

The overhaul of China's NIS after 1978 manifested itself in two major efforts: to overcome the legacy of the former system designed to serve the planned economic system, and to create a new institutional environment conducive to innovation. The revamped NIS in China, as depicted in Figure 2.2, now comprises seven interrelated components and displays a solid foundation on which the country can build to pursue its national goal of innovation development.

1   Policy formulation: this is the nerve brain of the system that sets the guiding principles, supporting policies and coordinating mechanisms.
2   Technological innovation: this component is concerned with innovation performers and their undertaking of innovation projects. The major elements in this component include the implementation of national projects of technological innovation, the building of enterprise innovation capability, and the development of new R&D organizations.

3 Knowledge innovation: this component is mainly concerned with improving learning, knowledge production and innovation at HEIs, implementing the Knowledge Innovation Project at CAS, and building of innovation capability and services in non-profit R&D organizations.

4 Defence technological innovation: two of the policy focuses are reforms of the S&T system in defence industries and the joined-up development of defence technologies and civilian technologies.

5 Technology intermediaries: this component is concerned with the development of institutions that bridges knowledge production and knowledge application. Policy measures have been taken to encourage the development of institutions such as technology markets, productivity promotion centres, innovation incubators, university science parks, demonstration projects of national technology transfer, and technology evaluation agencies.

6 S&T talent: this component embraces all elements concerning the supply of innovation talent in quantity and quality. Emphases have been placed on talent development in the HEI sector, use of expertise with returnees, and worldwide recruitment of top class scientists.

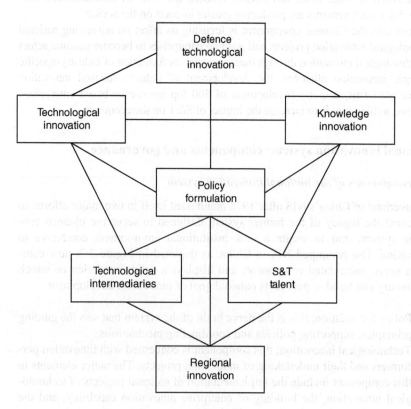

Figure 2.2 The national innovation system in China.

7   Regional innovation: this is a regional dimension of the NIS that is developed
    to reflect a region's innovation priorities and regional characteristics.

It has become clear from the MLNP that emphasis has now been placed on the
alignment of four key elements (enterprises, research institutes and HEIs, S&T
intermediaries, and government) in the innovation system.

Enterprises in national innovation system

Enterprises have always been a weak link in the NIS in China. The business
sector in the pre-reform era was dominated by SOEs that were virtually production units designated to fulfil mandatory tasks assigned by the government under
the directive planning regime. The traditional planned economic system in China
was not conducive to innovation, primarily due to: (1) a distorted macro policy
environment that featured artificially low interest rates, overvalued exchange
rates, low nominal wage rates, and low prices for living necessities and raw
materials, thereby distorting all necessary market signals; (2) a planned allocation mechanism for credit, foreign exchange, and other materials, thereby leaving
enterprises with few means of innovation; and (3) an ill-defined incentive structure that did not link performance with rewards (Ding, 1998; Lin *et al.*, 1996).
Clearly, this economic system equipped SOEs with neither the mission and
motivation nor capacity to undertake R&D. When it came to deal with imported
technologies, the system did not encourage SOEs to choose appropriate types of
technology, to use the imported technology efficiently, and to make adequate
assimilation efforts to build indigenous technological capabilities (Shi, 1998).

The profile of the business sector has undergone considerable changes since
1978, thanks to both reforms of the SOE sector and the emergence and thriving of
the private sector. The private sector is now composed of private enterprises,
foreign joint ventures, university and research institute spin-offs, and technology-
based enterprises/technology services agencies converted from former industry-
affiliated PRIs. The expansion of the business sector now means that the innovation
performance of this sector will strongly influence whether or not China will be able
to accomplish its mission of transforming itself into an innovation economy in
2020. Path dependence, however, also means that behaviours ingrained in the traditional system die hard. Hence, the Chinese government has specified that making
enterprises a key innovation player and raising their innovation capability and performance are the core elements of its innovation strategy.

This is a difficult task. As far as the SOE sector is concerned, its dominance
in the domestic strategic extraction and heavy industrial sectors presently dilutes
its motivation to innovate; the corporate governance may also give management
insufficient incentive to undertake long-term, risky investment in R&D. Innovation in the private sector faces different challenges. Lack of capital has been
identified as a barrier to innovation; institutional transition has also turned many
private enterprises into opportunists who act on making quick money through
means of duplicative imitation rather than innovation with genuine novelty.

In order to strengthen the role of enterprises as a true innovation player in the innovation system, the Chinese government has taken a range of measures. Apart from fiscal incentives that have widely been used by many other countries, China has also referred to a number of new policy instruments. For example, the 'Catalogue for Guidance of Key Technology Innovation Projects' was regularly updated and published to align business R&D efforts to national innovation priorities. Public procurement was used to help create markets for innovative businesses. High-technology zones and business incubators were established to provide an innovation-friendly environment for new and established businesses. Four industry-research strategic alliances were formed in 2007 to facilitate collaboration between industries, universities and research institutions.[8] Various public technology R&D and service platforms were constructed to provide services for enterprise technology innovation.

University and research institutions in the national innovation system

In 1998, the State Council, in its major reshuffle to resolve ten ministries, decided to convert 242 public research institutes affiliated to the Economic and Commercial Commission (ECC) into market-oriented entities. Similar measures were later taken by other ministerial departments and local governments. By 2005, 375 PRIs at the central government level and 1,000 PRIs at the local government level completed their conversion into market-oriented research institutes.[9] As a result, the public research system was downsized, rebalanced and better resourced. These research institutes continue to play a key role in supporting basic and strategic research, as well as mission-oriented research.

In the NIS, research institutions function as knowledge innovation, dissemination and transfer. Similarly, the main function of HEIs is knowledge dissemination, high-quality talent cultivation, and engagement in knowledge innovation and transfer. In order to build an innovative economy, the Chinese government has made constant efforts to strengthen the leading role of research institutions and to enhance the fundamental role of universities. Through implementing the Knowledge Innovation Project since 1998, the Chinese Academy of Sciences has made strategic adjustment to the layout of scientific research strength. As a result, scientific research conditions have improved remarkably; the personnel structure has been optimized; more achievements have been made in the fields of basic research, strategic high-tech research and research concerned with sustainable development. Through a different approach to reform, non-profit research institutions[10] optimized their structure, gradually developed core research teams with high competence and expertise, and increased remarkably non-profit innovation and service provision capability.

In short, the building of excellent research universities has won initial success; the quality of innovative talents churning from the HEIs has continuously improved; and the research capacity has been significantly increased. Various forms of cooperation in personnel training, scientific research and serving enterprises have been carried out between research institutions and HIEs.

S&T intermediaries in the national innovation system

In the market economy, S&T intermediaries link up industries, universities and research institutions, and bridge gaps between the needs of the economy and supply of S&T. There are a range of S&T intermediaries China are keen to encourage the development of, such as S&T information services, intellectual property services, asset evaluation institutions, investment and financing institutions, generic technology services, as well as various sorts of business incubators. These intermediaries link enterprises with universities and R&D institutions for the formation of networks beneficial to the application of innovation achievements and industrialization. They are important in improving innovation efficiency and reducing innovation risks.

As a conduit between various innovation actors, intermediaries play a crucial role in promoting knowledge dissemination and technology transfer among governments, innovators and markets.

In order to build an innovative country, S&T intermediaries are continuously encouraged to expand in business scope and capacity. For instance, institutions like productivity promotion centres[11] and innovation service centres (incubators) are directly involved in technology innovation; institutions like S&T evaluation centres and information centres provide consulting services for enterprises and society; institutions such as technology property rights exchange agencies and talent agencies provide services for innovation resource allocation.

Government in the national innovation system

In the NIS, governments facilitate the creation of a favourable environment for innovation through formulating policies and improving innovation institutions. As opposed to many other countries, the role of the government in the innovation system in China is rather broad and compelling. Similar to those developmental states as observed in many East Asian economies, the Chinese government takes more responsibility for guiding and stimulating innovation. This covers formulating development plans of the NIS; implementing monitoring, evaluation and regulation on organizations; providing support in the way of finance, taxation, financial and industrial policies for innovation activities; supporting the construction of infrastructure, which includes national information infrastructure, scientific research bases, educational infrastructure, technology service centres and so on; protecting appropriation of innovation through institutional arrangements, administrative or legal means; improving the legal system to maintain an orderly market for innovation activities; formulating innovative policies to stimulate innovative behaviour, to promote collaboration of innovative behaviours, and to promote the continuous increase of innovative investment; cultivating and improving an orderly and standardized technology market system to function as comprehensive and efficient mechanisms for innovative resource allocation; establishing a balance mechanism between private and public sectors to stimulate the private sector innovation while advancing social application of innovation achievements by maintaining enough public demands; correcting the deviation caused by market selection such as lack of coordination and the frustration of public welfare research, through the leverage of public investment.

Currently in China, under the organization and guidance of governments at all levels, an increasing number of innovative organizations, including enterprises, scientific research institutions and HIEs with their own advantages and characteristics, have emerged.

Governance of the national innovation system

The governance of the NIS in China consists of several major bodies sitting at various tiers. At the top level are three key institutions charged with making strategic decisions on the country's medium- and long-term priorities of science, technology and innovation. The second tier is a number of ministerial level agencies. The third tier is provincial and local governments. In addition, new mechanisms have been created to support horizontal coordination and coordination across different levels of government (see Figure 2.3).

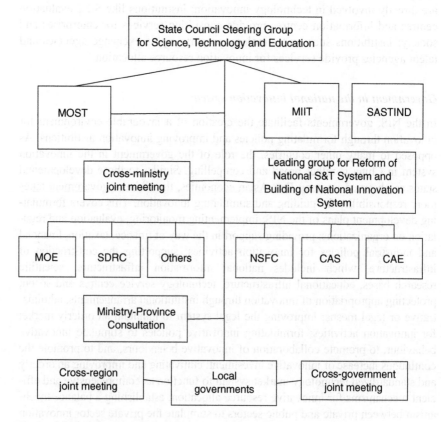

Figure 2.3 Governance in the national innovation system.

The State Council Steering Group for Science, Technology and Education

The State Council Steering Group for Science, Technology and Education headed by the Premier is a top-level decision-making and coordinating body on strategic matters. It is responsible for studying and reviewing national development strategy and major policies of science, technology and education; discussing and reviewing significant S&T and education tasks and programmes; coordinating important inter-governmental relationships related to science, technology and education between governmental departments and between central government and local governments.

Ministry of Science and Technology

The Ministry of Science and Technology (MOST) is a department under the State Council and is charged with the coordination and management of civilian-focused science and technology. It plays an important role in the NIS, functioning as a central government agent for researching and drafting S&T development plans and policies, regulations and departmental rules to promote innovation and socio-economic development; researching major S&T issues impacting on economic and social development; researching and formulating the significant layout and priorities of S&T development; promoting the construction of the NIS to improve national innovation capability; organizing the formulation of the medium- and-long term plans and annual plans for national civilian S&T development; researching and formulating policies and measures for strengthening basic research and high-tech development; overseeing the administration, implementation and management of national S&T programmes, mainly including three national major S&T programmes (Major Basic Research Programme, High-tech Research Development Programme and Science and Technology Pillar Programme), three plans for the construction of R&D conditions including key laboratory, science and technology infrastructure platform construction and international cooperation, as well as programmes for the industrialization facilities, such as Spark Programme, Torch Programme, Achievement Promotion, New Products and Technology Innovation Fund for Technology-based SMEs; strengthening the industrialization of high and new technology and the promotion of applied technology; researching the rational allocation of S&T talents, and proposing favourable policies for S&T personnel; promoting the popularization of S&T; and formulating guidelines and policies for international S&T cooperation and exchanges.

State Administration for Science, Technology and Industry for National Defence

In the NIS, State Administration for Science, Technology and Industry for National Defence (SASTIND) is the coordination and administrative agency of military S&T with responsibility for the drafting of plans, policies, standards and regulations of science, technology and industry for national defence, and supervising their implementation. SASTIND is a civilian ministerial department within the State Council and is a subordinate agency of the Ministry of Industry and Information Technology (MIIT). It was created to replace the Commission for Science, Technology and Industry for National Defence (COSTIND) under the Plan for Restructuring the State Council passed by the First Session of the Eleventh National People's Congress in 2008.

Ministerial bodies with S&T management function

1 Ministry of Education

In the NIS, the Ministry of Education (MOE) has main responsibility for supporting further and higher education institutions to develop skills students need to contribute to the innovative economy and supporting basic research to improve China's long-term competitiveness. Through a series of policies and measures like Project 211 and Project 985, MOE has supported a selected number of top research universities to perform knowledge creation, technology innovation and knowledge dissemination at the highest level.

2 State Development and Reform Commission

The State Development and Reform Commission (SDRC) in the innovation system is mainly charged with supporting the construction of innovation capacity infrastructure. During the 11th Five-Year Plan (2007–2012), for example, SDRC supported a series of major S&T infrastructure projects, creation of a number of national engineering research centres and national engineering laboratories, formation of a number of national centres for enterprise technology certification, and set-up of basic supporting platforms for independent innovation.

Besides supports to the construction of innovation capacity infrastructure, SDRC also supports industrialization of R&D outputs, such as organizing the implementation of a number of special projects of high-tech industrialization, such as full-scale manufacturing of new energy technologies. Moreover, it actively advances assimilation and re-innovation of heavy machinery like nuclear power, high-speed railway and the large complete set of ethylene technical equipment. Furthermore, it supports the building of a number of high-tech industry bases and formulates strategic high-tech industrial policies concerning integrated circuit and software, biology and so on.

3 Other ministries and commissions

In the NIS, other government departments such as Ministry of Information Industry, Ministry of Agriculture and Ministry of Public Health are mainly charged with overseeing S&T innovation activities within their respective remits.

In addition, Ministry of information Industry is in charge of the technology standard formulation in the information industry.

Other agencies

1 The National Natural Science Foundation of China (NSFC)

The NSFC is an institution responsible for the management of the National Natural Science Fund, with a particular emphasis on promoting and financing basic research and, to a lesser extent, applied research in China. In addition, NSFC cooperates with MOST to draw up principles, policies and plans for the development of basic research in China.

2 Chinese Academy of Sciences (CAS)

As the largest research institution in China, CAS plays an important role in the NIS. It is responsible for the Knowledge Innovation Project, which was implemented in three stages: the initial stage (1998–2000), the development stage (2001–2005) and the improvement stage (2006–2010). The overall objective of the Knowledge Innovation Project was: by 2010, CAS was to become the national knowledge innovation centre of natural science and high technology that conducts research of national strategic importance and at international S&T frontiers, the scientific research base of international excellence, the base of cultivating high-level talents and promoting the development of high-tech, and the national S&T knowledge library, scientific think tank and the S&T talent bank with international impact.

3 Chinese Academy of Engineering (CAE)

CAE is a consulting academic institution that bestows the highest honour of academician to Chinese scientists in the field of engineering technology. It carries out strategic research on important issues in national engineering S&T, provides consultations to policy-makers and promotes the development of engineering S&T. Its main task is to advance the solidarity and cooperation of the Chinese engineering S&T community, to advance Chinese engineering S&T, and to support the development of engineering S&T teams and outstanding talents so as to serve the sustainable development of the national economy.

Cross-government coordination mechanisms

1 Leading Group for Reform of National S&T System and Building of National Innovation System

The Leading Group was formed in July 2012 as a new high-level, cross-government platform for overall policy coordination. It is headed by State

Councillor Liu Yandong and brings together representatives of 26 different ministries, the military and non-governmental organizations to deal with policies concerning reform of the national S&T system and building of the NIS. It is specifically charged with deliberating new major policy measures, coordinating critical issues with broad implications, and generalizing and promoting good practices.

2 Cross-government joint meeting

This is a platform for horizontal coordination of a wide range of government departments on major issues of STI policies and implementation. Recent years have seen a proliferation of cross-government joint meetings. They have been established at three different levels. At the central government level, an example is the establishment of Cross-Ministerial Joint Meeting for the Implementation of National Intellectual Property Strategy in August 2008. Members of the Joint Meeting consist of representatives of 28 ministerial departments. At provincial level, for example, Ningxia Province set up a joint meeting system in 2013 that is represented by the heads of 12 provincial departments. At cross-region level, the best known example is the Joint Meeting on Building Innovation System in the Yangtze River Delta that has representatives of 22 cities in the region and has been fully functional since 2003. We will return to this type of coordination mechanism in greater detail in Chapter 7. The tasks of cross-government joint meetings generally are to improve the coherence of cross-departmental S&T programmes through coordinated and joined-up actions on policies, policy and regulation fine-tuning and implementation, coordinated resource allocation, and policy impact assessment.

3 Ministry-province consultation

The pilot of ministry-province consultation system as a vertical coordination mechanism across different levels of government started in 2002 when MOST set up a consultation platform with Anhui, Shanghai and Tianjin for joined-up actions on the building of national key laboratories. This institutional set-up was formalized and rolled out in 2007. In this consultation system, innovation policy is more of a joint responsibility, and policy deliberation and implementation are tailored in accordance with national priorities and regional conditions.

National innovation system and regional innovation system

China is a country with a vast territory. Regions in the coastal, middle and western parts of China display unmistakable differences in conditions, stages and strengths of economic development. The 'super-vast territory', as referred to by Zhang (2012), clearly indicates that needs for, and conditions of, innovation vary considerably between regions and that treating the NIS as a homogenous spatial system of innovation can be dangerous. In fact, China has a long tradition of central and local governments both playing a complementary role in planning and driving economic growth. This rare positive legacy of the planned economic regime was summed up illustratively by the late Mao Zedong as "walking on two legs", meaning central planning with a scope for local adaptation. In this sense, the effectiveness of the regional innovation system at the sub-national level matters a lot more than many other small countries in the performance of the NIS.

The regional innovation system is a networked system consisting of various innovation subjects and their associations, operating mechanisms and institutions within a region. Its purpose is to stimulate knowledge development, knowledge acquisition and knowledge application at the regional level. As part of the NIS, the regional innovation system is the building blocks of the NIS, following the national strategy and contributing to the NIS. In another word, the national system of innovation acts as a coordination mechanism for achieving the national mission of innovation and growth, whilst regional systems of innovation function as an implementation mechanism.

Differences in function and positioning

Composed of various innovation subjects within a particular region, a regional innovation system features more specific institutional arrangements and displays more unique regional culture. The exemplars of such differences in regional culture include marine culture in the coastal areas, Beijing culture, Shanghai culture and Shaanxi inland culture in the geographical sense, as well as entrepreneurial culture in Shenzhen thanks to the large-scale inflow of venturing immigrants since the start of reform and opening up. All of the above mentioned have a strong impact on the formation of a regional innovation system. A recent study on Chinese innovation conducted by the NESTA, the UK's innovation foundation, finds visible diverse models of innovation among China's coast hotspots and labels this diversity as "many Chinas, many innovation systems" (Bound *et al.*, 2013: 39).

Compared with the NIS at the macro level and the enterprise innovation system at the micro level, regional innovation systems are functioning at the meso level, displaying differences in function and positioning from the NIS.

At the national level, China uses the development of the NIS to serve four essential functions: (1) National innovation strategy formulation function. Through this function, national priority of innovation is identified and corresponding national strategies are drawn up. Examples of overarching national strategies include independent innovation strategy, the Knowledge Innovation Project of CAS, Project 985 of Ministry of Education, technological innovation for national defence purposes (e.g. the manned spacecraft programme), etc.; (2) Leapfrogging function. This is to push indigenous innovation to the frontier of technological developments in order to catch up and overtake innovation leaders in selected fields. Examples include the '863 Program', the 'Biotechnology Industry Power Project', etc.; (3) Balancing function. This is to use the development of the NIS to counter regional inequality. Key balancing initiatives have included the 'Westbound S&T Innovation Programme' that aims to channel resources westbound across the country to support innovation-led growth in the western region, 'Revitalizing the Traditional Industrial Bases of the Northeast' that aims to facilitate new industrial development to replace declining traditional manufacturing industries, and the 'Growth of the Central Region' that aims to help provinces in the central region to fulfil their growth potential; (4) Guiding function. This is to use resources earmarked for the building of the NIS as a lever to guide regional innovation and involve regions in the implementation of major R&D projects, so as to achieve a win–win situation in S&T development for the country as a whole and regions involved.

At the regional level, regional innovation systems function in a much more specific manner, since there is no provision of such public goods as national defence. It mainly aims to seek sources of innovation and promote their dynamic integration with the local economy so as to encourage S&T to better serve regional economic and social development. In addition, the regional innovation system also owns the following functions:

1 Rational allocation of innovation resources within the region. For instance, in Beijing, the incredible development of R&D industry and S&T parks has promoted clusters of S&T in the Zhongguancun Science Park, involving CAS, Peking University and Tsinghua University, which enables Beijing to fully play its comparative advantage as the national S&T centre. Similarly, Guangdong attracts R&D resources from other regions and foreign multinational companies to cluster through building a regional innovation system with enterprises as the pillar.

2 Implementation of objectives and tasks of the NIS. For instance, based on the national S&T layout within the region, provinces like Sichuan and Shaanxi assist and support the realization of national innovation strategy objectives through measures like building S&T infrastructure, matchfunding in resources and management to advance regional innovation capacity as well as the economic and social development.

3 Coordination of inter-regional and regional innovation activities. For instance, the building of regional innovation systems in Beijing needs not only to cultivate sources of innovation within the region, but also to create favourable conditions for dissemination. In addition, labour division and cooperation with the surrounding areas like Tianjin are also being taken into account.

In terms of positioning, the NIS aims to set up a comprehensive system of knowledge and technology innovation, dissemination and commercialization/industrialization, while regional innovation systems are concerned with regional comparative advantage/resources and strengthening the technological capability of local leading industries, through technology development, application and diffusion for commercialization and industrialization within the region. Regional innovation systems are also concerned with support to the growth of industrial clusters with regional characteristics. For instance, three emerging innovation poles in China, including Pearl River Delta, Yangtze River Delta and Beijing-Tianjin region, have different core innovation capabilities. In Pearl River Delta, innovations are driven by core capabilities in the industries of electrical power, machinery, electronic and information technology. In Yangtze River Delta, innovations are driven by specialization of industrial sectors, while in the Beijing-Tianjin region, innovation capabilities are underlined by the intensity of science and technology research.

Goals sharing and complementarity

Despite differences in functions and positioning, there is a close relationship between the NIS and regional innovation systems. Simply put, neither the regional innovation system nor NIS exists totally independent of each other.

A common feature of innovation systems on both levels in China is that they are government-led. Different from enterprises that undertake innovation activities under the rules of the market to pursue profit maximization, governments play a critical role in shaping both NIS and regional innovation system in order to maximize the public interest. On the one hand, regional innovation systems led by regional (local) governments not only embody regional comparative advantages and characteristics, but also serve the strategic objective and overall layout of the NIS. On the other hand, the NIS led by the central government achieves its overall objective through regional innovation, with one of the aims to promote regional development and inter-regional coordinated development.

The national and regional innovation systems complement each other. In other words, regional innovation systems emerge from the NIS, and constantly adapt to the development of the NIS. The enhancement of regional innovation capacity and the realization of regional innovation system objectives need common, key and significant technologies and some infrastructure platforms. Many of them are offered and should be offered by the NIS, since regional innovation subjects do not have the necessary capability and conditions to offer them. For instance, as the innovation poles in different regional innovation systems, 53 National High-tech Industrial Development Zones have been supported to some degree by central government agencies such as MOST. Many national significant S&T programmes like 'The National Key Technology R&D Programme', 'Spark Programme' and 'Torch Programme' are undertaken by regions (locals), which not only resolved the problem of insufficient funds in regions but also improved the regional innovation capacity.

However, lack of sufficient innovation resources, financing in particular, does exist in both the NIS and regional innovation systems. Undertaken by the national innovation subjects, the building of the NIS also needs platforms and resources supplemented by regional innovation subjects. While actively applying for and undertaking the national innovation projects and science and technology innovation programmes, regions (locals) usually support the national projects/programmes by adding them into the regional innovation project/programme list.

In order to better build an innovative country, a regional innovation system, tailored for regional characteristics and enhancement of regional innovation capacity, should be established under the guidance of the principles of the NIS. Currently, the Chinese government has approved the establishment of two national independent innovation demonstration zones, i.e. Zhongguancun in Beijing and East Lake in Wuhan, Hubei Province, and has deployed 53 national high-tech industrial development zones.

National innovation system and sectoral innovation system

The sectoral innovation system is a networked system consisting of various innovation subjects and their associations, operating mechanisms and institutions within an industry. Its purpose is to stimulate independent technological innovation and technological upgrading in a specific industry. As part of NIS building, a sectoral innovation system directly addresses the needs of national economic and social development, which not only reflects the national objectives but also provides S&T supports for industrial development. In short, it is an important part of the NIS.

In order to strengthen technology innovation of the non-profit industry, the MLNP explicitly requires to "attach importance to the building of the scientific research capacity of the non-profit industry, and establish a consistent support mechanism for science and technology in the non-profit industry". To this end, the Chinese government has set up a special fund for scientific research in the non-profit industry, specifically targeting sectors with a heavy load of non-profit scientific research tasks and supporting them in emergent, nurturing and basic scientific research. Up to now, pilot projects have involved 11 industrial sectors and relevant governmental departments, including Ministry of Agriculture, Ministry of Public Health, State Environmental Protection Administration and China Earthquake Administration.

In order to strengthen industrial technological innovation, the Chinese government has advanced the enterprise-oriented reform of research institutions in the field of technology development through the reform of the S&T system. Moreover, through policies and measures like continuing supports for them to undertake national science and technology programmes/projects, strengthening their infrastructure building, and extending preferential tax policy, the Chinese government supported institutions under enterprise-oriented reform to enhance their innovation capacity, to carry out industrial generic technology R&D and to take a more crucial role in technology innovation and industrialization of S&T.

During the 11th Five-Year Plan, the Chinese government has intensified its efforts to build key national laboratories and engineering technology research centres in institutions under enterprise-oriented reform. In addition, through the 'Technology Innovation Guidance Project', the Chinese government selected several key areas, linked by the generic technology and important standard research, to guide the formation of a variety of strategic industry-university-research institution alliances with leading enterprises, so as to further promote universities and scientific research institutions to better serve the advancement of industrial technology.

Through all these initiatives, China has developed and applied a number of key generic technologies of national significance. The independent development capability, the level of domestic manufacturing and comprehensive engineering capacity of important technology equipment have considerably improved. The technological capability of basic industry and processing manufacturing industry has been further strengthened. A number of emerging industries such as electronics and information technology, biomedicine, new energy and advanced manufacturing have been vigorously developed. The scale of high-tech industry has been continuously expanding and a large number of dynamic high-tech enterprises have rapidly grown.

National innovation system and economic opening-up

In recent years, S&T internationalization has become an integral part of globalization. The worldwide effective allocation of S&T resources has brought considerable changes in the organizational structure and ways of innovation in scientific research, which provides opportunities for developing countries to tap into international S&T resources in order to speed up technology advancement. In the new era of globalization, building of the NIS with independent innovation as core is based on the strategic thought of constantly expanding and strengthening international S&T cooperation as well as making use of global S&T resources. Ever since China launched its MLNP in 2006, there have been suspicions in the international community as to whether the 'independent innovation' policy illustrates its misunderstanding of how global innovation now works (Crookes, 2012).[12] It is clearly not the case that China will revert to the closed system of the pre-reform era in its pursuit of independent innovation. The increasing integration of the innovation system in China with the global innovation system since 2006 suggests otherwise.

To strengthen national independent innovation capacity, the Chinese government deems it essential to make full use of international S&T cooperation and exchange. Measures includes: (1) encouragement of research institutions and higher education institutions to set up joint laboratories or R&D centres with overseas R&D institutions, and support for the implementation of international cooperation projects within the framework of bilateral and multilateral S&T cooperation agreements; (2) supporting Chinese scientists and research institutions to actively participate in important international scientific projects and academic organizations; (3) supporting enterprises to employ foreign scientists and engineers, and attracting excellent talents studying abroad to return home and attracting overseas high-level talents to serve China through attractive policies and measures; (4) supporting Chinese enterprises to 'go global' to increase exports of high-tech and their products as well as to set up overseas R&D branches or industrial bases.

In implementing an independent innovation strategy, China has shown no intention to exclude technology importation and sees innovation through assimilation and absorption of imported technology as an important path for strengthening independent innovation capacity. Technology imports have become an important avenue to learn advanced S&T knowledge from all over the world. As a developing country, China will continue to import overseas advanced technology and attach more importance to the digestion, absorption and innovation of the imported technology. At the same time, China will continue to create a favourable environment to attract multinational corporations to set up R&D centres in China, to encourage Chinese enterprises and research institutions to carry out international technological cooperation, so as to accelerate the building of an internationalized innovation system.

Notes

1 For a more detailed account of technology imports in this period, see Shi (1998).
2 The four special economic zones are Shenzhen, Zhuhai and Shantou in Guangdong Province and Xiamen in Fujian Province.
3 See '中共中央关于科学技术体制改革的决定' (Decisions on the Reform of Science and Technology System), available at http://cpc.people.com.cn/GB/64162/134902/8092254.html (accessed 14 June 2011).
4 The figure of 21 and 1 within the name 211 are from the abbreviation of the twenty-first century and approximately one hundred universities. The motivation for the project was to turn the country's top universities' research standards up to international excellence. Universities that fall under the scope of Project 211, which totalled 112 at the end of 2011, train 80 per cent of the country's doctoral students, two-thirds of its graduate students, half the international students and a third of undergraduates. In the first three phases of Project 211 between 1995 and 2011, the Central Government invested 17.7 billion yuan (US$2.81 billion) in the project. In 1998, China further concentrated its efforts to create elite universities by launching Project 985, named after the date it was launched on 5 May 1998. This project provided extra funding to ten universities, and it has expanded to cover 39 universities by 2012. See report 'An ambitious objective' in *Beijing Review*, 29 February 2012.
5 See Premier Wen's speech published on 28 March 2005, available at http://news.xinhuanet.com/newscenter/2005-03/28/content_2754996.htm (accessed 15 June 2012).
6 For more information about China's 'big plane' project, see 'China wants to rival Boeing, Airbus with its C919 "big plane"', *USA Today*, 15 October 2009.
7 See Fortune 500 2013 at http://money.cnn.com/magazines/fortune/fortune500/2013/full_list/ (accessed 10 August 2013).
8 Four industry-research strategic alliances were Strategic Alliance for Technological Innovation in Circularable Steel Manufacturing Process, Strategic Alliance to Blaze Trails of New Coal (Energy) Chemical Technology (SACCT), Strategic Alliance for Technology Innovation of Coal Development and Utilization, and Technology Innovation Strategic Alliance for Agricultural Machinery Industry.
9 See MOST (2006), *China Science and Technology Development Report 2005*, p. 37.
10 They refer to those organizations that undertake not-for-profit research activities in areas of agriculture, forestry, medical care, environmental protection, meteorology and earthquake.

11 In 2011, there were 2,274 productivity promotion centres (PPC) nationwide, with an employment of 38,666 people. The main services PPC provide are consultancy, S&T intelligence, technology services, and training.

12 Another common misperception of independent innovation is to interpret it as "products, technology, and brands that are designed, developed, and owned by Chinese companies", see *Issue Brief: New Developments in China's Domestic Policies*, US China Business Council, January 2010, available at www.uschina.org/public/documents/2010/domestic_innovation_policies.pdf (accessed 10 July 2012).

3   Fiscal incentives for innovation

Fiscal policies (government expenditure, tax and subsidy) in China have a major role to play in shaping how the national innovation strategy will be delivered and how the targets of the MLNP can be achieved by 2020. After China launched its long-term innovation strategy in 2006 and shifted its emphasis to independent innovation from exchange of market access for foreign technology transfer, the government's fiscal policies have been considerably overhauled in order to boost R&D spending and to deliver the STI strategy and policies. Broadly speaking, domestic R&D spending in China comes from four sources: government expenditure, enterprise investment, foreign investment, and other funds (including financial institutions). In addition to their own expenditure on S&T and direct investment in R&D, the Chinese government has used policies of tax incentives to achieve a number of aims: to increase the overall level of R&D spending throughout the economy; to affect the distribution of R&D across sectors so as to channel investment into the more promising sectors and to loosen constraints, such as the supply of S&T workers; to directly support the development of selected technologies in fields with greater long-term social returns; to encourage capital investment in imported plants and equipment to promote technology absorption; and to draw FDI into selected industries to serve as a conduit for new technological innovation and possibly also as the axes for cluster development in technology zones. In this chapter we will examine China's government expenditure on S&T first and then analyse the system of tax incentives China has developed to support independent innovation. Government direct investment in R&D will be examined in the next chapter.

Government expenditures on S&T

Governments in China are always significant contributors to domestic expenditure on R&D, only second after enterprises in investment. As displayed in Figure 3.1, government expenditure made up 29.9 per cent of domestic investment in R&D in 2003. Despite a reduction in expenditure, governments still contributed 21.6 per cent from their budgets in 2012. As governments are changing their role as R&D investors to R&D investment facilitators, the increase of enterprise funds as a share of R&D expenditure from 60.2 per cent in 2003 to 74 per cent

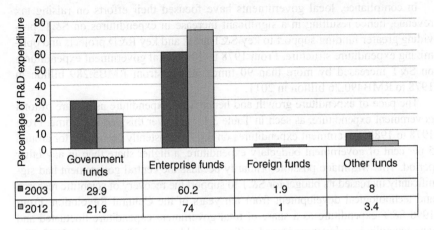

	Government funds	Enterprise funds	Foreign funds	Other funds
■2003	29.9	60.2	1.9	8
■2012	21.6	74	1	3.4

Figure 3.1 Expenditure on R&D by sources, 2003 and 2012 (source: *China Statistical Yearbook on Science and Technology 2013*).

in 2012 suggests the impact of public funding leverage. It can therefore be inferred that whether or not the target of domestic investment in R&D as a share of GDP as stated in the MLNP can be achieved will depend on both the quantity and quality of government expenditure on R&D as a catalyst for enterprise spending.

The guiding principle and government spending

To match the ambitious objectives of the national innovation strategy with necessary resources, China set forth a guiding principle on S&T expenditure in the Law on S&T Progress issued by the National People's Congress (NPC) in July 1993 and amended in December 2007. The Law stipulated that government expenditures on S&T should grow faster than regular government tax revenue in the same financial year. This has legally bound provincial and local governments in their S&T budgeting. Information available in the public domain suggests that some local governments have set specific growth target in their budget. For example, Zhejiang Province specified in the local S&T promotion regulations that expenditure on S&T at the provincial, municipal and county level should grow 8, 4.2 and 3.2 per cent faster than regular tax revenue in the same financial year respectively.[1] Hebei Province in its amended regulation on S&T progress stated that expenditure on S&T at all levels of government should grow 2 per cent faster than regular tax revenue.[2] The MLNP embedded the principle of S&T budgeting in the strategy by reiterating that governments of all levels should treat S&T expenditure as a top priority and ring-fence it in the budget and that they should distribute additional tax revenue in accordance with their legal obligation to ensure expenditure on S&T grows faster than tax revenue in the annual budget.

In compliance, local governments have focused their efforts on raising tax revenue, hence resulting in a significant increase in expenditures on S&T, providing greater funding support to key S&T areas and key R&D projects and optimizing expenditure structure. From 1978 to 2011, total government expenditures on S&T increased by more than 90 times, arising from RMB5.289 billion in 1978 to RMB490.26 billion in 2011.

The pace of expenditure growth and hence S&T expenditure as a share of total government expenditure, as seen in Table 3.1, vary over this period of time. From 1978 to 1988, government expenditures on S&T consistently accounted for around 5 per cent of government budgetary expenditure, a higher share than in any other period. This was made possible primarily because the central government had significantly increased its budget for S&T to support the recovery of scientific research and technological development from ten years of the Cultural Revolution. From 1990 S&T expenditure as a share of total government expenditure fluctuated and was generally in a downward trend, with a record low of 3.28 per cent in 2000. The causes of the observed relative decline of spending are two-fold. On the one hand, governments increasingly faced many competing demands in the budget to address pressing issues of economic and social development and they were susceptible to perceive the S&T budget as a non-core item because the impact of expenditures on S&T can take a long time to be seen. On the other hand, as the Chinese economy evolved to embrace the market economic system, governments have gradually aimed at playing as a facilitator of support for S&T activities rather than an enforcer of compulsory administrative directives and a principal funder of S&T activities. Direct support for innovation had accordingly changed by reducing the budget for operating costs of research institutes and increasing the budget for project-based funding. At the beginning of the twenty-first century, when China launched its new innovation strategy and pledged for independent innovation, policies were readjusted, leading to an increase in government expenditures on S&T. The ratio started to pick up again, rising to 4.49 per cent of government expenditure in 2011.

As shown in Figure 3.2, the growth pattern of government expenditures on S&T roughly is in alignment with the overall government expenditure. It grew relatively fast from 1978 to 1984, then until 1990, at a rate of no more than 10 per cent, with the lowest of 1.08 per cent in 1988. From 1991 to 1997, the growth rate was above 15 per cent except for 12 per cent in 1992, and followed by sharp rise and fall in the next five years from 1998 to 2002. It has grown even faster since 2004.

For many years, central government was the principal contributor to expenditures on S&T. As in Table 3.2, central government's S&T budget made up two-thirds of the overall expenditure, while local governments contributed one-third to the budget. China's expenditures on S&T reached a significant milestone in 2007 when local government's share in the budget rose to 50.7 per cent, reflecting the impact of decentralization and local government's growing significance in funding S&T. Similarly, local government expenditures on S&T as a percentage of its total government expenditure rose from 2 per cent in 1997 to 2.62 per cent in 2011, indicating local governments' greater support for S&T activities.

Table 3.1 Government expenditure and government expenditures on S&T: 1978–2011 (unit: RMB billion)

Year	Total government expenditure	Growth of government expenditure (%)	Expenditures on S&T	Growth of expenditures on S&T (%)	% of total government expenditure
1978	112.2	32.56	5.3	27.51	4.7
1979	128.2	14.23	6.2	17.77	4.9
1980	122.9	-4.13	6.5	3.69	5.26
1981	113.8	-7.36	6.2	-4.66	5.41
1982	123.0	8.05	6.5	6.02	5.31
1983	141.0	14.59	7.9	21.04	5.61
1984	170.1	20.68	9.5	19.85	5.57
1985	200.4	17.83	10.3	8.31	5.12
1986	220.5	10.01	11.3	9.73	5.11
1987	226.2	2.60	11.4	1.08	5.03
1988	249.1	10.12	12.1	6.44	4.86
1989	282.4	13.35	12.8	5.57	4.53
1990	308.4	9.20	13.9	8.80	4.51
1991	338.7	9.83	16.1	15.50	4.74
1992	374.2	10.50	18.9	17.78	5.06
1993	464.2	24.05	22.6	19.21	4.86
1994	579.3	24.78	26.8	18.90	4.63
1995	682.4	17.80	30.2	12.72	4.43
1996	793.8	16.32	34.9	15.30	4.39
1997	923.4	16.33	40.9	17.28	4.43
1998	1,079.8	16.94	43.9	7.27	4.06
1999	1,318.8	22.13	54.4	24.01	4.10
2000	1,588.7	20.46	57.6	5.83	3.62
2001	1,890.3	18.99	70.3	22.19	3.70
2002	2,205.3	16.67	81.6	16.06	3.70
2003	2,465.0	11.78	94.5	15.73	3.83
2004	2,848.7	15.57	109.5	15.95	3.84
2005	3,393.0	19.11	133.5	21.88	3.93
2006	4,042.3	19.13	168.9	26.49	4.20
2007	4,915.1	21.59	211.4	25.17	4.25
2008	6,259.3	27.35	258.2	22.16	4.12
2009	7,630.0	21.90	322.5	24.91	4.23
2010	8,987.4	17.79	411.4	27.52	4.58
2011	10,924.8	21.56	490.3	19.16	4.49

Sources: *China Statistical Yearbook on S&T; China Statistical Yearbook.*

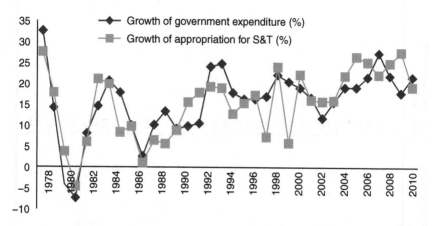

Figure 3.2 Changes of government expenditure and expenditures on S&T: 1978–2011 (sources: *China Statistical Yearbook on S&T*; *China Statistical Yearbook*).

The structure of government expenditures on S&T

Governments spend their public funding on S&T in a number of targeted areas. As suggested by the government budgetary revenue and expenditure classification which was used until 2007 (Figure 3.3), China's direct government S&T expenditures in the budget had gone to four areas: (1) Expenditures on new product development, trial production of new products, and major research project subsidy. This category of spending[3] was by far the most important source of funding from both central and local governments to support R&D projects in mission-oriented programmes, the Torch programme, Spark programme, commercialization of research output programme, and social development programme. (2) Research expenditure. Budgetary spending under this heading was mainly earmarked for covering operating costs of both public research institutes and university-based research institutes, projects in basic scientific research and research related to technology development, social welfare and agricultural development, social science research, and public communication of S&T. (3) Capital investment in research infrastructure. (4) Other research expenditure. The last category was primarily related to the budgetary spending administered by other ministerial departments within their respective remits to support innovation. In 2005, local government expenditure on S&T totalled RMB52.7 billion, of which, expenditures on new product development, trial production of new products, and major research project subsidy made up 56 per cent, research expenditure 27 per cent, capital investment in research infrastructure 4 per cent and other research expenditure 13 per cent.[4] At the local level, a significant share of expenditures on new product development, trial production of new products, and major research project subsidy was used as match fund for national key STI projects in the region.

Table 3.2 Percentage of central and local government expenditures on S&T

Year	Central government expenditures on S&T as % of government expenditures on S&T	Local government expenditures on S&T as % of government expenditures on S&T	Central government expenditures on S&T as % of total central government expenditure	Local government expenditures on S&T as % of total local government expenditure
1997	67.2	32.8	10.81	2.00
1998	66.1	33.9	9.27	1.94
1999	65.4	34.6	8.56	2.08
2000	60.7	39.3	6.33	2.18
2001	63.2	36.8	7.7	1.97
2002	62.6	37.4	7.55	2.00
2003	64.5	35.5	8.62	1.95
2004	63.2	36.8	8.77	1.96
2005	60.5	39.5	9.20	2.10
2006	59.8	40.2	10.3	2.20
2007	49.3	50.7	7.87	2.75
2008	49.8	50.2	9.63	2.63
2009	51.1	48.9	10.8	2.58
2010	49.7	50.3	12.8	2.80
2011	50.4	49.6	15.0	2.62

Sources: *China Statistical Yearbook on S&T; China Statistical Yearbook.*

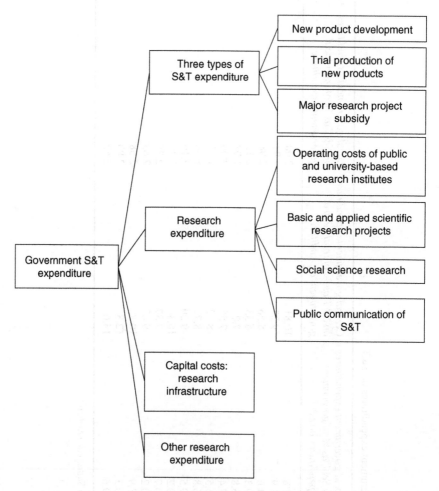

Figure 3.3 The government revenue and expenditure classification in China before 2007.

In 2005, China implemented a budgetary reform to institute a new classification system for revenue and expenditure in the budget and to establish a mechanism for controlling and promoting more efficient use of public funds. The new classification system, in effect in 2007, brings all S&T-related expenditure under one inclusive item of S&T. Under this heading, there are now nine categories of expenditures on S&T as seen in Figure 3.4. It is worth noting that government expenditure on S&T is not the only source of spending, albeit the predominant one in the government budget. Additional expenditure can include special appropriation earmarked for S&T projects, fiscal credit that is not included under the category of S&T expenditure, other governmental expenditure which may have a component of S&T spending, and S&T-related financial transfer payment from

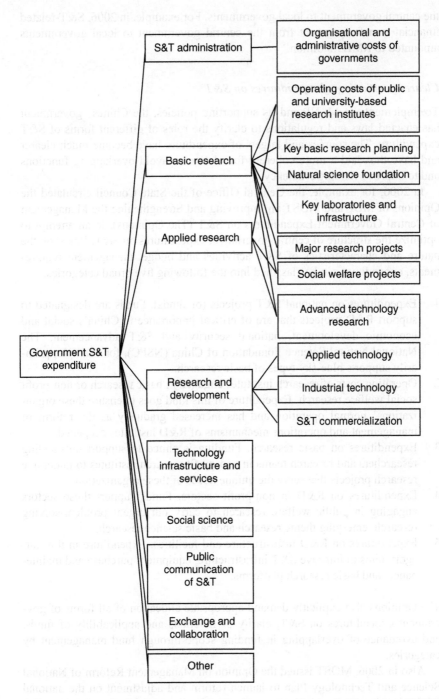

Figure 3.4 The government revenue and expenditure classification in China since 2007.

the central government to local governments. For example, in 2006, S&T-related financial transfer payment from the central government to local governments amounted to RMB3.8 billion.[5]

Clearer positioning of expenditures on S&T

To implement the MLNP and its supporting policies, the Chinese government has enacted laws and regulations to clarify the roles of different forms of S&T expenditure. The sources and targets of expenditure have become much clearer and have thus laid a more coherent foundation to avoid overlapping functions and to improve funding efficiency.

In 2006, for example, the General Office of the State Council circulated the Opinions of MOF and MOST on Improving and Strengthening the Management of Central Government Expenditures on S&T (The Opinions), in an attempt to optimize the structure of central government expenditures on S&T. Based on the nature and characteristics of S&T activities and budget management requirements, expenditure can be classified into the following five broad categories:

1   Expenditures on national S&T projects (or funds). Funds are designated to support R&D projects that are of critical importance to China's social and economic development, national security and S&T advancement. The National Natural Science Foundation of China (NSFC), for example, primarily supports blue-sky types of basic research.
2   Operating costs of research institutes engaged in basic research or non-profit social welfare research. Expenditure of this kind goes to ensure these organizations' normal operation and has increased gradually as the reform of management and operations mechanisms of R&D institutes deepened.
3   Expenditures on basic research. Funding is aimed to support outstanding researchers and research teams in non-profit research institutes to undertake research projects that serve the unique needs of these organizations.
4   Expenditures on R&D in non-profit sectors. Funds support those sectors engaging in public welfare research to carry out urgent problem-solving research, emerging theme research and basic science research.
5   Expenditures on R&D infrastructure and facilities. Expenditure in this category aims to improve S&T infrastructure, equipment purchase and maintenance, and basic research platforms.

The Opinions also explicitly demand appropriate allocation of all forms of government expenditures on S&T, clarity of functions and applicability of funds, and avoidance of overlapping in funding scope through fund management by categories.

Also in 2006, MOST issued the Opinion on Management Reform of National Science and Technology Plan to launch reform and adjustment on the national S&T planning system and to clarify the funding focus of each plan. The revamped national S&T planning system was made up of general plans and major special programmes. The general plans are the basic vehicles through which the state budget funds technological innovations, including the basic research project, national key technology R&D programme, high-tech research and development plan, fundamental research platform development plan, policy-led S&T plan, etc. Major special programmes cater to the needs of national development strategies and are designed to facilitate breakthroughs in critical areas to achieve leapfrogging development in a few key sectors.

Optimizing expenditure structure for innovation activities

Since the later period of the 10th Five-Year Plan (2001–2005), and the 11th Five-Year Plan (2006–2010) in particular, in reflection upon experiences of public funding of innovation at home and abroad, the government had endeavoured to restructure and optimize S&T expenditure to support public S&T activities where markets cannot function effectively, such as basic research, advanced technology research, research with social impacts and major key general purpose technology research. These efforts redressed the weaknesses observed in the previous S&T expenditure structure.

As can be seen in Table 3.3, in 2011 the top six areas of central government expenditures on S&T were the National Science Foundation (RMB14 billion), National Key Technology R&D Programme (5.5 billion), Innovation Fund for S&T SMEs (4.6 billion), 973 programme (3.1 billion), State Key Laboratory Development Programme (3.0 billion) and Programme on Key International S&T Cooperative Projects (3.0 billion).

There are a number of noticeable changes in the expenditure structure. First, the growing emphasis on international collaboration has seen a significant spending increase of 30-fold in the Programme on Key International S&T Cooperative Projects between 2001 and 2011, the biggest winner of central government expenditures on S&T. Second, research infrastructure investment has received a huge funding boost over the same period with a spending increase of 23-fold. Third, government expenditures on three basic research programmes grew from RMB3.24 billion in 2001 to RMB22.6 billion in 2011, a seven-fold increase. Of which, the National Natural Science Foundation received the biggest funding boost with its budget rising nearly nine-fold from 2001 to 2011. Additionally, during the 11th Five-Year Plan period, the national S&T planning system was adjusted. Under the new system, the State Programmes of S&T Development were changed to the National Key Technology R&D Programme. Correspondingly, central government expenditure was significantly raised from RMB1.1 billion in 2001 to RMB5.5 billion in 2011. The new programme focuses on key technologies that could promote public welfare or solve common problems faced by industries through developing technologies that could break through bottlenecks in the areas of energy, environment and health, etc., bolstering a sustainable and harmonic social and economic development. Fourth, a shift of focus to supporting innovation in SMEs has seen spending in Innovation Fund for S&T SMEs grow six-fold. Finally, support for public welfare research activities has

Table 3.3 Central government expenditures on key national S&T programmes (in million RMB)

Programmes	2001	2002	2003	2004	2005	2006	2007	2008	2009	2010	2011	2001–2011 growth (%)
Basic Research Programmes												
National Science Foundation	1,598.4	1,968.4	2,049.4	2,250.0	2,701.3	3,620.1	4,331.0	5,358.5	6,427.0	10,381.1	14,043.4	878.6
National Programme on Key Basic Research Project (973 Programme)	589.3	685.9	800.0	897.00	982.97	1,354.2	1,645.8	1,900.0	1,899.8	2,718.1	3,092.5	524.8
State Programmes of S&T Development/ National Key Technology R&D Programme	1,053.4	1,338.4	1,345.4	1,614.4	1,624.4	3,000.0	5,441.2	5,065.6	5,000.0	5,000.0	5,500.0	522.1
National S&T Infrastructure Programme												
R&D Infrastructure and Facility Development Programme	n/a	n/a	100.0	592.6	573.3	753.7	685.6	23.5	21.3	n/a	246.0	246.0
State Key Laboratories Development Programme	130.0	130.0	130.0	130.0	133.6	216.4	1,600.0	1,605.0	2,917.0	2,759.2	2,960.8	2,277.5
National Engineering Technology Research Centers Development Programme	50.0	50.0	50.0	85.5	59.5	83.5	85.5	n/a	103.0	105.0	195.0	390.0
S&T Basic Work Programme	199.7	200.0	200.0	n/a	n/a	102.7	178.4	150.0	150.5	155.2	183.5	–9.1
Spark Programme	100.0	100.0	100.0	105.0	117.0	101.6	150.0	200.0	218.9	200.0	300.0	300.0
Torch Programme	70.0	70.0	70.0	70.0	70.0	108.3	138.8	151.8	227.7	220.0	320.0	457.1
New National Key Product Programme	140.0	140.0	140.0	140.0	140.0	139.0	140.0	150.0	200.0	200.0	298.5	213.2
Innovation Fund for S&T SMEs	783.3	540.2	663.8	827.2	988.5	842.9	1,256.2	1,462.1	3,483.6	4,297.1	4,640.0	592.4
Agricultural S&T Achievement Transformation Fund	400.0	200.0	200.0	250.0	300.0	300.0	300.0	300.0	400.0	500.0	500.0	125.0
Programme on Key International S&T Cooperative Projects	100.0	120.0	140.0	160.0	180.0	300.0	300.0	400.0	2,917.0	2,759.2	2,960.8	2,960.8
Technology Development Fund for Research Institutes	158.3	213.9	193.0	182.6	186.0	200.0	250.0	250.0	103.0	105.0	195.0	123.2

Sources: *China Statistical Yearbook on S&T; China Statistical Yearbook.*

Note
Programmes listed here are from the 11th Five-Year Plan National S&T Planning System. The State Programmes of S&T Development was renamed the National Key Technology R&D Programme in 2006.

also been strengthened. Since 2006, the central government has gradually raised the level of financial support for institutes engaged in social welfare research, and set up special funds for basic research activities at central government financed research institutes and universities and for research activities at non-profit sectors. These measures strongly push forward the ongoing optimization of government expenditure structure for S&T.

Increased funding for operating costs

Institution-based funding for operating costs and competitive project-based funding are two basic forms of government expenditures on S&T. Institution-based funding for operating costs is the direct funding to research institutions for staffing, capital costs for research infrastructure building and maintenance, and indirect costs to keep S&T research institutes function normally, e.g. costs of administration, such as personnel, finance, library, etc. Alternatively, competitive project-based funding is mainly for projects that address research priorities in particular disciplines.

After the reform and opening-up in 1978 and especially since the S&T system reform in 1985, China's government expenditures on S&T have gone through a paradigm shift from a single mode of administrative rationing to a dual mode where institution-based funding for operating costs and competitive project-based funding coexist. Yet, for a long time, a big gap existed in funding for operating costs because other complementary reforms had lagged behind. Competitive project funding not only financed target-specific research programmes, but also became an important channel to compensate the inadequacy of funding for operating costs and for a long time the primary way of S&T funding.

The proper balance between these two forms of funding to ensure normal operation of research institutions and to stimulate moderate competition between them was deemed to be very important for the steady and healthy development of S&T. Since the commencement of the 11th Five-Year Plan (2006–2010), the central government has taken a range of measures to boost funding for operating costs. These measures included: an increase in funding for organizational and administrative costs of S&T institutes; creation of a basic research fund for central government-funded research institutes and a special fund for non-profit sectors; a significant increase in spending on S&T infrastructure, including the set-up of state (key) laboratories programmes and an increase in financial support for R&D bases; and allocations of project funds for the coordinated development of projects, research bases and talents. These measures have helped redress the imbalance observed in the previous system, namely a relatively high proportion of competitive project funding and inadequate normal operations funding.

Tax incentives for innovation

Undoubtedly, government expenditures on S&T have been an important way of funding S&T to advance national S&T progress. In recent years the Chinese government has stepped up its effort to explore multiple ways of government support for S&T while ensuring the growth of its own expenditure. It has paid more attention to the basic role of markets in resource allocation, explored a range of funding mechanisms, and experimented with use of public finance to guide and facilitate investment in S&T from all other sources. As a result, different sources of investment are channelled in different ways to support different innovation activities in alignment with innovators' needs.

Underpinning all this change has been the central government's endeavour to make enterprises the mainstay of independent innovation. It is the common practice in countries around the world to encourage innovation by employing appropriate tax incentive policies, and China is no exception. The MLNP and its supporting policy measures have specified explicitly the use of tax incentives to encourage independent innovation. Currently, China deploys measures such as preferential corporate income tax rate, additional R&D tax credits and import tax exemption on R&D facilities, etc. to support independent innovation with positive results.

Tax incentives are commonly justified by knowledge spillovers and innovation risk. Research evidence shows that innovation, R&D activities in particular, has a much higher social return than private return, which means the society benefits more from the R&D effort of enterprises and R&D bears the characteristics of public goods (Hu and Mathews, 2005). As a consequence, enterprises are reluctant to invest in R&D when they have concerns about appropriation of their R&D results. Hence, the government, as a guardian of the public interest, has a responsibility to ensure that enterprises at least get a fair return on their investment in R&D. In China, this is regarded as the government shaking its 'visible hand' with the 'invisible hand' of the market to ensure enterprises have both the incentive and ability to innovate. Moreover, tax incentives can reduce the cost of innovation and offset the expenses enterprises have to pay to innovate. For independent innovation to happen and thrive, governments not only need to intervene through direct funding support but also to motivate through incentive tax policies. In contrast with grants and subsidies, tax incentives are neutral and can improve the domestic environment for R&D expenditure without any sectoral or technological targeting, thereby reducing administrative costs. Fiscal incentives also allow companies to reduce their tax bills as a reward for carrying out innovative activities, thus enabling them to reduce the total costs of such investments (Atkinson, 2007).

Under the public finance framework, government spending and tax incentives are the two major fiscal incentives to encourage independent innovation of enterprises. Government spending guides the direction of enterprise independent innovation and encourages them to innovate independently and to 'digest' imported technologies and re-innovate. It focuses on supporting and encouraging innovation through investments, subsidies and guarantees. Government spending matches the characteristics of the innovation policy with such features of policies as democracy (open tendering of grants), independence (self-regulation on use of grants) and directness (sectoral, regional or technological targeting).

However, it also has the weaknesses of exposing the government to too much risk due to the government spending rigidness and use of grants as a way of disbursement. Compared with government spending, tax policies focus on building a favourable environment for independent innovation and on areas where market functions effectively. They are indirect and embody the preferences of government and its willingness to cooperate with micro-economic agents to innovate. Moreover, tax policies are more flexible and can be used either to reward or to punish economic agents. Furthermore, they tend to function in an ex post manner, reflecting the combined forces of government, enterprises and market while exposing government to lower risk. Simply put, only with the balanced drive of tax incentives and government spending, will enterprises have the incentives to innovate and will the strategy of building an innovative country turn to actions.

Research grants and subsidy

Government grants and subsidy have been a major way of government support for S&T, and the policy tools in use include ex ante subsidy, ex post subsidy, subsidized loans and government subsidy. Research grants in the mode of ex ante subsidy are the most widely employed government subsidy and are mainly used in the 973 Programme and 863 Programme. Payments of a grant are made based on the scheduled progress of the project after the funding application is awarded and its costing is approved.

Grants in the forms of *ex post* subsidy and subsidized loans are also important types of government subsidy which give special attention to product-oriented projects with a clear commercialization outlook. Both the National New Product Programme and the Innovation Fund for S&T SMEs have employed these forms of subsidies. They have been influential in leveraging investment from all other sources into relevant S&T areas, supporting high-growth technology-based firms, increasing the stock of S&T SMEs, accelerating the restructuring of regional industries, and creating high-end job opportunities. In the Interim Regulation on Key Civil Science and Technology Programme Fund Management issued jointly by MOF, MOST and NCDR in 2009, the specially designed *ex post* subsidy is split into two categories: *ex ante* approval with *ex post* subsidy and *ex post* approval with *ex post* subsidy, in accordance with the unique features of commercialization of the state key projects.

Local governments were also very active in exploring ways of public funding support for S&T and have made some progress. Zhejiang Province, for example, revamped its ways of government financial support for S&T in 2007 through establishing three new modes of S&T funding in its budget: payments of grant in instalment, *ex post* subsidy and subsidized loan. In adopting *ex post* subsidy, the local government was experimenting with replacing subsidy with financial reward after a project was completed and evaluation was done. The new method of funding appeared to have achieved good and immediate effect. In Jiangsu Province, *ex post* subsidy was used for projects with good prospect for

generating immediate economic benefits at trial, demonstration or commercialization stages.

With regard to special key projects, both grants (*ex ante* subsidy) and *ex post*
subsidy are now used. While grants apply to basic research and non-profit
research projects, *ex post* subsidy primarily applies to key applied research projects with clearly defined deliverables in either new product development or full-
scale manufacturing. *Ex post* subsidy is also employed to support key applied
research projects with a suite of related research activities focusing on one major
theme and undertaken by different collaborative teams. The *ex post* subsidy
approach differs from China's conventional funding model in which grants were
made available to projects in advance. Anecdotal evidence shows that *ex post*
subsidy is appropriate to special key applied research projects and has led to the
more efficient use of public funds. In promoting indigenous innovation diffusion, governments have sought new ways of support. One of such new methods
in some pilot projects has been to subsidize users for their adoption of new products rather than producers of such new products as in the past. For example, in
2009, the central government initiated a new energy demonstration programme,
entitled the Ten Cities, Thousand Vehicles Programme. The programme tasked
each of the selected ten cities with rolling out pilots of at least a thousand electric vehicles. To give consumers an incentive to purchase electric vehicles, the
central government offered a subsidy of RMB60,000 per vehicle for Battery
Electric Vehicles (BEV) and RMB50,000 per vehicle for Plug-in Hybrid Electric
Vehicles (PHEV). Through this incentive scheme, the programme aimed to use
large-scale pilots to help car-makers to identify and address technology and
safety issues associated with electric vehicles and to accelerate market development for electric vehicles. The same approach has also been used in another
similar scheme called the Ten Cities, Ten Thousand Semiconductor Lighting
(LED) programme launched by MOST and Ministry of Housing and Urban Construction in 2009. The purpose of the programme was to pilot LED application
and demonstration in ten cities with each aiming to achieve an adoption of
10,000 LED.

Corporation income tax unification

In alignment with the development of S&T strategy, the innovation-oriented
taxation system has undergone two significant shifts since the reform and
opening up (Ding *et al.*, 2008). One was a shift to a unified taxation system that
applies equally to all domestic and foreign enterprises from a taxation system in
which two different income taxes applied to domestic and foreign enterprises
separately with preferential tax mainly oriented to foreign enterprises. Since ini-
tiating reform and opening to the outside world, China had long adopted the
'dual-track' income tax model under which two separate income tax systems
existed side by side for domestic and foreign funded enterprises respectively.
The underlying reason for the design of such a system was that China placed
needs for overseas capital, technology and talents as a priority. So, in 1980, the

Income Tax Law for Sino-Foreign Joint Venture was enacted and it was followed by the Income Tax Law for Foreign Enterprises that came into effect the following year. In 1991, these two separate laws for wholly foreign owned enterprises and joint venture enterprises were merged into the Income Tax Law for Wholly Foreign-owned Enterprises and Foreign Enterprises. For domestic enterprises, the State Council issued successive regulations, including the Interim Regulations on Income Tax for State Owned Enterprises in 1984, the Interim Regulations on Income Tax for Collectively Owned Enterprises in 1985 and the Interim Regulations on Income Tax for Private Enterprises in 1988. In 1993, these three regulations were merged into Interim Regulations on Corporate Income Tax that took effect in 1994. This marked the formation of the two separate income tax systems, referred to as a 'Dual Track' income tax system, under which domestic and foreign enterprises were treated differently in terms of pre-tax deductions, preferential policies and effective tax rates.

As regards pre-tax deduction, domestic enterprises were imposed a ceiling on the amount of pre-tax deductions for payroll expenses, charitable donations, advertisement fees, staff training expenses, employee benefits and employee union fees, whereas foreign funded enterprises were allowed to deduct all such costs before tax without any restriction.

In respect of preferential taxation treatment, to boost the policy initiatives of attracting foreign investment, the state adopted a series of preferential taxation policies, mainly including an incentive of "income tax exemption for two years and tax reduction by 50 per cent for another three years" for foreign funded production enterprises, an incentive of 'income tax exemption for five years and tax reduction by 50 per cent for another five years' for foreign funded enterprises investing in port/harbour and energy sectors, and a reduced tax rate of 15 per cent and 24 per cent for foreign funded production enterprises located in special economic zones and economic and technology development zones respectively. Evidently, the Chinese government offered a broad range of generous incentives to foreign funded enterprises with preferential policies aiming to attract foreign direct investment, encourage export and utilize advanced technology, etc. In comparison, domestic enterprises were only entitled to a narrower band of preferential taxation treatment.

With regard to effective tax rates, domestic enterprises were subject to a statutory baseline income tax rate of 33 per cent and a reduced tax rate of 18 per cent or 27 per cent in the case of taxable income falling in the range of RMB30,000~100,000. Foreign funded enterprise were subject to a proportional income tax rate of 30 per cent plus a local income tax rate of 3 per cent (total tax rate: 33 per cent). While the nominal income tax rates applicable to domestic funded and foreign funded enterprises may appear to be the same, the effective enterprise income tax rates (burdens) were in effect below nominal tax rates after adjusting for allowances offered by preferential policies under different tax laws and regulations. For example, 3 per cent local income tax included in foreign funded enterprise income tax was exempted in most areas of China. As mentioned earlier, domestic and foreign funded enterprises were subject to different preferential taxation treatments, which allowed foreign funded enterprises to have a far lower actual tax liability than that of domestic enterprises. According to the findings of a nationwide survey on corporate income tax, the actual average tax burden was approximately 25 per cent for domestic enterprises and approximately 15 per cent for foreign funded enterprises, i.e. 10 per cent additional tax burden for domestic funded enterprises (Ding *et al.*, 2008).

From a historical perspective, the 'dual-track' income tax model played a positive role in promoting China's technological progress and innovation, attracting a huge amount of foreign investment, and importing advanced technologies and management methods, while promoting China's openness and science and technology progresses. Given China's greater emphasis on independent innovation after the turn of the century, however, the discrepancies between the two separate tax regimes for domestic and foreign enterprises were in contradiction with China's S&T development strategies. Nor would they deliver a unified fair and normative tax policy environment for all forms of enterprises and created a tax policy environment for independent innovation. Therefore, it was inevitable that China moved to unify the income tax regimes for domestic and foreign funded enterprises.

A new Corporate Income Tax Law in China was enacted at the 5th Meeting of the 10th National People's Congress in 2007 and became effective on 1 January 2008. Under the new law, domestic and foreign funded companies are all subject to a unified income tax system. The general income tax rate for all enterprises is 25 per cent, and low profit-making micro and small businesses matching certain pre-set criteria are eligible for a favourable tax rate of 20 per cent; rules and regulations for pre-tax deductions are uniformed, and reasonable actual expenses for income-making are deductible when calculating taxable income; preferential tax policies are unified, the focus of which has shifted from region-orientation to industries-orientation so as to reflect the government's industrial policies and encourage energy and resource conservation, environment protection and high-tech development.

In effect, the new corporate income tax law was designated to create a unified, equitable tax environment for all forms of enterprises and to incentivize domestic enterprises to pursue independent innovation.

VAT reform

Another significant change in tax incentives was to switch from production-based value added tax (VAT) to consumption-based VAT. Reforming the VAT system aimed to eliminate double taxation, encourage investment, and assist in industrial restructuring by improving firms' technology level and competitiveness (Shi, 2009). VAT was initially piloted in three industrial sectors in 1979 and expanded to other sectors gradually. From 1994, VAT was widely applied to sectors such as industry, commerce and trade and in activities of import, manufacture, maintenance and repair. The inherent drawback of the production-based VAT regime was that it did not allow enterprises to deduct taxes levied on fixed assets when purchased. The tax policy design of this nature was intended in order to embed a countermeasure against a cyclical overheated economy through a link-up between fiscal revenue and excessive investment. Over time, VAT had become the most important tax in China and accounted for 50 per cent or so of the overall tax revenue most years. At the end of the last century, the economic circumstances in China had changed dramatically. Domestic demand had replaced resources to become the major economic development constraint. The priority of economic development was to increase investment and consumption and to combat deflation. After China joined the WTO, market competition among enterprises started to focus on capital availability and the high-tech sector, and the enhancement of technology became the key to business growth. However, production-based VAT became an inhibitor in this process since it discouraged enterprises from investing and innovating. High-tech industries generally require more investment in fixed assets such as machinery and equipment, but production-based VAT did not allow deduction of VAT paid in the purchase of fixed assets, which means it is more expensive for enterprises to invest. So enterprises were reluctant to invest in equipment renewal and technology innovation. To rectify this problem, China started reforming its VAT regime from the production-based VAT to the more innovation-friendly consumption-based VAT.

In 2004, China launched the first pilot programme offering a broader scope of VAT deductions to eight industries in three provinces (Heilongjiang, Jilin and Liaoning) and one city (Dalian) in North-East China as the first step of reform of the VAT regime. In 2007, MOF and the State Administration of Taxation jointly promulgated the Provisional Regulations on Expanding the Scope of VAT Deductions in Central China to expand the pilot programme to eight industries in 26 traditional industry-base cities in central China. VAT reform aimed to shorten the investment payoff period and reduce investment risk exposure, boost capital expenditure, technological progress and equipment upgrade, promote technology-intensive and capital-intensive enterprise development, push Chinese enterprises to pursue technological innovation, enhance enterprise product upgrade, and create favourable conditions for building an innovative economy. The VAT reform was completed in 2009 when the new VAT regime was rolled out across the country.

Tax incentives for R&D

In addition to creating a unified income tax system applicable to all enterprises, the 2007-enacted Corporate Income Tax law embraces many tax incentives targeting technological innovation. These incentives include: (1) High and new technology enterprises (HNTEs)[6] nationwide are entitled to a 15 per cent preferential tax rate, which used to be exclusively available to those locating in national high-tech development zones only. (2) R&D expenses for new technology, new product and new technique can be deducted when calculating the taxable income. (3) Venture capital investment in key areas supported and encouraged by the government can be deducted as a proportion of investment from taxable income. (4) Fixed assets which need to accelerate depreciation due to technology advancement can shorten their depreciable life or accelerate the depreciation. (5) Income tax of technology transfer income subject to certain criteria can be exempted or be proportionally deducted.

In the implementation of MLNP, the whole set of fiscal incentives have been modified and updated alongside the introduction of new regulations in order to help shape the innovation system. Table 3.4 provides a summary of current tax incentives for innovation in China.

Characteristics of fiscal incentives

After many years' adjustment and improvement, China's fiscal and tax policies on S&T development have now better fit for purpose. Overall, the STI-oriented fiscal policies display the following characteristics.

First, governments play a pivotal role in the development of S&T and have created a diversified and multi-channel of S&T funding system. Through direct expenditure and tax incentives, the Chinese government has played a leading role in providing funding for S&T development and mobilizing additional resources from other non-governmental organizations. Public expenditure is mainly used to support public S&T activities that cannot be effectively resolved through market mechanisms, such as basic research, cutting-edge technological research, non-profit research for common goods, and major research programs for the development of generic and key technologies. Public expenditure is also used to channel capital from the private sector and other sources into S&T development. The central and local governments at all levels have all abided by the Law on Science and Technology Progress to ensure that the growth of S&T spending is significantly higher than that of regular tax revenue, so as to meet the target of R&D spending as a share of GDP by stage. In the meantime, governments regard enterprises as the mainstay of S&T investment and encourage them to increase their investment in R&D, thus driving the formation of the diversified and multi-channel system of S&T funding.

Second, China has gradually shifted emphasis from use of direct budgetary expenditure to use of R&D tax incentives in support of independent innovation, albeit the scale and importance of government S&T expenditure. Support for enterprise R&D through the tax system has become an integral part of a broader set of policies to support investment in R&D. It is estimated that since China established a compound/multiple taxation system in the 1980s, preferential tax clauses (about 600 articles) are spread in all 20 taxes currently levied. There are 118 S&T-related preferential clauses in total, among which 48 are under turnover tax, 58 under income tax and 12 under property tax. As a whole, China has already put in place a large number of tax incentives for S&T. The number of S&T-related taxation preferential policies in the taxation system is only second to the number of those for civil affairs. International widely adopted indirect tax incentives such as tax exemption, tax deduction and accelerated depreciation,

Table 3.4 Design of tax incentives for innovation in China

Tax treatment of R&D

Type	Incentive	Policy
Current expenditures	Pre-tax deduction applicable to the wages, salaries, bonus, allowances and subsidy of research personnel	企业研究开发费用税前扣除管理办法 (试行) (2008) (Interim regulations on pre-tax deduction applicable to R&D expenses)
Capital expenditures	(1) An immediate or accelerated write-off of expenditures on R&D equipment and facilities	企业研究开发费用税前扣除管理办法 (试行) (2008) (Interim regulations on pre-tax deduction applicable to R&D expenses)
	(2) Shorten depreciation or accelerated depreciation methods for key fixed assets due to technological progresses	关于企业固定资产加速折旧所得税处理有关问题的通知 (2009) (Notice on corporate income tax treatment of accelerated depreciation of fixed assets)
	(3) Tax deduction for investment in special purpose equipment for environment protection, energy and water conservation and safety production	关于环境保护节能节水 安全生产等专用设备投资抵免企业所得税有关问题的通知 (2010) (Notice on corporate income tax deduction applicable to capital expenditures on special purpose equipment for environment protection, energy and water conservation and safety production)
Tax allowances/ Tax credits	*Income tax*	
	(1) 150% tax allowance against taxable profits on the level of R&D expenditures in a given year and unused tax allowance may be carried forward up to five years to offset future tax	关于研究开发费用税前加计扣除有关政策问题的通知 (2013) (Notice on pre-tax deduction applicable to R&D expenses)
	(2) Cash prizes awarded by agencies at government ministerial level or by international organizations for science, education, technology, culture, health, sports, or environment protection, etc., are exempt from individual income tax	《中华人民共和国个人所得税法 (修正) (2011) (Individual income tax law) (Amendment)

continued

Table 3.4 Continued

Tax treatment of R&D

Type	Incentive	Policy
Tax allowances/ Tax credits *continued*	*Income tax continued*	
	(3) 100% tax allowance against taxable profits on donations to R&D foundations	《中华人民共和国个人所得税法 (修正)》(2011) (Individual income tax law) (Amendment)
	(4) High and new technology firms HNTEs are subject to the corporate tax rate of 15%	《国家税务总局关于实施高新技术企业所得税优惠有关问题的通知》(2009) (Notice on the implementation of corporate income tax incentives concerning high and new technology enterprises)
	(5) Overseas income of HNTEs is taxed at a 15% reduced enterprise income tax (EIT) rate	关于高新技术企业境外所得适用税率及税收抵免问题的通知 (2011) (Notice on income tax rates and tax credits applicable to foreign income of high-tech companies)
	(6) Enterprises investing in technical renovation can get 10% deduction of income tax for investment in domestic equipment in the year of purchase, or deduction can be carried forward up to five years	企业所得税法 (2007) (Corporate income tax law)
	(7) The first RMB5 million of income from qualified technology transfers is exempt from EIT; any income from technology transfers in excess of RMB5 million is taxed at a 50% reduced EIT rate	关于居民企业技术转让有关企业所得税政策问题的通知 (2010) (Notice on corporate income tax policies concerning technology transfers of private enterprises)
	Tariff and import duties	
	(1) Major S&T special projects are exempt from import duty and VAT on imported items for R&D purpose	关于科技重大专项进口税收政策的通知 (2010) (Notice on major special S&T import duty policies)
	(2) Foreign R&D centres are exempt for import duty, VAT and consumption tax on imported items for R&D purpose	关于科技重大专项进口税收政策的通知 (2010) (Notice on major special S&T import duty policies)

	(3) Small R&D service providers are exempt for import duty, VAT and consumption tax on imported items for R&D purpose	关于国家中小企业公共技术服务平台适用科技开发用品进口税收政策的通知 (2011) (Notice on import duty policies applicable to appropriate technology goods imported by national small and medium-sized service providers for common technology and demonstration platforms)
	VAT Domestic research institutes and foreign R&D centres can have VAT rebate on procurement of home-made equipment	关于继续执行研发机构采购设备税收政策的通知 (2011) (Notice on the continuity of taxation policies concerning equipment procurement by R&D organizations)
	Other From 1 January 2008 to 31 December 2010, real estates and land owned by or used by qualified university S&T parks and leased to incubator clients are exempted from property tax and urban land use tax; incomes from land and real estates leasing and incubating services are exempted from business tax	关于国家大学科技园有关税收政策问题的通知 (2007) (Notice on taxation policies concerning national level university-affiliated science parks)
Targeting		
Special for investment in start-ups	70% tax deduction for venture capital firms for investment in unlisted HNTE firms, and unused tax allowance can be carried forward to offset future tax	关于实施创业投资企业所得税优惠问题的通知 (2009) (Notice on the implementation of corporate income tax incentives concerning venture investment firms)
Special for commercialization of research output	Income from environment protection, energy and water conservation projects and the income from technology transfer subject to certain criteria is exempted or proportionally deductible	

continued

Table 3.4 Continued

Tax treatment of R&D

Type	Incentive	Policy
Special for R&D service providers	(1) The reduced rate of 15% from 1 July 2010 to 31 December 2013 applies to qualified Technology Advanced Service Enterprises in designated cities with over 50% revenue derived from providing qualified technology advanced services outsourced by foreign entities (2) A full deduction of training expenses based on 8% of salaries paid against taxable profits in the year incurred	关于技术先进型服务企业有关企业所得税政策问题的通知 (2010) (Notice on corporate income tax policies concerning advanced technology service companies)
Special for software and integrated circuit industries	Software and integrated circuit enterprises are exempt from corporate income tax in their first two profit-making years, and are taxed at a reduced 25% from the third to fifth year	关于进一步鼓励软件产业和集成电路产业发展企业所得税政策的通知 (2012) (Notice on corporate income tax policies to further encourage the development of the software industry and integrated circuit industry)
Special for patent filing	Eligible individuals can defer payment of 85% of application fee, application review fee and annual fee and 80% of annual review fee and reexamination fee; for eligible organizations the deferral rates are 70% and 60% respectively	专利费用减缓办法 (2006) (Measures of patent fee deferral)

Source: compiled by the authors.

which are cost-effective and indicative for high-tech R&D, are all in place. In short, China, in line with the features of the innovation system, has established an S&T-oriented tax system in which corporate income tax is dominant while personal income tax, value added tax (VAT) and business tax are complementary. Many of the tax incentives that used to be entitled only by high and new technology enterprises (HNTEs) located in the state-approved high and new technology development zones have become universal R&D tax incentives for all enterprises, regardless of their locations. Tax incentives for innovation include expenditure-based tax incentives and income-based tax incentives. China also applies a system that targets specific areas of R&D activities and R&D investment.

1   Current and capital expenditure. China allows for current expenditure (wages, salaries, bonus, allowances and subsidy of research personnel) to be deducted from income in the year they are incurred as a form of business expenses. Deduction of other forms of current expenditures (e.g. training) is also offered to S&T services providers (deduction of training expenses based on 8 per cent of wages and salaries paid against taxable profits in the year incurred). Likewise, China allows a 100 per cent immediate write-off of expenditures on R&D equipment and facilities (costs of equipment and facilities) and accelerated depreciation for fixed assets.

2   Tax allowances and tax credits. The main form of tax allowances and tax credits in China is volume-based, namely they are based on the level of R&D expenditures in a given year. Currently, China offers a generous 150 per cent super deduction for eligible R&D expenditures. According to MOST, in 2010, 18,000 enterprises were the beneficiaries of this policy with tax credit worth RMB20.97 billion.[7] China also allows tax allowances to be claimed against tax in future years under tax allowance carry-forward rules (e.g. specially for investment in start-ups).

3   Purpose-built incentives. China has given R&D tax incentives to particular targets in order to achieve policy goals such as venture investment, commercialization of research outputs, R&D service provision, and the development of software and integrated circuit industries.

Third, S&T development and economic development are more coherently integrated. With the deepening of reform and opening up, governments have paid more attention to the role of S&T in supporting economic development. This is epitomized by the doctrine that national economy should be developed through the means of S&T and S&T should aim to serve the development of national economy. Fiscal policies have thus been adjusted to solve the serious discord between S&T and economic development. In 1985, China started to reform the S&T system, setting an overarching goal of commercializing S&T achievements quickly and widely so as to promote social and economic development. Accordingly, the patterns and structures of S&T spending have changed, and funding schemes for research institutes have been categorized according to the characteristics of S&T activities and the respective strengths of research institutes. Government expenditure on operating expenses of research institutes primarily engaged in technology development was completely or almost completely phased out within five years; for research institutes primarily engaged in basic research or research that does not have short-term prospects for practical applications, government expenditure has now covered their operating expenses only, and their research will mainly rely on competitive funding programmes; for those engaged in non-profit research and agricultural S&T research, the government has continued to fund their operation and research using a pre-agreed funding formula; for those involved in research activities of different types, their funding will come from different channels in accordance with the type of research undertaken. The new funding scheme by category has moved S&T institutes to reduce their funding dependence on their superior administrative bodies, pushing them to engage more closely with the market to find alternative sources of funding. At the same time, the formation of a market-oriented economy has changed the layout of S&T resources, expanding private investment in S&T and accelerating commercialization of S&T achievements. The MLNP enacted in 2006 further emphasizes reliance on technological progress and innovation to bring about a qualitative leap of the national economy, to promote the comprehensive, coordinated and sustainable development of society and economy, and to establish an enterprise-centred innovation system with closer cooperation among industries, universities and research institutes. Correspondingly, the central government introduced a series of policies to promote closer cooperation among industries, universities and research institutes. These policies include: (1) improvement in ways of supporting national S&T programmes (funds); (2) national S&T plans to reflect major S&T needs of enterprises, which should involve enterprises, universities and research institutes in areas where clear application prospects can be identified; (3) more supports for closer cooperation among industries, universities and research institutes through full use of a variety of funding methods, ranging from grants, subsidized loans, venture capital, etc.

Fourth, governments have endeavoured to incentivize enterprises to become the mainstay of innovation and have enacted a series of fiscal policies to motivate enterprises to innovate. In terms of public expenditure, governments have reformed expenditure mechanisms, integrated government funding schemes, and strengthened funding supports to guide and encourage large-scale key enterprises to undertake R&D on major equipment and technologies of strategically importance for their future competitive advantages, to build an R&D service system for enterprises' technology innovation, and to increase funding contribution to the Innovation Fund for Technology SMEs. As for tax policies, measures taken include VAT reform, uniform corporate income tax for domestic and foreign enterprises, 100 per cent plus R&D expenses exemption, and accelerated depreciation. The new system seems to be working. Statistics from the State Administration of Taxation indicate that over the period 2008–2010 all HNTEs paid RMB1.34 trillion of tax against RMB139.2 billion of tax reduction, almost ten times higher than the tax benefit they had received.[8] In short, these fiscal and taxation policies have charted the direction of innovation for enterprises and have strengthened their R&D capability. In their empirical research on the impact of fiscal incentive policies on business R&D investment, Yang and Nie (2011) find that overall there was a significantly positive relationship between fiscal incentive policies and R&D investment by large and medium-sized enterprises.

Complementary fiscal incentives of local governments

Since the 1990s, as the central government continuously refined national fiscal incentives on S&T, local governments have played their part in designing and implementing their own fiscal incentives to promote S&T development. This has been made possible by the decentralized fiscal system China has adopted over the past few decades. It is also because national laws and regulations often set forth only general principles rather than clear prescriptions and local governments are allowed leeway to formulate and implement their own policies. While local governments are expected to take on board and fully implement the national policies in respect of fiscal incentives, they are allowed to offer additional incentives in taxes accruing to local tax revenue. For example, Jiangsu Province in its Circulations on Several Policies on Encouraging and Promoting S&T Innovation and Entrepreneurship stated that enterprises, in addition to 150 per cent of R&D expense reduction, are entitled to a local tax rebate by a certain percentage if they spend more than 5 per cent of their annual sales revenue on R&D. Incentive for patent filing is another example where local policies supplement the central government policy. To encourage patent filing, the State Administration of Intellectual Property issued the 'Measures of Patent Fee Deferral' in 2006. Many local governments have since issued additional incentives for patenting. For example, Beijing's fiscal incentives include a subsidy of up to RMB2,150 for an invention patent application, and RMB150 for a utility and design patent application; cash award of up to RMB1 million to the recipients of national best patent award; and a grant of up to RMB300,000 to patent commercialization.[9]

Improved S&T system and innovative approaches to S&T funding

The Science and Technology Department of Zhejiang Province, for example, made a few changes regarding resource allocation. Starting from 2008, the department focused its support on four top priority plans, i.e. innovation environment, innovation platform, innovation talents and innovation projects. In 2008, these four plans received respective funds of 10 per cent, near 10 per cent, 30 per cent and more than 50 per cent from an overall budget of RMB1.886 billion. Built on this funding policy, they moved to focus their efforts more on the aspects of innovation talents and innovation platform. RMB150 million of budgetary spending was estimated to have been appropriated for human resource development in

2009, so as to ensure resource allocation reflecting the characteristics of the public finance and to promote the effectiveness of public expenditure.

Jiangsu Province has established an S&T Knowledge Transfer Fund to support S&T transfer and industrialization. Funding is made available in three forms, including grants, subsidized loans and repayable financing, with each having a budget of over RMB10 million. The fund started with a budget of RMB300 million in 2004, rising to RMB500 million in 2005, RMB800 million in 2006 and RMB1 billion per annum from 2007 to 2009. Government expenditure strengthened entrepreneurs' confidence of commercialization and effectively boosted their investment, thereby helping the transfer of S&T achievements and nurturing emerging industries in Jiangsu Province. For instances, Yozosoft, a Wuxi-based software company that started in 2000, received a funding of RMB20 million from the province's Knowledge Transfer Fund and has since grown to become Asia's leading office software developer, providing customers in China and abroad with a suite of office software products, industry solutions and application services.

Ensured smooth transition of local public research institutes

Reform of public research institutes as a national policy to overhaul the national innovation system has wider implications. Policy-makers are therefore expected to consider policies and their implementation that can address the concerns of all those involved at the local level and to adapt local fiscal policies to local conditions. In this regard, local governments have experimented with innovative approaches with positive outcomes. For example, in Jiangsu, Chongqing and Qinghai Provinces, research institutes in the process of change from public ownership to non-public ownership could allocate up to 30 per cent of re-evaluated assets (excluding the government-funded part) to award technical and management personnel, subject to the approval of the local state-owned assets management authorities. Qinghai and Dalian also allowed organizations to use assets as equity to compensate employees for their change of employment contract or for redundancy payment in the course of public research institute reform. Jiangsu, Yunnan, Liaoning, Sichuan and Qinghai allowed employees of research institutes to invest in shares, and encouraged employees, especially technical staff, to buy out entire or part of the state-owned assets individually or collectively. The buyout could be paid in instalments, and different preferential terms would apply according to the methods of payment. Jiangsu, Zhejiang, Anhui, Qinghai, Shanxi and Dalian allowed employees over a certain age or with length of service over 30 years to retire, whose retirement pension policy would be the same as those of public institutions. Tianjin allowed some centres specialized in quality control, standard and metrology to be treated as legal persons of public institutions after the reform and continue their functions. Inner Mongolia, Chongqing and Tianjin set up S&T asset management companies to deal with the state-owned assets of S&T research institutes and to provide services to these institutes.

Attracting needed talents for innovation and commercialization

Yunnan, Tianjin, Dalian, Xiamen, Qingdao, Fujian and Chongqing have set up special purpose Talent Funds to support enterprises, research institutes and universities to attract talent and to provide match funds to the central government-supported talent recruitment projects. For example, Shenzhen set aside RMB30 million each year to support returned overseas students (returnees) to start businesses in Shenzhen. Statistics shows that 21 out of 28 provinces and municipalities surveyed have introduced local measures similar to the Law to Promote Commercialization of S&T Achievements, the Decisions on Innovation and the Rules on Promoting Commercialization of S&T Achievements jointly issued by MOST and six other ministries. These measures award people who have contributed to the commercialization of S&T achievements in certain ways, ranging from a share of incomes of S&T commercialization, a lump sum cash bonus to equity shares. As such, many universities, research institutes and enterprises have moved to take advantage of these incentives. In some provinces and municipalities, the incentive is even more generous than what the central government has proposed, and new incentive methods are introduced. For example, Heilongjiang allowed R&D staffs to be awarded a share of sales revenue or profits. Tianjin and Dalian provided a cash award up to RMB500,000 to S&T talents. Many enterprises in Tianjin also established their own rules to award S&T commercialization.

Increased government expenditures on S&T infrastructure and facilities

In recent years, many local governments regard the construction of first-class S&T infrastructure and facility as a priority task to build regional innovation system. Guangdong, Jiangsu, Zhejiang, Hubei, Gansu and Sichuan have set up their own special fund for S&T infrastructure and facility development respectively. For instance, Zhejiang provincial government sets aside RMB100 million each year for equipment procurement, laboratory construction, R&D initiation and international cooperation. Since the year 2004 when MOF and three other ministries jointly issued the Outline for National S&T Infrastructure and Facility Development 2004–2010, local governments have increased their inputs in S&T infrastructure and facility such as key laboratories, pilot testing bases and large scientific instruments. In many areas, regional observation and monitor networks have been established, efforts to protect and utilize seed sources and specimen have been strengthened, and the work of co-construction and share of large scientific instruments and library resources in S&T fields has been promoted.

Challenges in fiscal incentive for innovation

As an important macroeconomic control instrument, tax policies can promote technological innovation in supplementing the market mechanism for resource allocation. In support of S&T development strategies, China has undergone a series of transformations and adjustment in R&D tax incentives over the years. First, there has been a shift from the dual-track income tax system in favour of foreign funded enterprises to the unified income tax system for domestic and foreign funded enterprises to pay the same income tax rate; second, there was a transformation from the production-based VAT system to the consumption-based VAT system; third, there was adjustment and fine-tuning of preferential policies in respect of R&D expenditure pre-tax deduction, accelerated depreciation, etc. We will assess the impact of China's programmes of incentives for innovation in Chapter 8. Here, some challenges concerning fiscal incentives are highlighted.

First, the system of R&D tax incentives needs to be simpler, more transparent and cost-effective. China has made a lot of effort in recent years to make its fiscal incentives for innovation less complicated and more coherent, and the combination of national and local tax incentives for R&D expenditures can certainly reduce the cost of business investment in R&D. Nevertheless, the provision of many such incentives remains subject to many administrative requirements that impose significant transaction costs. Hence, companies may find access to tax incentives highly bureaucratic and burdensome. Experiences from OECD countries suggest that the overall costs associated with the R&D tax incentives schemes depend both on the uptake of the scheme by firms and on the design of the tax incentives in a country (OECD, 2011). Removing some of the administrative hurdles would be a positive step. China has fully appreciated the need to simplify its R&D tax incentives, judging by the remarks of Wan Gang, Minister of MOST, in his press conference held in Beijing on 11 October 2013. Moreover, tax incentives for innovation can incur substantial intended and unintended tax revenue losses, since they might support R&D activities that would have taken place even in the absence of support. Currently, there is no public official assessment of this so-called 'crowding-out effect' associated with R&D tax incentives. It is clearly necessary to put in place a system that rigorously examines the cost-effectiveness of the design of the R&D tax incentives schemes in China.

Second, the structure of government expenditure needs further optimization to tackle the obvious problems such as lack of basic research and S&T commercialization. In spite of a better clarity in the targets of public expenditures on different S&T activities, the problem of overlapping exists to some extent. Spending for normal operations needs to be further enhanced. Structures of the expenditure of national S&T programmes still need adjustment. Further, the impact of government expenditure needs further improvement. Despite a significant increase in government expenditure and business investment in R&D and an improved innovation environment in recent years, a large number of S&T outputs remain ending up on the shelf and difficult to commercialize, while many enterprises lack the support of advanced and applicable technologies.

Third, the leading role of government expenditures on S&T is not strong enough. Funding schemes and management of government expenditure are yet to be further driven by the market. The situation that most expenditure is free of charge and the funding channel is rather limited has not changed. In short, the leveraging effect of the government expenditure can still be maximized. New ways of funding other than subsidies are still under pilots so that no common applicable model for certain stages has been formed. The issues such as the division of interests and risk sharing among different stakeholders in funding schemes, the security of government funds, etc. need to be more clearly defined. Certainly, there is still a long way to go to reach the goal of effective allocation of funds to the different parts of the entire innovation value chain.

Fourth, from the perspective of enterprise technological innovation mechanism, no tax and fiscal incentives have been tailored to the whole innovation process of enterprises. Preferential tax policies lack systematic management and its legal status is rather low. Although a number of taxation preferential policies are in place, most of them are modification or supplement of certain clauses of basic taxation laws. They are scattered in various taxation laws or rules, and only a handful are in the form of regulations. Many of them are notices, circulars and instructions, which are low in terms of legal status.

Notes

1 See MOST (2012), *China Science and Technology Development Report 2011*, p. 32.
2 See MOST (2011), *China Science and Technology Development Report 2010*, p. 66.
3 This category of spending was usually referred to as the "three items of S&T expenditure" (科技三项经费) in official documents.
4 From MOST (2007), *China Science and Technology Development Report 2006*, p. 65.
5 From ibid., p. 61.
6 The status of high and new technology firms (HNTEs) must be applied for and renewed every three years. Prospective HNTEs must meet six qualification criteria to be granted the status. These six criteria mainly demand that enterprises should conduct R&D activities that fall into the national priority of technology development, that they have developed R&D capability and have obtained core IPRs, and there is a close link between the enterprise's core business and its R&D and commercialization. See policies on the authorization of HNTEs (高新技术企业认定管理政策) at www.most.gov.cn/kjzc/zdkjzcjd/gxjsqyssyhzc/ (accessed 16 December 2013).
7 See MOST (2012), *China Science and Technology Development Report 2011*, p. 34.
8 Ibid.
9 For the detail of information, see www.qianyan.biz/patent/sangaoyongxin/youhuizhengce.htm.

4 Financial policies for innovation

While fiscal policies have played a significant role in leveraging public and private funding into R&D and motivating firms to innovate, it is clear that innovative firms will be seriously constrained if they have to rely on internal capital to invest in R&D and full-scale commercialization. Hence, it is imperative that they should be able to access the capital market to meet their finance needs as innovations move forward. This presents a new challenge to China as its monobank system inherited from the pre-reform system was ill-equipped to meet enterprises' unprecedented needs in financing of innovation. Under the monobank system, all cash (deposits) from enterprises, mainly state-owned enterprises (SOEs), must be held by the People's Bank of China (PBOC) and all credits (loans) to SOEs and state projects were extended by the PBOC. In short, the PBOC became the centre of settlement for both deposits and credits. It thus means that China needed to transform its monobank system into a modern banking system and to build a modern financial system from scratch. It is in this area that China's financial institution-building and financial innovations have been impressive.

The framework of innovation-oriented financial policies

China's economic reform over the past three decades has led to significant changes in the financial sector. The foremost important steps of reform in the financial sector have included the replacement of a monobank system in 1984 with a multi-tiered one in which central banking functions are separated from the rest. This was epitomized in the separation of commercial banking activities from policy lending banks in 1994, the enactment of a new Commercial Banking Law in 1995, the enactment of a new charter for PBOC in 1995, and the creation of the *China Banking Regulatory Commission* (CBRC) in 2003 to separate PBOC's responsibilities for monetary policy and banking supervision. These changes in the financial sector have opened up new opportunities for governments in China to exploit new financial tools for resource mobilization in support of innovation. They have however posed new challenges for governments in building new institutions and seeking financial innovations. In the development of a new framework of financial policies, three critical documents have set the tone and spelled out the principles of innovation-oriented financial policies. The first is the Communist Party Central Committee's 'Decisions on Reform of the Science and Technology System' issued in 1985. The decisions signalled a departure from the previous system that relied primarily on government direct funding to support innovation to one that all alternative options were encouraged. More specifically, governments at all levels were encouraged to seek out other sources of funding, to bring on board other governmental departments, enterprises and public organizations to invest in S&T, and to consider using venture capital (VC) to support highly uncertain, risky high-tech enterprises. Banks were also encouraged to extend more credit to S&T-related activities and to monitor and supervise the use of S&T funds on behalf of governments. The second is the Law on Science and Technology Progress (LSTP) – China's basic law on science and technology, promulgated in 1993 and amended in 2007. It is stipulated in the General Provisions of LSTP that the State shall ensure a steady and continuous growth of funding for STI through greater financial support and the development of industrial policy, taxation policy, financial policy and government procurement policy to encourage and guide enterprise investment. Meanwhile, the LSTP also states that the State shall leverage state funding to provide enterprises with loan interest subsidy and loan guarantee for their independent innovation and commercialization of innovation outputs. Furthermore, the LSTP specifies the guiding principles for the innovation-related business operation of policy-oriented banks, capital markets and venture capital (fund-of-funds). The third is the Outline of Medium and Long-term National Plan for Science and Technology Development (2006–2020) promulgated in 2006. This document was thus far the most comprehensive in its scope for outlining policies concerning financial support for S&T. Step by step, the framework of financial policies for supporting innovation in China has taken shape (see the milestones of reforms in Figure 4.1). Currently, the policy framework for innovation-oriented financial support comprises seven streams of initiatives.

Mobilizing policy-oriented financial institutions to support innovation

China at present has three policy-oriented financial institutions,[1] i.e. Agricultural Development Bank of China (ADBC), the Export-Import Bank of China (EximBank) and China Export and Credit Insurance Corporation (SINOSURE). They are charged with using the considerable financial resources under their control to fulfil their respective policy functions. Measured by financial capacity, China Development Bank (CDB) is the biggest of three policy-oriented banks. In 2011, CDB had total assets of RMB6.2 trillion with a loan balance of RMB5.5 trillion. Comparatively, the respective total assets of ADBC and EximBank were RMB1.95 trillion and 1.36 trillion, and their respective loan balance was RMB1.86 trillion and 1.08 trillion.[2] These policy-oriented financial institutions have been given the mandate to prioritize policy loans to key national special S&T projects, large-scale financing of key national S&T industrialization

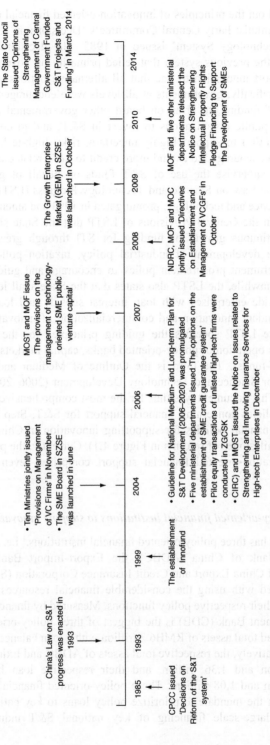

Figure 4.1 The milestones of innovation-focused financial policies in China.

projects and commercialization projects of S&T achievements, high-tech industrialization projects, import and absorption of foreign technologies and high-tech products exports. CDB, for example, makes soft loans in the form of equity financing to high-tech enterprises, and EximBank provides finance to support import and export of core technologies and key equipment necessary for the development of high-tech enterprises. Similarly, ADBC supports commercialization and industrialization of agricultural innovations.

Leveraging commercial financial institutions to support innovation

Policies in this regard concern the use of public policy instruments, for example, public funds, interest subsidies and guarantees, to leverage more lending from financial institutions to projects of independent innovation and full-scale industrialization. Policies, for example, are targeted at key high-tech projects of national and regional importance. Both central and local governments have used a tendering system and publication of their approved project lists as a filtering mechanism for identifying high-quality projects before encouraging commercial banks, in full compliance with the country's investment policies and credit policies, to lend to those projects. Policies are also targeted at support for export of high-tech products arising from independent innovations. With particular regard to firms with profitable products and debt repayment capacity, commercial banks are encouraged to prioritize credit arrangements to meet these firms' working capital need. They are also encouraged to provide value-added financial services, e.g. credit provision and clearing services, to those exporting firms with excellent credit rating.

Improving financial services for technology-oriented SMEs

One of the focuses in this area has been the development of a nation-wide business and the general public credit reference system. Despite decades of reform, the market system in China remains a project in progress. In particular, the credit rating system for businesses and individuals was both rudimentary and segmented. The focus of efforts hence has been to encourage the development of various types of credit reporting agencies on the one hand and to convert a disjoined credit system into a nationally integrated one on the other. It was hoped that a relatively robust credit reference system would become a supporting pillar for credit risk control of commercial banks, on which they can better service the needs of technology-based SMEs. PBOC and its regional branches have been charged with the task of facilitating, supervising and regulating the development of a national credit reporting system. Another important development has been the construction of a national loan guarantee system. The key policy driving developments in this area was the Opinions on the Construction of SME Credit Guarantee System, issued by NDRC in conjunction with four other ministerial departments in November 2006. Governments at all levels have since acted upon this policy agenda and the private sector was encouraged to participate in the establishment of SME credit guarantee institutions. The purpose was to create a variety of guarantee methods to make up for SMEs' lack of secured collateral. Measures have also been taken to address issues such as channels of raising equity capital for guarantee agencies and the development of a multi-level risk-sharing mechanism. Policy lending banks, commercial banks and other financial institutions have also piloted business services on pledge over intellectual property rights.

Developing the venture capital sector

Policies related to the development of the venture capital sector were first concerned with the improvement of the legal and regulatory environment for the sector. An important development was the circulation of the 'Interim Measures for the Administration of Venture Capital Firms' drafted by ten ministerial departments and approved by the State Council in 2005. The interim measures, which came into effect in 2006, define regulations concerning incorporation, registration, business operations, policy support, and supervision and regulation of venture capital firms. In addition attention has been paid to involving governments in setting up public venture capital funds as a way of leveraging private capital to invest in entrepreneurial firms at the seed and start-up stages. Early spontaneous pilots at the regional level were later consolidated through the release of 'Guidance on the Establishment and Operation of VC Guiding Funds' by the State Council in 2008. Correspondingly, regulations were relaxed to allow insurance companies and securities companies to invest in VC funds and to allow VC firms to boost their fund under management through use of debt financing. Related changes were also made on the foreign exchange management system to regulate foreign exchange administration of venture investment enterprises.

Establishing a multi-level capital market for financing of innovation

Policies in this area were two-fold. First, focus was to help eligible high-tech SMEs to raise funds through listing in China's main stock markets as well as in the secondary board markets. For the latter, the first breakthrough came on 25 June 2004 when the SME Board in the Shenzhen Stock Exchange (SZSE) opened with eight companies making their debut. The SME Board has since become an indispensable and independent segment in China's multi-tier capital market system and has contributed to the growth of China's technology industries, thanks to many high quality IPOs. As of 30 December 2011, there were 646 companies listed on the SME Board with a total market capitalization of RMB2.7 trillion (US$428.6 billion).[3] The success of the SME Board was soon followed by the opening of ChiNext, the Growth Enterprise Market (GEM), in SZSE on 23 October 2009. As of 30 December 2011, there were 281 companies listed on the ChiNext, of which 93 per cent were high-tech firms. The total market capitalization of ChiNext listed companies reached RMB743.4 billion

(US$118 billion).[4] Policies have since been fine-tuned to reduce the timescale of pre-listing tutoring and to simplify the approval process in order to smooth the way of IPOs for technology-based SMEs. Both GEM and ChiNext in SZSE serve SME issuers in both traditional and innovative sectors. The SME Board adopts almost the same listing rules as the Main Board and gears toward traditional manufacturing businesses like the Main Board. It has nevertheless offered an important channel for growth companies seeking financing support from capital markets. ChiNext, in comparison, offers less stringent listing rules and requires shorter operational history and less profit for potential issuers. ChiNext is positioned to be more accessible to new and high-tech enterprises from innovative sectors. Table 4.1 summarizes the comparative listing criteria in the Main Board, SME Board and ChiNext Board in SZSE.

Second, emphasis has been placed on the development of the equity transaction market for unlisted high-tech companies. In January 2006, securities companies opened a pilot platform to unlisted high-tech enterprises in Zhongguancun Science Park, Beijing, to broker equity transactions. A similar pilot was later rolled out to other National High-Tech Industrial Development Zones.[5] A pilot has also been carried out in many regions to develop regional equity transaction markets, using local government pump-priming funds, so as to broaden the venture capital exit routes. In 2013, the State Council issued the Decisions on the National System of Equity Transaction for Unlisted High-tech SMEs to simplify the procedure of approval and the administration of the system.

Developing insurance services for high-tech enterprises

Two government policies set the foundation of developments in this area. The first was the issuance of the Notice on the Strengthening and Improvement of Insurance Services for High-Tech Enterprises by MOST and CIRC in December 2006. The second was the Notice on Further Support to Export Credit Insurance for New and High-Tech Firms issued by MOF in the same year. Six cities (Suzhou, Chongqing, Wuhan, Beijing, Shenzhen and Tianjin) and four insurance companies were soon selected as the first cohort of regions and financial institutions to pilot insurance services aiming at technology-based firms. Pilot insurance services were particularly focused on the development and provision of six types of insurance products, i.e. product liability insurance, key R&D equipment insurance, business interruption insurance, export credit insurance, directors and key R&D employees' liability insurance, and accident insurance.

Improving foreign exchange management policy for high-tech enterprises

Policy developments have been concerned with changes in foreign exchange management to meet the needs of domestic high-tech firms in their international trade of goods and services, in the set-up of overseas R&D centres and in acquisition of foreign R&D institutes or high-tech companies.

Table 4.1 Comparative listing criteria of the Main Board, SME Board and ChiNext Board in SZSE

	Main Board	SME Board	ChiNext Board
Targeting companies	Large-scale companies which intend to solicit large amount of public funds	Companies with a smaller scale for equity flow	Companies engaged in independent innovation businesses and other growing venture enterprises to solicit public funds
Track record requirement	A minimum of three years track record requirement Positive net profits for the last three fiscal years, and cumulative net profits for the last three fiscal years exceed RMB30 million Cumulative net cash flows for the last three fiscal years from business operation exceed RMB50 million or cumulative business revenues for the last three fiscal years exceed RMB300 million The total value of its stocks before the offering is no less than RMB30 million The proportion of its intangible assets at the end of its most recent fiscal period in its net assets does not exceed 20% No unrecovered loss at the end of its most recent fiscal period		A minimum of two years track record requirement Cumulative profits for the last two years exceed RMB10 million or profits for last year exceed RMB5 million An operating income for the last year exceeds RMB 50 million; the annual growth rate for the last two years exceeds 30% The total value of its stocks after the offering is no less than RMB30 million No unrecovered losses
Minimum market capitalization	The total share capital before the share offering shall be no less than RMB50 million		The total share capital after the listing shall not be less than RMB30 million
Shareholding requirements	The shares offered to the public shall not be less than 25% of the total shares of the listed company, and if the total value of the shares of the listed company is more than RMB400 million, such ratio must not be less than 10%		The shares offered to the public shall not be less than 25% of the total shares of the listed company, and if the total value of the shares of the listed company is more than RMB400 million, such ratio must not be less than 10%

Source: compiled from SZSE documents.

The framework of innovation-specific financial policies clearly shows that governments of all levels in China have now had a variety of financial policy instruments to support S&T innovation activities. As explained in Chapter 2, R&D projects in China are categorized under two types of national S&T programmes: (1) major special national S&T programmes, and (2) basic programmes. To support key national S&T programmes, governments can now employ appropriate means from options of financial instruments and funding mechanisms such as grants, loan interest subsidy, repayable assistance and venture capital, in accordance with the features of projects and types of organizations involved in delivering the projects. For technology-oriented SMEs, the Innovation Fund for Technology-based SMEs (InnoFund) can match R&D projects of SMEs with a variety of supporting methods, ranging from loan interest subsidy, grants, to equity financing.

Policy instruments for financing innovation

International experiences suggest that financing innovation needs a well-functioning financial system that makes equity and debt financing available to innovators and innovation projects and that have an efficient loan guarantee system to complement bank lending (Commission of the European Communities, 2009). Under the framework conditions as described in the preceding section, governments at the central and regional levels in China now have a variety of policy instruments under their disposal to allocate resources, and the principles guiding the use of policy instruments have changed to mobilizing private funds for innovation. Broadly speaking, the policy instruments currently in use can be grouped into the categories of direct funding, indirect funding, credit enhancements and technical, infrastructural or knowledge support.

Direct funding

This is a form of financing that is provided by governments and public agencies, in line with their broader social objectives of innovation and economic development. Three forms of direct funding can be identified, namely co-investment through public venture capital funds, equity financing by policy-oriented financial institutions, and incentive grants for stock market listing.

In the technological innovation life cycle, the early-stage innovation segment is commonly underfunded due to the lack of clarity of technologies and product markets as well as a high degree of uncertainty about the ultimate market potential of innovations. The situation was even more challenging in China, despite the development of capital markets during the economic reform period. This has called for measures to address financial market failures in order to ensure adequate funds for young innovative firms. In addition to merit-based funding awards (e.g. grants) as described in the previous chapter, the Chinese government has used measures of setting up government-backed venture capital funds at both central and regional levels, in the name of public venture capital guiding funds, to co-invest with private VC firms in early-stage innovations. Through this vehicle, more private capital investment has been leveraged to firms at the seed and start-up stages. This direct form of funding will be examined in more detail in Chapter 5.

Repayable subsidy, venture capital and equity capital investment also fall into this category. The central government has made breakthroughs in developing new ways of financing national key S&T projects, managing government-backed venture capital funds, and co-funding S&T infrastructures and facilities with enterprises. In February 2007, for example, the State Council decided to set up a state-controlled large passenger aircraft corporation to push forward research and development of this key project. It was intended that the project would be financed in accordance with the principles of market mechanism and interests of various stakeholders. In 2007, MOF and MOST jointly initiated the first national venture capital fund to support S&T SMEs. The central government allocated RMB100 million to this fund to support enterprises involved in innovation projects in the start-up stage. More specifically, the fund supports four types of start-up S&T SMEs, namely venture capital funds focused on start-up firms, venture capital management firms, SMEs service facilities with venture capital functions, and technology firms at early stage. The fund lends its support through the means of equity shares at different stages, follow-up investment, risk subsidies and investment insurance. Based on the successful experiences of Pudong S&T Development Fund, the Shanghai New Pudong District further improved the S&T development fund operations. The new financial supporting facility was mostly repayable. Repayable schemes such as guarantees and venture capitals have been added gradually to ensure the long-term sustainability of the fund. Over time, more and more local governments have become interested in venture capital funds, and many provincial/municipal governments have already set up venture capital funds.

Local governments have also created an initial public offering (IPO) readiness scheme to incentivize local enterprises to seek equity financing from capital markets through IPOs. For instance, Hangzhou Municipal Government provides financial support to companies at the stage of pre-listing preparation. It provides an incentive of RMB200,000 for companies before and after the shareholding reform, RMB300,000 for those in the share transfer system, RMB500,000 for those listed on GEM, RMB1 million for those listed on the Main Board and RMB2 million for those listed on foreign capital markets.

Indirect funding

Indirect funding in China takes forms of incentive schemes for lending to R&D projects and high-tech SMEs and fund-of-funds programmes. In these indirect funding programmes, the government involvement is more remote and there is a certain degree of separation from the financing decision-makers.

Reward schemes for additional lending to R&D projects and
technology-based SMEs

Reward schemes were designated to use fiscal policy instruments to encourage financial institutions to increase their lending facility to S&T activities and to provide more credit to S&T projects and small enterprises. In Jiangsu, for example, the provincial government launched a reward scheme in 2009 through its Incentive Funds for Compensation of Risks from Additional Loans. Funds for the scheme primarily came from the provincial government's budget with some match funds from other levels of local governments. The scheme was used to compensate policy-oriented banks, commercial banks and rural cooperative financial institutions for their assuming higher financial risk as a result of additional lending they commit to technology-based small firms. More specifically, if a financial institution has increased its lending to S&T enterprises by 20 per cent over the previous year, all its province-wide sub-branches would receive an award of risk compensation from the Provincial Department of Finance, at equivalence to 1 per cent of additional S&T loans of the same year. If, however, the financial institution has not met the target of lending increase by 20 per cent, then, only those sub-branches with an increase of 20 per cent of loans would receive an award. In addition, the scheme gives each banking financial institution the autonomy to use, according to its own circumstances, up to 5 per cent of the reward to award their bank managers who have performed well in lending to S&T projects or small enterprises.

Direct funding through co-investment has a substantial administrative and decision burden associated with the selection and support of the recipient enterprises. Over time, policy instruments have shifted to an emphasis on the sharing of financial burden indirectly. As will be explained in the next chapter, for all the options for funding enterprises at the seed and start-up stage through public VC guiding funds, fund-of-funds have become the preferred option in order to let markets play a greater role in selecting, evaluating, investing and monitoring innovative enterprises.

Credit enhancements

Financing innovation requires a funding system that provides potential rewards to financiers for assuming the risks involved. International experiences show that venture capital is an important part of such a system. However, venture capital finances only a very small fraction of businesses. For early-stage enterprises, the most common form of external financing remains bank financing. Reforms of the banking sector in China since 1994 have endeavoured to establish a banking system that functions more closely to commercial principles, and banks in the revamped system have gradually placed profit consideration as key criteria in lending decisions. In response to changes in commercialization in the banking sector, governments in China have sought new measures to enhance credit availability and to encourage banks to lend to innovative enterprises.

Intellectual property rights pledge financing

As can be seen in Chapter 8, soaring patent filings in China mean that a growing number of technology enterprises have held intellectual property rights in their asset portfolio. Yet, banks consider intangible assets of intellectual property rights too difficult to value and hence are reluctant to accept them as collateral. Financial innovation in using the value of intellectual property as collateral has made it easier for high-tech enterprises to get loans.

Early experiments on intellectual property rights pledge financing started on an ad hoc basis in a few regional financial institutions in the 1990s. For example, the Shanxi Province Qizhou Branch of Industrial and Commercial Bank of China (ICBC) launched China's first ever banking services on intellectual property rights pledge financing in 1999. Banks such as Bank of Communications and Shenzhen Development Bank soon piloted similar services. Local financial innovations received a boost from the central government in August 2010 when MOF in conjunction with five other ministerial departments released the Notice on Strengthening Intellectual Property Rights Pledge Financing to Support the Development of SMEs. The Notice provided a more coherent framework for the initiative concerning service provision, risk control, evaluation of intellectual property rights pledge financing, and intellectual property transaction.

Financial innovations in this area have mainly been driven by the State Intellectual Property Office and its regional offices, and they share many common features of practices. Intellectual property rights pledge financing schemes operated by a city or region have adopted the following application eligibility criteria:

- business registration and operation locally;
- legal holders of patents granted by the State Intellectual Property Office with no less than ten years of legal protection period;
- meeting a threshold of registered capital (e.g. more than RMB15 million if application is made in Tianjin);
- in the stage of commercializing the patent(s) with a capacity of proceeding to mass production.

This government-led scheme has two modes. (1) Subsidized loan scheme. Under this scheme, governments set up a special fund in their budget earmarked to subsidize SMEs to reduce their borrowing costs from using intellectual property rights pledge financing facility. Banks and IP service providers who sign up with the scheme are responsible for independent IPR evaluation, lending decision and risk-taking of repayment default. For example, in Shenzhen, the subsidized loan scheme provided a government subsidy for 40 per cent of the total interest of a loan, subject to a cap of RMB2 million. Borrowers using an intellectual property rights pledge financing facility can apply for a grant against their actual repayment of the loan and the interest before a specified deadline each year. (2) Loan guarantee scheme. The scheme signed up local banks and provided a government guarantee against default on loans from the participating lenders. Under this scheme, governments would earmark a special fund in their budget and banks would set up the intellectual property rights pledge financing facility that matches the size of the special fund at a pre-agreed ratio. For instance, from 2006 to 2010 Shanghai Pudong District Government arranged RMB20 million in its loan guarantee scheme each year and the participating banks in the scheme provided the financing facility worth 2–2.5 times the size of the government funding. The scheme could guarantee a loan of up to RMB2 million for three years. In both schemes, businesses that meet the basic eligibility criteria do not have an automatic entitlement to receive intellectual property rights pledge financing. Decision-making on individual loans is fully delegated to the participating lenders and is integrated with the commercial decision to lend.

For over five years from January 2006 to June 2011 financial institutions in China provided RMB31.85 billion worth of intellectual property rights pledge financing to 3,361 applications.[6] Intellectual property rights pledge financing in 2012 alone was worth RMB14.1 billion.[7] Pilot financial services on intellectual property rights pledge financing were already undertaken in 28 provinces by the end of 2012.

Lending risk compensation funds

Banks are inherently conservative in lending to risky technology firms. To enhance credit availability, many governments at the local level have worked with local financial institutions to experiment with intellectual property right pledge loans. In October 2009, for example, Jiangsu set up a special risk compensation fund under the Provisional Regulations on the Administration of Special Fund on Risk Compensation for Commercialization of S&T Outputs. The fund was jointly managed by the Provincial Department of Finance and Department of Science and Technology. The Special Fund had earmarked RMB50 million from the provincial budget and was designated to achieve three objectives: (1) to mitigate difficulties in financing of S&T-oriented small enterprises; (2) to establish closer ties between S&T and financial resources; and (3) to accelerate the growth of emerging industries. This is a kind of loan guarantee scheme, designated to encourage financial institutions to extend more credit to commercialization projects that are ready for full-scale manufacturing after completing pilot testing. The Fund was entrusted to Jiangsu Provincial Productivity Promotion Centre (PPC) and focused on intellectual property right pledge loans for SMEs. Under this scheme, if PPC accepted a firm's intellectual property right pledge, a bank that has signed up to the scheme would issue a loan at the ratio of three times more than the intellectual property right pledge. In the event of bad loans incurred by the written-off lending in the failed project, the Special Fund would bear 70 per cent of loss in loan principal with other levels of local governments bearing the other 30 per cent of loss, and the lender would bear the loss of loan interest. A fund like this was expected to develop a mechanism for local governments, banks and enterprises to share risks.

Guarantee schemes

Guarantees have demonstrated to be a crucial measure to facilitate access to financing for early-stage innovative enterprises. Governments launched enterprise finance guarantee schemes to facilitate additional lending to viable S&T-oriented SMEs lacking adequate security or proven track record for a standard commercial loan.

For instance, in Nanjing, capital city of Jiangsu Province, the municipal government provided RMB8 million to establish an S&T Innovation Investment and Guarantee Management Company in 2002. The company increased its guarantee capacity to RMB90 million in 2008, with 39 per cent of contribution from private capital. Over 200 SMEs and 313 projects have been offered guarantee loans with a total value of RMB1 billion.

Hangzhou High-tech Guaranty Company is another example. The company is a state-owned policy-oriented guarantee company affiliated to Hangzhou Municipal Bureau of Science and Technology charged with providing guarantee and other financing services to S&T-oriented SMEs in Hangzhou. Since its establishment in March 2006, the company has increased its registered capital from RMB20 million to RMB125 million and has provided guarantee services to over 70 SMEs with a total value of RMB160 million. The guarantee company experimented financial innovations through the launching of five unique products, i.e. angel guarantee, guarantee option, intellectual property right pledge-based guarantee, pledge-based guarantee with order/accounts receivable and pre-guarantee with policy-oriented appropriation. This way, the company has helped SMEs of different types at different growth stages resolve their financing problems.

Guarantee risk compensation funds

Local governments have also established guarantee risk compensation funds to expand the business of guarantee agencies. For instance, Jiangsu Provincial Government used the proceeds repaid to the special fund of R&D commercialization as a guarantee risk compensation fund. Under the scheme, the government provides the loan guarantee agency a subsidy of up to 20 per cent of its risk reserves drawn in proportion to the agency's year-end average guaranteed balance (the reserves drawn as per up to 1 per cent of the responsible balance at the current year end and drawn pro rata of post-tax profits). For SME loan guarantee agencies, if they charge guarantee fees at 50 per cent lower than the bank loan interest rates in the same period, the government will provide a subsidy of up to 2.5 per cent of the guarantee premium. In the case of loan default, the provincial government will cover 70 per cent of the lender's loss, and other participating local governments will cover the remaining 30 per cent. As of the end of 2012, Jiangsu increased the capacity of the guarantee risk compensation fund from the original RMB50 million to RMB200 million.[8]

S&T banks (sub-branches)[9]

To increase lending to high-tech enterprises, China encourages banks to set up S&T-oriented branches. Such experiments first emerged in Sichuan Province in January 2009 when Chengdu S&T Sub-branch of CCB and Chengdu S&T Sub-branch of Bank of Chengdu were established. The pilot was facilitated by Sichuan Provincial Department of Science and Technology (SPDST) in collaboration with Sichuan Office of CBRC. The two sub-branches specialize in providing loans to S&T-oriented enterprises in support for the growth of high- and new-tech industries. Specifically, SPDST is responsible for establishing the experts system and conducting a technical review prior to the loan approval of S&T projects, while the two sub-branches, following independent due diligence, provide preferential support for the S&T projects recommended by SPDST. They developed innovative financing products such as intellectual property right pledge financing and joint factoring. As of 20 September 2009, Chengdu S&T Sub-branch of Bank of Chengdu had provided services for an additional 39 S&T-oriented enterprises, with a loan balance of RMB527 million.

In Zhejiang Province, the S&T Sub-branch of the Bank of Hangzhou was founded in Hangzhou in July 2009. As a financial institution focusing on S&T-oriented SMEs in Hangzhou, the sub-branch mainly provides financing support to Hangzhou-based provincial and municipal level high- and new-tech enterprises or S&T-oriented SMEs certified by Hangzhou S&T authority. Half of the capital in the S&T Sub-branch's capital was from over 30 private equity firms' entrusted deposits, and the other half came from corporate current account balance, government funding and raised capital of listed companies. As of the end of 2011, 354 local start-up and growth enterprises received loans worth RMB4 billion.[10]

R&D insurance

In December 2006, China Insurance Regulatory Commission (CIRC) and MOST issued the Notice on Issues related to Strengthening and Improving Insurance Services for High-tech Enterprises. This marked another attempt of financial innovation for credit enhancement. As a tentative measure, CIRC and MOST identified liability insurance product development of high-tech enterprises, key R&D equipment insurance, business interruption insurance, export credit insurance, key executives and R&D personnel group health, and accident insurance as the first six insurance products to develop. It was also stated that enterprises can list their expenses from any of these six R&D insurance policies as technology development costs and are eligible for tax incentives. In 2006, 12 cities, including Beijing, Tianjin, Chongqing and Suzhou National High & New-Tech Industrial Development Zone, were selected by MOST and CIRC to pilot R&D insurance.

As one of the second batches of pilot cities on R&D insurance designated by CIRC and MOST, Chengdu, the capital city of Sichuan Province, earmarked RMB10 million as a subsidy fund for the development of R&D insurance. The fund provided a subsidy of 40 or 50 per cent of their actual premiums, subject to the cap of RMB200,000 per year for each enterprise. This has promoted the rapid growth of R&D insurance in Chengdu. In Wuxi City and Suzhou high- and new-tech zones in Jiangsu Province, both as pilot areas for R&D insurance innovation, the relevant government units worked closely with insurance companies to encourage, support and guide various S&T-oriented enterprises in participating R&D insurance.

As can be seen in Table 4.2, policy measures to support R&D insurance in the first group of cities under the pilot programme vary. In Chongqing, participating enterprises in the scheme can expect to receive a subsidy of up to 70 per cent of the R&D insurance premium it pays. Shenzhen set the ratio at a maximum of 50 per cent but offers an enterprise the most generous subsidy capped at RMB1 million.

R&D insurance has also been actively explored in the non-pilot regions. Although Zhejiang Province was not listed as the national pilot area for R&D insurance, the provincial government coordinated with insurance companies to implement R&D insurance. In May 2009, Zhejiang Office of PICC Property & Casualty issued a product liability insurance policy for Hangzhou Honghua Digital Technology Co. Ltd., indicating the start of R&D insurance services in Zhejiang Province.

R&D insurance has been ushered into a stage of fast growth with the gradual expansion of the pilot projects. As of end 2008, four insurance companies were engaged in R&D insurance, i.e. SINOSURE, PICC Property & Casualty, Huatai Insurance and PingAn Endowment Insurance. Thirteen R&D insurance products including R&D product liability insurance for high- and new-tech enterprises have been launched, with a total premium of RMB107.7 billion, 57.23 per cent more than that of 2007; about 1,600 high- and new-tech enterprises have been entitled to S&T insurance services, up 45 per cent versus 2007; insurance premiums are more than RMB1.15 billion; and the claim amount exceeded RMB367 million, and up to RMB20 million has been subsidized for R&D insurance premiums by the pilot cities (zones). The function of R&D insurance in sharing risks has been enhanced, and thus effectively promoted commercialization of technical innovation and achievements.

Table 4.2 Policies of government support to R&D insurance

	Subsidy as % of insurance premium	Maximum value of subsidy (RMB)	Issuance of policy
Suzhou National High & New-Tech Industrial Development Zone	Up to 50	300,000	2009
Chongqing	30–70	100,000	2012
Wuhan	various	100,000–350,000	2012
Shenzhen	Up to 50	1,000,000	2007
Tianjin	30	100,000	2010

Source: compiled by the authors.

Innovation of trust products

To address the difficulty of commercial exploitation of patents, Wuhan International Trust and Investment Company launched a patent trust business on 25 October 2000, the first of its kind in China. Despite its failure two years later, it has provided some lessons for the trust sector with exploiting business opportunities in support of S&T development. Since the launch of the MLNP in 2006, the trust sector has been thrust into the limelight in the S&T area. In February 2009, China Zhongtou Trust, headquartered in Hangzhou, issued Hangzhou Cultural and Creative Industry Trust Fund of Creditor Rights, 'Bao Shi Liu Xia' (宝石流霞), raising RMB60 million to support 29 creative industry companies in the city. The raised capital comprised RMB10 million purchased by the Municipal Department of Finance, RMB47 million from the public and RMB3 million by a private equity firm. An insurance company provided a comprehensive policy that covered a loss of up to RMB60 million. This marks a new model of 'cooperation between government and trust company', integrating the special supporting fund of governments, bank funds raised by financial management products and investment funds of the professional investing firms. Later on, the trust service has received a positive response from many areas such as intellectual property right development, S&T-oriented SMEs' financing and corporate equity investments.

Technical, infrastructural or knowledge support

International experiences suggest that fund-raising systems, capital market provisions and entry and exit mechanisms are all important factors that encourage firms to innovate (Shi, 2009). In constructing the financial incentive structure for innovation, governments in China have taken important measures of institution building with regard to technical, infrastructural or knowledge support.

The multiple-layer capital markets as infrastructural support for innovation

Secondary board markets. As of 2009, five years after the SME Board was launched, 75 per cent of the 273 listed companies were S&T companies. The average R&D expenses of each listed S&T company increased from the original RMB15.30 million prior to their IPOs to RMB22.55 million, up 47.4 per cent; an additional 3,268 patents were granted, including 374 invention patents, and 180 companies have owned core patented technologies related to their major products.

Share transfer agent services. To help the growing number of unlisted shareholding high-tech companies to optimize their capital structure through unlisted share liquidity, Zhongguancun Science Park, under the support of MOST, CSRC and Beijing Municipal Government, launched the pilot unlisted share transfer agent service for non-listed companies in Zhongguancun in January 2006. By the end of 2011, 100 high tech companies had used the share transfer agent service for share transfer, of which, 48 per cent were IT companies; five companies had become fully listed in the main stock markets in China with another 15 in progression to IPO.[11] The share transfer agent services have become an important incubator from which firms can gain experiences with using the capital market. CSRC promulgated the restructuring schemes related to investor access, conditions of being listed for companies, transaction settlement, limited sales of shares and information disclosure, providing favourable conditions to expand the pilot project. As a result, the multiple-layer capital markets have become key platforms to nurture emerging strategic industries and enterprises with independent innovation.

Bond markets. Bond markets have also become a key channel for the national high- and new-tech areas and S&T-oriented SMEs to raise funds. In 1998 and 2003 respectively, MOST successfully issued the joint bond for enterprises in the national high- and new-tech areas to expand financing sources and enhance financing credibility and capacity of these areas. Zhongguancun Science Park, Shenzhen and Dalian, following the similar model, have also successfully issued joint bonds for SMEs within their areas. At present, CSRC is studying the issuance of corporate bonds of different credit ratings. The property trading markets in China provide a key platform for the asset transaction of enterprises of different ownership and the continuous equity trading of non-listed companies, which have satisfied the demand of non-listed companies in attracting investment to some extent and make it possible for the M&A of enterprises. So far, the benefits of the property market in terms of information gathering, price discovery and consulting service have been much appreciated by the business sector.

The establishment of a comprehensive platform for S&T-oriented financial services

To provide a service platform that bridges VC firms and start-up enterprises, Zhejiang Hangzhou Municipal Bureau of Science and Technology established the Hangzhou Venture Capital Service Centre, a not-for-profit financial service organization, in July 2008. The service centre was intended to be a venture capital services platform to help technology-oriented enterprises to raise fund and financial institutions to invest in, and provide added value to, promising enterprises in order to boost economic development in Hangzhou. The Centre was operated and managed by Hangzhou Municipal High-Tech Investment Co. Ltd. The centre provided four main financial service functions, namely financial advice, project brokering, intermediary services and start-up mentoring, and housed venture capital institutions, venture capital management companies, security companies, banks, law firms, accounting firms, patent offices and other institutions. As of November 2013, the centre had 65 registered members, of which 36 were investment management firms that managed over RMB10 billion of venture capital; 16 guarantee agencies with a guarantee capacity of over RMB2.5 billion; and 13 intermediary agencies engaged in patenting, legal counselling and accounting services. Thirty-three members have chosen either to locate their whole operations or to open an office in the Centre.

The creation of an information system that bridges high-tech enterprises and financial institutions

To address concerns of information asymmetry between financial institutions and S&T enterprises, Sichuan Provincial Department of Science and Technology and Sichuan Office of CBRC jointly sponsored and established the Sichuan Information Service Platform for Banks and Enterprises. The Platform was built upon two interactive websites, i.e. the Sichuan S&T-oriented Finance Website which was supported by the Sichuan Provincial S&T-oriented Finance Database System, and the official website of Sichuan Office of CBRC which releases updated data from its Information System of Banking and Financial Institutions. In addition, the Platform developed six sub-databases, including Sichuan S&T-oriented SMEs Database, High- and New-Tech Enterprise Database, Venture Capital Firm Database, and Sichuan Venture Capital Subsidy Application and Review Database. Through the process of enterprises application, expert review (assessment and recommendation), government monitoring, banks due diligence, and credit approval and feedback, the Platform publishes interactive business and finance information online in both websites on a regular basis, and builds a system of exchanging statistical analysis and reports. Many SMEs, banking sector, VC firms and relevant intermediary agencies are effectively connected by the online database to achieve interaction, information sharing and resources consolidation. When it was officially launched on 19 August 2009, information about more than 740 enterprises, 40 headquarters of banks and 161 sub-branches of banks was included in the database. By the end of 2010, more than 1,500 S&T-oriented SMEs in Sichuan Province were already covered by the database.

A summary of the financial instruments concerning innovation in China is provided in Table 4.3.

Policy coordination and complementarities

Alignment of financial policies with innovation policies

After many efforts over the last three decades, China has now established a financial system that is big in scale and that has a relatively sound structure and orderly competition. At the core of this system are the market-oriented financial institutions and a regulatory and supervisory body, comprising the PBC, China Banking Regulatory Commission (CBRC), CSRC and China Insurance Regulatory Commission (CIRC). This revamped financial system has the division of labour and cooperation between different types of financial institutions and offers a variety of avenues to financing innovation. These institutions complement each other and develop in a coordinated way. As a result, the financial market has seen a considerable improvement in the efficiency of financial

Table 4.3 A summary overview of the financial incentive structure for innovation in China

Mode of intervention	Instrument	Recipient(s)
Direct funding	Stock market listing incentive grants	High-growth enterprises
	Public VC funds	Enterprises
	Equity financing from policy-oriented financial institutions	Enterprises
Indirect funding	Incentive scheme for lending to R&D projects and high-tech SMEs	Financial institutions
	S&T banks	Enterprises
	Fund-of-funds programme	Private VC funds
Credit enhancements	Lending risk compensation scheme	Financial institutions
	SME credit guarantee	Financial institutions
	Guarantee risk compensation scheme	Debt guarantee agencies
	R&D insurance grants	Enterprises
	IPR pledge-based loans	Enterprises
	Patent trust funds	Enterprises
Technical, infrastructural or knowledge support	Share transaction platforms for non-listed high-tech firms	Enterprises
	Nation-wide business and individual credit reference system	Potential entrepreneurs/investors
	SME Board	High-growth enterprises/investors
	Growth Enterprise Market (GEM)	High-growth enterprises/investors
	Information dissemination	Potential entrepreneurs/investors

Source: compiled by the authors.

resource allocation, the emergence of innovative measures in financial markets, the development of new financial tools and financial products, and the significant expansion of financial markets. It can be argued that a financial market system that integrates the money market, capital market, foreign currency market and gold markets has taken shape.

Thanks to market reforms and market competition, financial institutions in China have turned their attention to providing financial services to SMEs in general, and technology-based SMEs in particular. As of end 2008, about four million small enterprises had been granted credit by financial institutions, up by 22 per cent compared on a yearly basis. The growth rate of the number of SMEs granted credit was higher than that of the average loan value. Over the recent years, banks have aligned their credit policy more closely with the government's industrial policy and S&T policies, resulting in positive impacts on economic development and restructuring. The multi-layer capital markets have become a key platform to nurture new strategic industries and enterprises undertaking independent innovation. Among 273 listed companies at SZSE in 2009, more than 75 per cent were S&T-oriented SMEs. In the pilot platform for brokering share transfers for non-listed companies in Zhongguancun, Beijing, 58 high-tech companies used the platform and successfully transferred their shares. Moreover, in the first batch of 28 enterprises listed on the ChiNext, 25 were high-tech new enterprises.

New cooperation mechanisms for governments and financial sectors

At the national level, a cooperation mechanism has been established among MOST and PBOC, CBRC, CSRC and CIRC. Moreover, MOST has established partnerships with many domestic banks including CDB, Huaxia Bank, ABC, EXIM Bank, CMB, CEB, PSBC and BOC. Cooperations between S&T and financial sectors are now in full swing, providing a solid foundation for deepening S&T financial reform and innovation.

At the local level, similar efforts were also made to use novel approaches to closer cooperation between the S&T and financial sectors. For instance, Sichuan Provincial Government, through its relevant governmental departments, signed strategic cooperation agreements with financial institutions to provide investment and financing services to S&T-oriented SMEs and improve the institutional environment. These agreements serve as platforms through which parties involved can take concerted action to support innovation. Examples of such institutional arrangements which involved Sichuan Provincial Government include an agreement with SZSE to help high- and new-tech enterprises in Sichuan to restructure and list in SZSE, a cooperation agreement with Sichuan Office of CBRC and SZSE to prepare candidates of high- and new-tech enterprises in Sichuan through training for stock marketing listing, a cooperation agreement with Sichuan Administration of Intellectual Property Rights and China Industrial Bank Chengdu Branch on intellectual property rights pledge financing, a cooperation agreement with Agricultural Development Bank of

China Sichuan Branch to enhance banking services to agricultural S&T, a cooperation agreement with Sichuan Provincial Department of Commerce and China Export & Credit Insurance Corporation Chengdu Office to leverage credit insurance to support the construction of innovation bases of high-tech exports, a cooperation agreement with Sichuan Provincial Department of Commerce and China EximBank to leverage financial means to support the construction of innovation bases of high-tech exports, and a cooperation agreement with Sichuan Office of CBRC on S&T and financial information exchange and cooperation.

In addition, S&T-oriented financial (service) groups and S&T venture capital groups have been established in high- and new-tech areas in Hangzhou, Zhong-guancun, Pudong, Suzhou, Wuxi and Chengdu, linking S&T with financial services.

Complementarity between central and local government policies

Optimizing the policy environment with regional characters

To support the national efforts to develop S&T-oriented finance, local governments have conducted many experiments in laying out the mechanism of cooperation between the S&T sector and financial sector and in developing the S&T-oriented financial system. The following good practices have been observed in Zhejiang Province.

Clarity in the role of S&T-oriented finance in the regional regulatory system

At the provincial level, Zhejiang Provincial Government has used the issuance of S&T-related regulations to clarify the development of the regional innovation system and define how it can be supported. Important provincial regulations have included regulations on progress of science and technology, the technology market, patent protection, and commercialization of scientific and technological innovations. Correspondingly, departments of S&T at city and county levels, e.g. Hangzhou, Ningbo, Shaoxing and Deqing, have developed and issued supporting policies. As a result, an S&T-oriented financial policy system has been initially put in place in the province.

The establishment of a coordinated mechanism

Zhejiang Provincial Department of Science and Technology, the main agency in charge of S&T, has taken responsibility for coordinating cross-institutional S&T-related efforts. For example, it has created respective coordination mechanisms with key provincial regulatory organizations, such as the Provincial Department of Finance, Zhejiang Office of CBRC and CIRC, etc. In the meantime, it has established partnership with some of the local financial institutions, including CCB Zhejiang Branch, and Zhejiang Office of PICC Property & Casualty. All these efforts have gradually put in place a working mechanism that integrates the S&T and financial sectors across the whole province.

Challenges for financial policies

Governments of all levels in China have been innovative in finding more effective ways of incentivizing banks and other financial institutions to boost their lending to technology-based SMEs, using fiscal policy instruments as a lever. The main areas of developments have been to provide risk subsidy to banks, set up compensation funds for bank loans, establish a mechanism for managing guarantee risks by the involvement of guarantee agencies, and set up S&T-oriented banks. These innovative schemes have expanded financing channels for technology-based SMEs.

As of end 2008, CDB, China EximBank and ADBC issued a total of RMB187.8 billion S&T-related loans to S&T-oriented SMEs, key S&T projects, national high- and new-tech areas, VC guiding funds, high- and new-tech products and enterprises under the strategy of 'going global', and agricultural S&T projects. In national high- and new-tech zones, loan arrangements for infrastructure development and implementation of loan interest rate subsidy policy have significantly enhanced the financing credibility and capacity of these zones. Some banks, working with local S&T authorities, carry out innovation and pilot projects on the development of lending facility for S&T-oriented SMEs, IPR pledge-based loan and energy conservation and emission reduction based credit. During the course of providing loans to the S&T-oriented SMEs, intermediary agencies including S&T guarantee firms set up by S&T authorities at various levels and the management committees of national high- and new-tech areas have played a key role and accumulated rich experiences in this regard.

Despite achievements of financial incentives for innovation, they have yet to meet the financing needs of technology innovation commercialization. Due to obstacles in management systems, system designs and operation modes, there is a lack of coordination and interaction among funds of different natures, such as enterprise funds, government investment funds, angel investments, venture capital, bank loans, equity financing and bond funds, etc., thus an absence in functions and maladjustments in policy. This results in insufficient start-up capital and vitality for technology innovation activities and the unsustainable follow-up funds for industrial development.

Financial incentives for innovation in China have been overwhelmingly focused on the supply side of funding. Comparatively, few measures have been taken to stimulate the demand side of funding through policies targeted at investment readiness training. Many early-stage innovative enterprises simply lack adequate knowledge of the nature and motives of venture capital. Demand-side policies such as investment readiness training programmes are important as they help enterprises with presenting their projects in ways that respond to the concerns of investors and hence increase the chances of matching available funding and innovative enterprises. Additionally, despite the financing gap in early-stage firms beings well recognized by policy-makers, policy initiatives in this area remain limited. Apparently, the launch of public venture capital guidance funds as can be seen in the next chapter has moved in the right direction. Other areas such as business angel investment and microcredit are surprisingly inadequately attended. Business angels primarily focus on early-stage investment. So a modest increase in business angel investment is likely to have a much larger impact on innovative firms in the seed phase and start-up phase than an equivalent increase in formal venture capital. In October 2010, Suzhou City in Jiangsu Province started a pilot initiative with focus on technology-oriented microcredit by creating Suzhou Rongda Technology Microcredit Company (RDKD). The company was founded by Suzhou Venture Investment Group, a leading financial institution specialized in equity investment, credit finance and equity investment services in China, and established itself in the mould of Silicon Valley Bank[12] with focus on venture debt financing. Venture debt, also known as venture lending, broadly covers loans to early-stage VC-backed companies. In return for the loan, the venture lenders receive principal and interest payments together with warrants and sometimes, depending upon the contract, the right to invest in a future round. Lending to early-stage companies can broadly take two forms, venture leasing and venture debt. As of October 2013, RDKD had provided venture debt financing in the value of over RMB1 billion to 70 high-growth, early-stage firms.[13] The experiment of this kind remains an exception.

Clearly the financial incentive framework has comprised many instruments. Ensuring coordination and synergies between these programmes will be crucial to maximize impact.

Notes

1 China Development Bank (CDB) used to be a policy-oriented financial institution but was converted into a commercial institution in December 2008. Nevertheless, it still assumes certain functions of a policy-oriented financial institution presently. It is for this reason that some scholars in China have called it to be reversed back into a fully fledged policy-oriented financial institution.
2 Data are from the 2012 annual reports of the three banks.
3 Quoted from information in the Shenzhen Stock Exchange: www.szse.cn/main/en/SMEBoard/ (accessed 13 February 2012).
4 Quoted from information in the Shenzhen Stock Exchange: www.szse.cn/main/en/ChiNext/ (accessed 13 February 2012).
5 As of April 2014, China has a total of 57 National High-Tech Industrial Development Zones. A full list of National High-Tech Industrial Development Zones is available on www.most.gov.cn/gxjscykfq/ (accessed 8 May 2014).
6 See news "知识产权质押融资在探索中成长" (The development of intellectual property rights pledge financing under pilot) on the State Intellectual Property Office of China, available at www.sipo.gov.cn/mtjj/2011/201109/t20110915_620308.html (accessed 22 March 2013).
7 From the China Intellectual Property News' commentary "知识产权质押融资缘何春来早" (Why spring came earlier with intellectual property rights pledge financing) on 18 February 2013, available at ip.people.com.cn/n/2013/0218/c136655-20515647.html (accessed 18 March 2013).

8 See "2012年江苏科技工作基本情况" (The highlights of S&T in Jiangsu 2012) from the Department of S&T, Jiangsu Province, available at www.jstd.gov.cn_kjxxgk_nrglIndex.action_type=2&messa (accessed 22 November 2013).
9 Large banks in China are structured in a hierarchical system with different decision-making power and financial responsibilities: bank head-office, first-tier branch (provincial capital-based), second-tier branch (city-based), first-tier sub-branch (city district-based or county-level), grassroots saving offices.
10 See report '杭州银行科技支行：打造杭州的硅谷银行' (Hangzhou Bank S&T Sub-Branch: creating a Silicon Bank in Hangzhou), available at www.zjsr.com/detail-8664.shtml (accessed 18 March 2013).
11 See China Galaxy Securities' 2011 report '中关村科技园区非上市公司股份报价转让系统研究报告' (A report of Zhongguancun Science Park unlisted share quoting and transfer system), available at www.chinastock.com.cn/yhwz_postdoc.do?methodCall=getResultsInfo&docId=2775986# (accessed 24 November 2013).
12 Silicon Valley Bank is the world's leading innovator of venture debt financing. It is the California bank subsidiary and the commercial banking operation of SVB Financial Group.
13 See '融达科贷：一家"硅谷银行"的园区实践' (RDKD: a science park-based financing experiment of a Chinese 'Silicon Valley Bank'), available at http://sz.xinhuanet.com/2013-10/25/c_117868416.htm (assessed 24 November 2013).

5 The public venture capital in China

As a late-comer economy, China has attached great importance to technological innovation and entrepreneurship. A big shift in China's thinking on innovation policy was manifested in President Hu Jintao's keynote speech in the National People's Congress meeting in 2006 when he called for China to transform itself into 'an innovation-orientated society'. With such an aspiration come a series of policy initiatives concerning the development of the venture capital sector. Leading these initiatives is the release of the 'Directives on the Establishment and Management of Venture Capital Guiding Funds (VCGFs)' by NDRC, MOF and MOC in October 2008. The Directives were intended to provide a framework for consolidating many spontaneous local experiments in government-backed VC and aimed at adopting a relatively hand-off approach to addressing both the supply-side and demand-side conditions impacting on the VC sector. Similar to efforts to set up public venture capital elsewhere,[1] the Chinese initiative was underpinned by two assumptions: (1) the traditional financial sector is unable to provide sufficient capital to match the needs of new technology-based firms, and (2) governments can use a pump-priming fund to maximize the availability of risk capital from financial intermediaries and private investors towards areas of strategic importance, thereby yielding higher social and/or private returns. Internationally, while these efforts have proliferated, consensus on how to structure such programmes remains elusive. As Lerner (2009) states, the challenge centres on how to structure such programmes to ensure their greatest effectiveness and to avoid political distortions.

The evolution of Chinese public venture capital initiative

The concept of venture capital was not fully introduced into any mainstream policy initiative in China until in March 1985 when the central government endorsed the establishment of venture capital funds to support highly uncertain, risky high-tech enterprises in the major government policy – 'Decisions on Reform of the S&T System'. This new development can be understood in the context of China's pursuit of deepened reform with renewed vigour after Deng Xiaoping's tour of South China in January 1984. Deng used his tour in Shenzhen and Zhuhai to openly endorse the unprecedented but controversial special economic zone (SEZ) policy. Soon afterwards, similar policies previously only available in SEZs were extended to another 14 coastal cities and Hainan Province. Under these circumstances, new ideas of reform, including the experiment of venture capital investment, were sought and put into action. The manifestation of such new developments was the launch of China New Technology Venture Capital Corporation (CNTVC) in 1986 under the approval of the Chinese government. On board in China's first venture capital firm were two biggest government shareholders: the State Science and Technology Commission and MOF, with each contributing 40 per cent and 23 per cent respectively to the fund which had a registered capital of US$10 million. CNTVC's remit was to create a new financing vehicle to assist with the implementation of the 'Torch Plan'.[2] Unfortunately, the experiment in VC, despite a promising start, ended with failure. CNTVC was liquidated in June 1998 primarily as a result of its financial misconduct (speculative investment in the stock and future markets) and a senior executive's embezzlement of the corporation's funds. Nevertheless, the setback in CNTVC did not sap the momentum. In March 1991, the State Council released the 'Provisions of Policies for National High-Tech Development Zones'. The Provisions reiterated that local governments could establish VC funds in high-tech development zones and that well-established high-tech development zones could set up their own venture investment enterprises. This mandated local governments for pursuing their VC policy agenda.

The development of public venture capital received another boost in August 1999 when the Communist Party Central Committee (CPCC) and State Council issued the 'Resolutions to Enhance Technological Innovation, Develop High Technology, and Realise Commercialisation' in an attempt to encourage the development of VC mechanisms, venture investment enterprises and VC funds. Subsequent policies from the central and local governments followed. For example, in December of the same year, MOST and other six ministries issued the 'Opinions on Establishing Venture Capital Mechanism'. With these encouragements, local governments stormed to set up venture capital organizations with funding either entirely from their own budget or from partnerships with large state-owned enterprises. Meanwhile, local governments enacted local policies to attract private or foreign funds to get involved in venture capital. Without a template to follow, public venture capital initiatives launched by local governments in this period were experimental and on an ad hoc basis. The first experiment of this kind occurred in 1999 when Shanghai municipal government launched a scheme with a particular emphasis on leverage of private venture capital to provide seed capital investment in high-tech SMEs.

The establishment of Innovation Fund for Small Technology-based Firms (InnoFund) in 1999 represented an important milestone in the central government's effort to redress problems in financing of high-tech SMEs. The InnoFund was designated to support technological innovations of small technology-based firms and R&D commercialization. InnoFund differed from other nongovernmental funds or commercial venture capital in three respects. First, it was policy-oriented with a particular emphasis on playing the government's macro policy guiding role in promoting innovation of technology-based SMEs and the development of new- and high-tech industries. Second, it served as a 'priming-pump' fund to leverage additional investment towards technology-based SMEs from local governments, corporations and financial institutions. It was an attempt to facilitate the development of a new investment mechanism conforming to the principles of market economy for technological innovations of SMEs. Third, it embraced a much broader agenda in innovation, i.e. GDP growth and job creation, thereby contributing to the restructuring and growth of the national economy. InnoFund used grants, loan interest subsidy and equity investment to finance innovations of technology-based SMEs. As far as equity investment was concerned, InnoFund could invest up to 20 per cent of the registered capital of the investee company but in reality the equity investment tool was rarely used.

At the turn of the twenty-first century, the development of the VC sector continued to gain momentum. First, the State Council's 'Provisions of Setting up Foreign Venture Investment Enterprises' took effect in September 2001. It removed the entry barriers of foreign VCs to China. Second, the Small and Medium Enterprise Board (SME Board) in Shenzhen Stock Exchange was launched in May 2004. Zhejiang NHU, a specialized producer of pharmaceutical chemicals, medications, health products, food additives, feed additives and flavours, became the first company to list on the SME Board in June 2004, signalling the official operation of the SME Board. The SME Board offers VC firms an important exit route to their venture investment.

Alongside the development of the VC sector were considerable improvements of legal environments as manifested in the issuance of an amendment to three laws – 'Securities Law', 'Corporate Law' and 'Partnership Law' – from October 2005 to August 2006. Under these law amendments, venture capital firms were permitted to raise funds through issuing non-publicly trading shares and to invest by instalment or in full; VC funds could be incorporated as limited partnerships. In November 2005, ten Ministries jointly issued the 'Interim Measures for the Administration of Venture Investment Enterprises'. The key regulations comprised:

1   A new venture investment enterprise should contribute no less than RMB30 million to the actual capital raised or should pay a deposit of no less than RMB10 million for its capital contributions provided that all investors commit to paying off the balance of actual capital contributions in a sum of not less than RMB30 million within five years of registration.
2   The number of investors should not exceed 200 persons, or 50 persons for a venture investment enterprise incorporated as a limited liability company.
3   A single investor's investment in a venture-backed enterprise should be no less than RMB1 million.
4   No venture investment enterprise may engage in any guarantee business or real estate business except for the purchase of real estate for its own use.
5   A venture investment enterprise should invest no more than 20 per cent of its total assets in a single venture-backed enterprise.[3]

The enactment of the Interim Measures marked the inclusion of venture investment enterprises into the legal framework and was of great significance for the development of the venture capital sector in China.

In August 2006 the State Council released the 'Notice on Supporting Measures for Implementing the National Medium and Long-Term Science and Technology Development Plan (2006–2020)'. The document lays out grounds for central government departments and local governments to establish venture capital guiding funds (VCGF) in order to attract more private capital contribution to venture investment enterprises and encourage venture capital firms to invest in seed or fledging businesses. The major push to address financing gaps came when the MOF and MOST co-issued 'the Interim Measures for Administration of the Venture Capital Guiding Fund for High-tech SMEs' (the Interim Measures) in 6 July 2007 and set up the first ever state-level Venture Capital Guiding Fund for Technology-based SMEs. The new initiative represents China's tremendous effort to identify the most suitable means of intervention in the venture capital market to support innovative firms. Also, in 2007, the MOF and State Administration of Taxation issued the 'Notice on Tax Policy in Support of Venture Investment Enterprises'.

In October 2008, NDRC, MOF and MOC jointly issued the 'Directives on the Establishment and Operation of VCGFs'. As promulgated in the Directives, the objectives of guiding funds were to leverage fiscal pump-priming funds to increase the supply of venture capital and to overcome market failures. Venture investment enterprises were encouraged to invest in enterprises in the seed or start-up stage alongside their general practice of investment in fledging and mature enterprises or merger and acquisition (M&A). Central government also made it clear that guiding funds should manage funds in the forms of fund-of-funds (equity shares), guarantees and co-investment on four principles that VCGFs are guided by government (government guiding), are run in compliance with the market-based VC model (market-based operation), follow the due diligence process in decision-making (scientific decision-making) and take calculated risk (controlled risk-taking). As a public VC fund, guiding funds would be brought into the evaluation system of public finance performance. Moreover, when withdrawing shares from fund-of-funds or co-investment projects, VCGFs should decide exit routes and prices in alignment with public finance principles and the VCGF's remit. Finally, Guiding Funds would not be allowed to invest in such areas as loans or stocks, futures, real estates, mutual fund, corporate debts, financial derivatives, sponsorship or donation. Unused capital should be deposited in banks or be used to buy treasury bonds only.

In October 2009, after a long debate and deliberation on the legality and practicality of setting up the Growth Enterprise Market (GEM) for an additional exit route for VC investments, China's GEM, or ChiNext Board, was launched in Shenzhen Stock Exchange. This was made possible after a significant hurdle was removed after China Securities Regulation Committee promulgated the 'Interim Measures on Initial Public Offering and Its Listing on the Growth Enterprise Board' in April 2009. Twenty-eight growth enterprises received approval of

IPOs in September and were listed in the GEM in October. The establishment of Growth Enterprises Board further expanded options of exit route for venture capital, thereby injecting strong stimulus to the development of China's venture capital sector. Highlights of the evolution of the VC industry and public VC schemes in China can be seen in Figure 5.1.

The VC Guiding Funds (VCGF) initiative

Like many public venture capital initiatives observed in other countries, VCGF's broad aim is to address the equity gap in financing of new high-tech firms by increasing the amount of risk capital available to affected businesses, both through direct investment and by attracting private investors. As stated in 'the Interim Measures for Administration of the Venture Capital Guiding Fund for High-tech SMEs' (VCGF for HTSMEs), for example, VCGF for HTSMEs is designated to guide venture investment enterprises to invest in technology-based SMEs in the seed and start-up stage. The Interim Measures define this group of SMEs as those engaging in research, development, production and servicing of new- and high-tech products and those unquoted companies with the prospect for becoming quoted within five years. The Chinese approach emphasizes risk sharing among all VC investors, including the government as a shareholder, in both seed-corn investment in the commercialization of S&T and co-investment in early-stage high-growth and often technology-based companies. It also aims to take a lead in financing high-potential, but high-risk projects, in which private equity providers are reluctant to become involved until later stages. In addition, it intends to share costs in financing of small firms, since most venture capital companies find the costs of investing small sums to be prohibitive. The language of the late 1990s was thus less about 'market failure' but more about developing new forms of public-private partnership to realize high potential opportunities which are associated with high levels of risk at their earlier stages. It is also much more about bringing different types of partners on board with contribution in different ways at various stages in the investment cycle of a new venture.

The government set out two important principles for the establishment of VCGFs in the 'Directives on Establishment and Operation of VCGFs' released jointly by the NDRC, MOF and MOC in October 2008.

1   *Government guidance.* This implies that governments will not assume the role of lead investors and that governments are to use public finance to leverage and guide more private capital toward investment in the national priority areas of strategic importance. Under such institutional arrangements for public and private sector involvement, VCGFs are expected to speed up the industrialization of indigenous innovation and the development of emerging, strategic industries.

2   *Market-based management.* This means that in VCGF invested funds, fund managers of venture investment enterprises are given full responsibility for

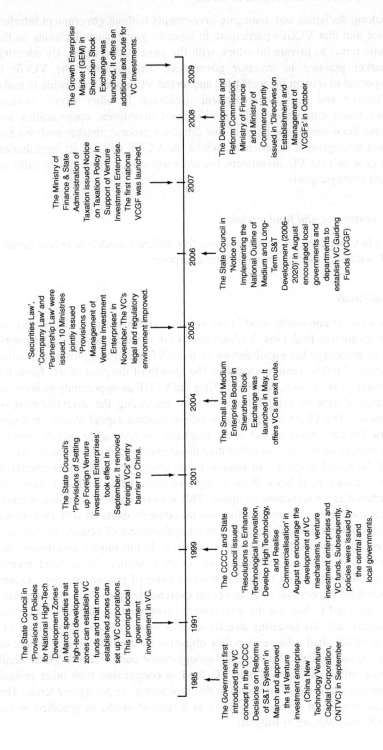

1985 — The Government first introduced the VC concept in the 'CCCC Decisions on Reforms of S&T System' in March and approved the 1st Venture investment enterprise (China New Technology Venture Capital Corporation, CNTVC) in September

1991 — The State Council in 'Provisions of Policies for National High-Tech Development Zones' in March specifies that high-tech development zones can establish VC funds and that more established zones can set up VC corporations. This prompts local government involvement in VC.

1999 — The CCCC and State Council issued 'Resolutions to Enhance Technological Innovation, Develop High Technology, and Realise Commercialisation' in August to encourage the development of VC mechanisms, venture investment enterprises and VC funds. Subsequently, policies were issued by the central and local governments.

2001 — The State Council's 'Provisions of Setting up Foreign Venture Investment Enterprises' took effect in September. It removed foreign VCs' entry barrier to China.

2004 — The Small and Medium Enterprise Board in Shenzhen Stock Exchange was launched in May. It offers VCs an exit route.

2005 — 'Securities Law', 'Company Law' and 'Partnership Law' were issued. 10 Ministries jointly issued 'Provisions on Management of Venture Investment Enterprises' in November. The VC's legal and regulatory environment improved.

2006 — The State Council in 'Notice on Implementing the National Outline of Medium and Long-Term S&T Development (2006–2020)' in August encouraged local governments and departments to establish VC Guiding Funds (VCGF)

2007 — The Ministry of Finance & State Administration of Taxation issued Notice on Taxation Policy in Support of Venture Investment Enterprise. The first national VCGF was launched.

2008 — The Development and Reform Commission, Ministry of Finance and Ministry of Commerce jointly issued in 'Directives on Establishment and Management of VCGFs' in October

2009 — The Growth Enterprise Market (GEM) in Shenzhen Stock Exchange was launched. It offers an additional exit route for VC investments.

Figure 5.1 Evolution of the VC industry and public VC schemes in China.

making decisions and managing investments without government interference and that VCGFs participate in investor governance decisions on the same terms as private investors, with the same voting rights. By adopting market practice in investor governance arrangements, the VCGF is expected to rely on the well-tried and tested VC model worldwide to make effective and sensible investment decisions. In other words, venture investment enterprises will identify good investment opportunities and make decisions on the basis of due diligence process, market analyses and fund management experiences, whilst the VCGF will use its contribution to gear private VC investment toward early-stage companies to fulfil its own strategic goal.

Public venture capital fund models

VCGFs in China have experimented with five different models of public venture capital, with each model serving different purposes.

Fund-of-funds

This is a model commonly used in the venture capital industry. The benefits of this model are two-fold. First, it allows the VCGF to use its equity capital contribution to encourage the establishment of more VC funds and thus to maximize the impact of public venture capital on the growth of the pool of VC funds for new- and high-tech firms. Second, it offers the VCGF an opportunity to invest in a number of venture capital funds thereby increasing the diversification of investments. The Chinese approach to public venture capital shows similarity with the Israeli Yozma model in its emphasis on leveraging private venture capital through co-investment rather than direct public equity investment.[4] At the core of the model is the use of fund-of-funds whereby it makes investments in private venture capital funds. Prior to any investment being made, a fund would be structured as a stand-alone company. This is to ensure that government could distance itself from risk and liability for investments made. It will also ensure the fund's independence in decisions about appointment of venture capital fund managers and in individual investment decisions. In this model, investments are structured as equity and can be bought out by investors. Government investments in the funds are on the same terms as those of private investors, except that each fund is provided with an option exercisable up to the end of the fifth year of the fund to buy out the government investment on the basis of capital plus interest only. By investing directly towards many new and stand-alone VC funds, a VCGF shall achieve its policy objective by multiplying the amount of venture capital available for new, technology-based companies. A VCGF shall contribute initial capital to a new VC fund in conjunction with other private founders and shall sell off its shares in due time under the pre-agreed terms. The particular conditions involving VCGFs in a fund-of-funds, as specified in the Interim Regulation, are as follows:

- A VCGF shall not contribute more than 25 per cent of the subscribed sum of capital to the new VC fund, and shall not become the largest shareholder of the fund.
- The new VC fund should invest in early-stage high-tech SMEs no less than twice as much as the VCGF's contribution to the fund.
- A VCGF shall not hold its shares in a fund for more than five years.
- A VCGF should plan to exit whenever it receives a proposal from other shareholders or external investors to buy out its shares. In the meantime, under no circumstances should any other VC shareholders make their exit from the fund before the VCGF does. In the fund's first three years of operation, if the shareholders or external investors decide to buy out the VCGF's shares, they shall pay for the price equivalent to the SVGF's initial contribution. After three years, they shall pay the VCGF for the price equivalent to the VCGF's initial contribution and interest calculated at the benchmark one-year lending rate of the Central Bank.

Co-investment

This model of public venture capital means that both the VCGF and the venture investment enterprise co-invest in early-stage SMEs. The main purpose of this approach is to bring existing, decent size private venture investment enterprises on board to invest in high-tech start-ups and to share investment risk with the VC investors. The particularities of co-investment are specified in the Interim Regulation as follows.

- Venture investment enterprises can apply to a VCGF for co-investment within one year of identifying prospective investment targets or completing investment in the targeted project. The VCGF shall invest in conjunction with the venture investment enterprises in those projects that meet the VCGF's due diligence exercises. Nevertheless, the VCGF shall not invest in one project more than 50 per cent as much as the venture investment enterprise's investment, and the VCGF's contribution to one investment shall not exceed RMB3 million.
- The VCGF entrusts the venture investment enterprise with managing its investment and shall use up to 50 per cent of its capital gains to pay the venture investment enterprise management fees and bonuses.
- A VCGF shall not hold its shares in the invested project for more than five years. Under no circumstances should the venture investment enterprise withdraw from the co-invested project ahead of the VCGF.

VC investment subsidy

The purpose of this approach is very similar to co-investment except that VCGFs subsidize a venture investment enterprise's investment costs with a non-repayable grant without having any shareholding in the venture-backed company. In this way,

VCGFs help the venture investment enterprise to withstand risks arising from its investments in early-stage ventures. Subsidy is open to all venture investment enterprises who have invested in early-stage firms. VCGFs disburse a successful applicant a grant of either up to 5 per cent of the venture investment enterprise's actual sum of investment in one project or a maximum of RMB5 million.

Investment guarantee

The main purpose of this approach is to encourage venture investment enterprises to monitor investment opportunities and nurture early-stage high-tech firms. In practice, venture investment enterprises first select prospective early-stage high-tech firms named as 'firms under supervision' and then apply to a VCGF for a grant for these firms. The VCGF can provide a grant of up to RMB1 million to a firm of this kind to subsidize its R&D expenses. As a binding condition, the venture investment enterprise shall first provide free supervisory services to the candidate company for the duration of one year to a maximum of two years and then invests in the company when the supervisory period ends. In parallel with the venture investment enterprise's investment, the VCGF shall offer to the venture-backed company a second grant of up to RMB2 million to subsidize the costs of mass production of the new product.

Financing guarantee

This is to support VC funds to borrow money through debt financing. In this way, VCGFs help reduce creditor risk and encourage small investors and banks to invest in high-growth ventures through the platform of VC funds. VC funds can also improve their financial performance as debt creditors will only receive relatively low fixed rate interest. Using information from credit rating agencies, VCGFs can provide financing guarantee to those VC funds that have excellent credit record in support of their debt financing to consolidate their funding resources.

Governance of VCGFs

The state level 'Venture Capital Guiding Fund for Technology-based SMEs' (VCGF for TSME) co-founded by MOF and MOST is the exemplary of VCGF governance and the model has been emulated by those at the local government level. The VCGF for TSME adopts a three-tier governance structure to ensure an orderly and risk-controllable operation.

On the top tier of governance are MOF and MOST who are responsible for setting rules for fund management, making decisions on directions of strategic investment, and determining capital allocation. On the second tier is the Expert Review Committee (ERC). Members of the committee are appointed by the MOF and MOST and are responsible for reviewing applications and short-listing projects for consideration of the MOF and MOST. On the third tier is the Innovation Fund Management Centre (IFMC) which is charged with the following responsibilities: (1) managing funding applications, conducting initial screening, and recommending candidates to the Review Committee; (2) managing VCGF for TSME's shares in all invested interests on behalf of MOF and MOST; and (3) monitoring VCGF for TSME's invested or supported projects and reporting periodically to the MOF and MOST.

More specifically, VCGF for TSME's decision to invest in a fund managed by a venture investment enterprise will follow after completing an extensive selection and due diligence process to determine whether the fund proposal is 'investment grade'. The initial screening is done by the IFMC, followed by an outside assessment by the ERC, an independent specialist advisory board. A standard methodology and fixed criteria are used to assess and rank all applications. Following the completion of external due diligence, short-listed candidates are recommended to MOST and MOF. Both departments select those applications and signs funding agreements with them after a satisfactory full disclosure. The flowchart of the selection process can be seen in Figure 5.2.

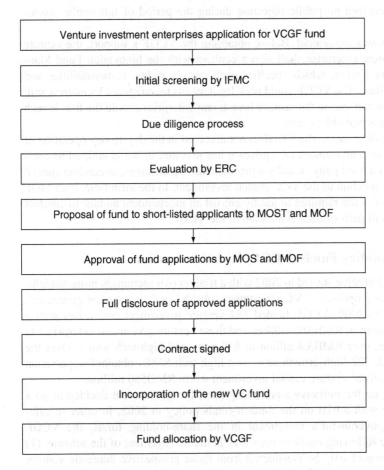

Figure 5.2 The flowchart of the fund-of-funds.

When using the vehicle of either fund-of-funds or co-investment, VCGF for TSME would use a bundling strategy to package together investments from both the VCGF for TSME and the venture investment enterprise into one bundled solution. The strategy is such that the VCGF shall only use its equity capital investment to leverage more similar investment from other parties and that it shall not commit an investment of more than 25 per cent of the total sum of sub-scribed funds. This is deliberate in order to achieve two objectives – sharing the venture investment enterprise's investment risk and reinforcing the firm's responsibility. Moreover, VCGF for TSME takes an additional three measures to ensure an appropriate management system in place.

- *Full disclosure.* Information about the short-listed venture investment enter-prises is disclosed on the official websites of both MOF and MOST and other public media outlets. MOF and MOST shall only proceed to invest in conjunction with venture investment enterprises in those firms after they have received no public objection during the period of full public disclo-sure.
- *Contractual agreement.* Before obtaining the VCGF's support, the venture investment enterprise shall sign a contract with the Innovation Fund Man-agement Centre, which specifies each party's rights, responsibilities and obligations. The VCGF could seek legal means to safeguard its interest and/ or name and shame the venture investment enterprise should the firm breach its contractual obligations.
- *Independent audit.* The VCGF is not involved in the day-to-day operation of the venture investment enterprises it has invested in but is entitled to com-mission a third party, usually a professional organization, to conduct special audit inspection of the VCs' annual investment. In the meantime, both MOF and MOST are required to jointly entrust an independent auditor to conduct an overall performance evaluation of the VCGF.

The VC Guiding Funds (VCGF) initiative in action

The VCGF initiative started in 2007 with a trial on two seemingly more straight-forward policy options – 'VC investment subsidy' and 'investment guarantee'. From 2007 to 2009, VCGF funded 154 venture investment enterprises with a total investment of RMB350 million, and these venture investment enterprises in turn invested over RMB3.8 billion in 830 new- and high-tech SMEs. Over the same period, 222 high-growth new- and high-tech SMEs obtained supervision and later received venture capital investment worth RMB550 million.

Building on the initiative's promising start, the government decided to go a step further with a trial on the fund-of-funds policy in 2008. In order to safe-guard the government's investment in the share-holding funds, the VCGF imposed the following cautious measures in the management of the scheme: (1) candidates would only be considered from those prospective domestic venture investment enterprises that had shown a proven track record of successful fund-raising and management so that the new VC funds would have good prospects of making a profit and fulfilling the VCGF's policy objectives; (2) funds to the new jointly set-up venture investment enterprises would not be released until all other investors had met their investment commitment in full; (3) banks were entrusted to manage the financial affairs of the venture investment enterprises in an attempt to strengthen supervision of fund use, prevent moral hazards such as misuse of funds, and standardise investment behaviour; (4) restrictive covenant was put in place in the agreement for newly established VC funds; (5) a clear measure to deal with the fund's loss-making was specified, for example, the founding venture investment enterprise should buy out the VCGF's share or the fund should be liquidated if the new fund makes more than 20 per cent loss.

The trial on fund-of-funds was formally launched in selected provinces in November 2008. Fifteen venture investment enterprises handed in their applications and six of them were eventually chosen to become partners of the VCGF after passing the initial eligibility checking and interview, review and evaluation of the Expert Committee, and the joint examination of MOST and MOF. As can be seen in Table 5.1, the central government offered RMB159 million of equity investment, resulting in a match-funding of RMB1.045 billion from six firms.

The establishment and experiment of the VCGF for TSME generated widespread interest and prompted many local governments to set up similar funds. As of the end of 2009, local government had contributed to local VCGFs a total of RMB25.5 billion.

There were three types of local government-backed VCGFs. The first type of local VCGFs was one backed by provincial governments. Up to 2009, 17 provinces had set up province-level VCGFs with a pledged investment of RMB15.1 billion. The second type of local VCGFs was one supported by municipal governments, such as Wuhan, Hangzhou, Shenzhen and Wuxi. Local VCGFs under this category had a total capital of RMB2.3 billion. The third type of local VCGFs was one established by state-level new- and high-tech development zone administrations. At this level 23 local governments had set up VCGFs with a total capital of RMB8.1 billion. Key parameters of illustrative Venture Capital Guiding Funds in all levels can be seen in Table 5.2.

According to a 2011 nation-wide survey conducted by MOST, 55 VCGFs were established at all levels between 2006 and 2010 with a possible total fund of RMB43 billion (see Table 5.3).[5] 2009 represented a dip in the overall upward development primarily due to the national economic slowdown under the impact of the global financial crisis. Despite a greater number of newly created VCGFs, capital contribution from governments of all levels was significantly smaller: total contribution dropped by more than one-third to RMB6.9 billion in 2009 year on year, an average size of VCGFs shrank by more than half of the previous year to RMB383 million. This was reversed in 2010 when capital contribution to VCGFs almost tripled to RMB17.2 billion.

Of all 58 VCGFs, there were three super funds involving the central government. As mentioned earlier, the VCGF for High-Tech SME was set up jointly by the MOST and MOF in June 2007 with the funding entirely coming from the

Table 5.1 Projects in the VCGF's trial on fund-of-funds in 2008

	Capital under management (RMB million)	VCGF contribution (RMB million)	Per cent of VCGF contribution
Shanghai Venture Capital Company	175	25	14.29
China-Singapore Suzhou Industrial Park Venture Capital Company	150	20	13.33
Jiangsu Govtor Capital Group	221	55	24.89
Shandong High & New Technology Venture Capital Company	100	20	20.00
Wuhan Huagong Venture Capital Co., Ltd	206	16	7.77
Hefei Technological Innovation Venture Capital Co. Ltd	193	23	11.92
Total	1,045	159	

Table 5.2 Parameters of VGFs by region

Region	Objectives	Year commenced	Fund size	Source of fund	Funding target
Provincial and first tier municipality level					
Beijing	Supply of financing	July 2008	n/a	Industrial development budget, fund earnings, and others	Early-stage high-tech firms; innovative SMEs
Shandong	The development of venture investment enterprises and small and medium-sized innovative ventures	September 2009	n/a	Special budgetary revenue; fund and guarantee proceeds; slack deposit in bank and securities earning; donations	High-tech SMEs in seed or early stage; high-tech SMEs
Zhejiang	Industrial restructuring and upgrading	March 2009	500 million	n/a	Early-stage high-tech SMEs; growth SMEs
Fujian	n/a	August 2008	n/a	Budgetary revenues	Venture investment enterprise subsidy; subsidy of ventured firms using VC investment and management; grants for bridging prospective firms and venture investment enterprises
Anhui	n/a	September 2009	Originally 500 million with a target of 1 billion	Budgetary revenue of RMB500 million	50 per cent of capital to set up fund-of-fund; 50 per cent to support Hefei, Wuhu and Benbo in the establishment of municipality-level VCGFs

continued

Table 5.2 Continued

Region	Objectives	Year commenced	Fund size	Source of fund	Funding target
Inner Mongolia	Industrial restructuring and upgrading; job creation; disposable income increase; economic stability and development	2009	n/a	Special budgetary revenue; fund and guarantee proceeds; donations	Early-stage high-tech SMEs; growth SMEs
Shanxi	n/a	2008	200 million originally with a target of 1 billion	150 million from Department of Finance; 50 million from Development and Reform Commission	Early-stage high-tech SMEs; SME M&A
Chongqing	VC system building; R&D commercialization; high-tech industry development	August 2008	n/a	Special budgetary revenue; investment of financial institutions and large SOEs; central government policy funds	n/a
Provincial capital city level					
Nanjing	The development of a VC market and an innovative city	December 2009	200 million	Special budgetary revenue; fund earnings; central and provincial VCGFs	Growth ventures
Hangzhou	The development of a VC market and an innovative city	April 2008	200 million	Budgetary revenue	Early-stage ventures
Shijiazhuang	The development of high-tech industries	September 2009	300 million	Equity capital of Shijiazhuang Development Investment Ltd; fund earnings, and others	Early-stage high-tech SMEs; SME M&A

Wuhan	High-tech industrial upgrading	October 2008	n/a	Budgetary R&D special fund; fund proceeds; public donations	Early-stage high-tech SMEs
Changsha	R&D commercialization	June 2009	20 million	n/a	Early-stage high-tech SMEs; R&D commercialization
Kunming	n/a	June 2008	n/a	Kunming InnoFund; fund proceeds; public donations	High-tech SMEs
City level					
Haidian, Beijing	The development of venture investment enterprises and small and medium-sized innovative ventures	June 2007	70 million with a target of 500 million in five years	Special budgetary revenue; enterprise development grants from central and Beijing government; fund proceeds; donations	Early-stage and growth stage enterprises
Yangpu, Shanghai	n/a	November 2008	n/a	Budgetary revenue; fund exit proceeds and earnings; donations	Incubators; early-stage SMEs
Minghang, Shanghai	Industrial upgrading	May 2010	100 million with a target of 500 million in five years	Budgetary revenue; operating public asset earnings; fund exit proceeds and earnings; donations	n/a
Binghai, Tianjin	The development of a national modern manufacturing and R&D commercialization base	March 2007	2 billion	1 billion from Binghai Management Commission; 1 billion from China Development Bank	Fast-growth high-tech firms

continued

Table 5.2 Continued

Region	Objectives	Year commenced	Fund size	Source of fund	Funding target
Changzhou, Jiangsu	Industrial development	May 2008	n/a	Budgetary revenue; investment of financial institutions; national and provincial VCGF and grants; fund earnings; donations	New- and high-tech enterprises
Yuhang, Hangzhou	The development of an innovative city	July 2008	30 million	Budgetary R&D special fund; fund exit revenue and earnings	Early-stage enterprises
Xiaoshan, Hangzhou	The development of entrepreneurship and innovation	June 2009	100 million	Budgetary revenue; fund exit revenue and earnings	Early-stage enterprises
High-tech Development Zone, Hangzhou	n/a	September 2008	30 million with a target of 500 million	Budgetary revenue; fund exit revenue and earnings	Early-stage enterprises
Jinxing, Zhejiang	n/a	August 2009	40 million with a target of 100 million	n/a	Early-stage SMEs; high-tech enterprises
Shaoxing, Zhejiang	Implementation of an entrepreneurship and innovation strategy	September 2008	200 million	Budgetary revenue; existing budgetary enterprise development funds, and others	Business ventures
Pinghu, Zhejiang	Industrial restructuring and upgrading	January 2010	30 million	n/a	Early-stage high-tech SMEs; high-tech enterprises

Jiangde	n/a	September 2008	5 million	Budgetary revenue; existing budgetary enterprise development funds, and others	Early-stage high-tech SMEs
Fuyang	The development of an innovative city	December 2008	20 million	Budgetary revenue; existing budgetary enterprise development funds	Early-stage high-tech SMEs
Quzhou	Industrial restructuring and upgrading	August 2009	50 million	n/a	Seed stage and early-stage SMEs
County level					
Tonglu	n/a	August 2008	5 million	Budgetary revenue; existing budgetary enterprise development funds	Early-stage SMEs
Anji	n/a	January 2009	30 million	Budgetary revenue; existing budgetary enterprise development funds; fund exit revenue and earnings	Seed stage and early-stage SMEs
Nanhu, Jiaxin	Implementation of an entrepreneurship and innovation strategy	October 2009	15 million	Budgetary revenue; existing budgetary enterprise development funds; fund exit revenue and earnings	Business ventures

Sources: compiled from respective government documents.

Table 5.3 VCGFs, 2006–2010

	(A) Number of VCGFs	(B) Promised capital, billion	(C) Actual contribution, billion	(B)/(A), billion	(C)/(B), per cent
2006	5	3.621	1.955	0.724	54
2007	8	5.35	2.515	0.669	47
2008	13	10.375	5.706	0.798	55
2009	18	6.896	5.172	0.383	75
2010	11	17.2	3.784	1.564	22

Source: 2011 nation-wide survey conducted by MOST.

central government budget. By the end of 2010, the central government's cumulated capital contribution amounted to RMB1.159 billion. In October 2009, NDRC and MOF set up the New Industry Venture Capital Programme (NIVCP) with an initial contribution of RMB1 billion from the national fund for industry and technology research and development. In December 2010, the China Development Bank (CBD), in conjunction with Suzhou Ventures Group (SVG), set up China Development Finance (CDF), a wholly owned subsidiary of CBD, with a registered capital of RMB5 billion for investment mainly in early-stage and high-growth ventures. Due to the demonstration effect of the super-size state-level funds, local governments' enthusiasm with the public venture capital initiative was evident. From 2006 to 2010, 35 VCGFs were established by governments at the city level and 21 VCGFs by provincial governments (Table 5.4). In terms of the distribution of fund size, city-level VCGFs overall were smaller with near half having a total capital of less than RMB500 million. Province-level VCGFs were better resourced with nearly two-thirds owing capital of more than RMB500 million.

Fiscal special fund from government budget was the main source of capital in VCGFs. This is fund from special accounts set up by MOF or departments of finance at the local level for earmarked, transitory activities. It was involved in

Table 5.4 VCGFs at three different administrative levels, 2010

		All	State level	Provincial level	City level
Number of VCGFs		58*	3	21	35
Promised capital, billion		45.21	7.16	15.47	22.58
Fund scale distribution, per cent	More than 1 billion	35	100	33	32
	500 million–1 billion	22	0	29	20
	100–499 million	33	0	33	34
	Less than 100 million	10	0	5	14

Source: 2011 nation-wide survey conducted by MOST.

Note
* Includes three VCGFs that were established before 2006.

the establishment of 51 VCGFs and contributed almost two-thirds of capital in all VCGFs. As can be seen in Table 5.5, banks contributed another 15.73 per cent to VCGFs. These mainly refer to CDB's contribution to three VCGFs and EximBank's contribution to the Chengdu VCGF.

The VCGF initiative in China started with a more conventional approach to investment subsidy but over time fund-of-funds have gradually become the main form of financing. As of 2010, 93 per cent of VCGFs had used this method to make an impact on the private VC sector (Table 5.6). Capital contribution-wide, this approach even has a much higher percentage of VCGF involvement. 2012 statistics from the Torch Centre of MOST show that VC investment in the forms of financing guarantee and investment subsidy continues to shrink. In 2012, VCGFs contributed RMB1.4 billion to investment subsidy and RMB748 million to financing guarantee.[6] Clearly, the greater emphasis on use of fund-of-funds and co-investment in VCGFs is a very positive sign of development in the public venture capital sector.

The challenge of VCGFs

The development of the venture capital sector has been impressive since 1999 after the Communist Party Central Committee (CPCC) and State Council issued the 'Resolutions to Enhance Technological Innovation, Develop High Techno-logy, and Realise Commercialisation' in an effort to speed up the development of the VC market in China. The government statistics show that the number of

Table 5.5 Source of capital in VCGFs, 2010

	VCGF		Capital	
	Number	Per cent	Billion	Per cent
Fiscal special fund	51	79.69	34.30	63.49
Listed/non-listed companies	6	9.38	0.33	0.60
Solely state-owned investment companies	2	3.13	5.9	10.92
Banks	4	6.25	8.5	15.73
Other	1	1.56	5	9.26

Source: 2011 nation-wide survey conducted by MOST.

Table 5.6 Forms of financing by VCGFs, 2010

	Use of fund	Per cent	Capital allocation, billion	Per cent
Fund-of-funds	54	93	44.95	99
Co-investment	34	58.62	31.26	69
Financing guarantee	5	8.62	1.6	4
Investment subsidy	7	12.07	4.46	10

Source: 2011 nation-wide survey conducted by MOST.

VC firms reached 942 in 2012 from 323 in 2001 and that these firms managed a total fund of RMB331.3 billion in 2012, up from RMB61.9 billion in 2001 (Table 5.7). By the end of 2012, VC firms in China invested a total of RMB235.5 billion in 11,112 high-tech companies. However, the venture capital market development has displayed an extraordinary uneven geographical distribution. Data from Zero2IPO Research Centre in China for example shows that over the period 2002–2008 domestic and foreign VC institutions made a combined venture capital investment of US$13.1 billion, of which US$9.9 billion, three-quarters of investment, was invested in deals in six municipalities and provinces (Beijing, Shanghai, Guangdong, Jiangsu, Zhejiang and Shandong) (Zero2IPO, 2010).

Accordingly, the distinctive VCGF contribution lies in financing smaller companies, high-tech companies and start-ups in China who have difficulty in raising equity funding from the private sector. A critical area that Chinese government targeted was enhancing innovation, and encouraging venture capital was a critical aspect of this goal. In light of limited activity in the local market, the government sought to accelerate the growth of the venture capital market through co-investment with private investors.

Performance against objectives

Evidence seems to suggest that VCGFs have started satisfactorily in terms of overall increase in the availability of venture capital. By the end of 2009, there were 43 venture investment enterprises applying for setting up fund-of-funds from the VCGF for TSME. After a prescribed procedure of preliminary evaluation, due diligence survey, project presentation and Q&A, final evaluation by the Evaluation Committee, the VCGF placed RMB309 million in 14 new venture

Table 5.7 The VC sector in China, 2001–2012

	VC firms		Funds under management	
	Number	Growth (%)	RMB billion	Growth (%)
2001	323	29.7	61.9	21.0
2002	366	13.3	68.9	11.2
2003	315	−13.9	61.7	−10.5
2004	304	−3.5	61.8	0.2
2005	319	4.9	63.2	2.3
2006	345	8.2	66.4	5.1
2007	383	11.0	111.3	67.7
2008	464	21.1	145.6	30.8
2009	576	24.1	160.5	10.3
2010	720	25.0	240.7	49.9
2011	860	19.4	319.8	32.9
2012	942	9.5	331.3	3.6

Source: MOST Touch Centre.

capital funds. These 14 funds raised a further RMB2.382 billion, making a total of RMB2.691 billion potentially available. Local governments follow the central government to establish VCGFs. By June 2009, 23 provinces had set up 50 local VCGFs, 19 of which operated at provincial level and 31 at city level. All the local funds possess total capital of RMB25.2 billion. This was a remarkable growth in terms of the number of funds and the venture capital they managed. According to the Hong Kong-based China Venture Capital Research Centre report (Chen, 2008), there were only three VCGFs in 2006 with a capital of RMB2.5 billion and 16 VCGFs with a capital of RMB8.85 billion in 2008 in China.

Performance evaluation with focus on overall increase in the availability of venture capital can be rather narrowly focused, however. A study of the public venture capital funds in the UK suggested that a broader approach could be used to measure performance, comprising indicators: (1) the extent that the government funding does not crowd out other investment; (2) evidence of focused targeting of the equity gap; (3) evidence of overall increases in the availability of risk capital; and (4) the rate of return of funds, the level of successful exits to date and the cost of managing funds relative to the investment (NAO, 2009). Nevertheless, as can be seen in Table 5.7, VCGFs in China have often set multiple aims but these aims have not been defined as clear measurable objectives. In particular, none of the funds had an explicit financial performance objective. This does not appear to be a unique Chinese problem with the VCGF initiative. Similar concerns were raised by the National Audit Office of the United Kingdom in its evaluation of seven venture capital funds involved with the Department for Business, Innovation and Skills in 2009 (NAO, 2009). The NAO (2009) report found evidence of a structured process to measure performance but admitted that it is not clear how performance was measured against its objectives. In late 2008 MOST commenced an interim evaluation of the economic benefits of VCGFs. None of the VCGFs have reached the end of their life and hence the matter of financial performance evaluation is yet to be on the top of those funds' agenda. It will be important, though, that robust evidence to measure achievement of all of the stated objectives is produced by the time when funds come to the end of their life.

The VCGF design

The performance of VCGFs can be impeded by their design. Recent academic research (e.g. Lerner, 2009) identifies a number of factors which tend to improve the chances of a successful public venture capital fund, including a flow of good quality deals, the timing of investments, broad geographic coverage, larger fund sizes, and the ability to make follow-on investments and to exit individual investments on a timely basis. Comparatively, VCGFs in China appear to display weaknesses against all of these criteria to varying degrees. The pool of viable business propositions targeted by the funds was restricted in some cases by investment criteria, which restricted the size of initial and follow-on investments.

There is also evidence that local government policy-makers made decisions based on 'buzz'. Many local governments started the public venture capital scheme to promote high-tech industries, in hope of creating a cluster of activity. Realistically, only a handful of these regions had the base of scientific resources and the supporting infrastructure to support a successful cluster, so the bulk of these funds could be ineffective. Concerns were expressed about whether it is desirable for a city at the county level to set up a VCGF.[7] We might be sceptical about whether smart selection is a feasible task for governments. Entrepreneurship is an intensely unfair activity: there are powerful forces that lead firms to cluster in particular places. Thus, much of the impact can be diluted as funds that could be very helpful in a core area end up where they are not helpful.

Local governments' enthusiastic replication of the state-level VCGFs at the local levels came with caveats. In many local initiatives, VCGFs have been conditional on funds investing in specific regions, local registration and the threshold of registered capital for a new fund-of-fund. For example, in the 2011 survey conducted by the Torch Centre of MOST, it was found that 87 per cent of local VCGFs demanded their venture investment enterprise partners to invest a certain sum or a certain percentage of investment of the fund locally, that 68 per cent of VCGFs requested the new fund to be registered locally, and that 61 per cent set the minimum size of a new fund. The survey also found that 49 per cent of VCGFs had included all three restrictive clauses in their initiatives, that 25 per cent had included two restrictive clauses, that 24 per cent had one restrictive clause, and that only 3 per cent did not set any restriction. There was a tendency that the further down the local levels the more restrictions were placed on the VCGF's partners in obtaining local government's contribution. In a separate survey in 2011 conducted by Zero2IPO, it was found that a condition on a fund-of-fund to invest 60–70 per cent of its subscribed capital locally was a common practice.[8] This local protection tendency counters against one of the principles of VCGFs, namely, market-based operation. The extent that a local VCGF can impact on the local economy should be considered from a demand-side perspective. It is reasonable to suggest that not every region has a large group of high-potential firms that are capable of earning the exceptionally high returns sought by venture capital investors. By placing restrictions on the venture capital fund in regions where a strong deal flow of attractive, high-potential firms is lacking, these VCGFs are in danger of creating a mismatch between demand and supply in a specific region and compromising fund performance. Clarity concerning intellectual property rights is one of the key issues for venture capital investors during the due diligence process.

Some schemes shared one considerably problematic feature: financial 'ground rules' that were inconsistent with their basic missions. On the one hand, the schemes operated under the rule that its investments be undertaken profitably. This requirement has been interpreted as meaning that its returns each year were expected to be above the inflation rate. These requirements seem quite out of line with the funds' ultimate objectives of addressing failures in early-stage venture capital markets. The Finnish experience showed that this requirement led to the Finnish Industry Investment Ltd (FII) to emphasize later-stage investing, in the hope that a more steady profit flow would allow the fund to remain in compliance with its ground rule (Lerner, 2009).

Notes

1 Public venture capital is also called 'hybrid' venture capital schemes that are backed by both private and public sector funding.
2 Launched in August 1988, the Torch Programme is China's most important programme with specific focus on promoting innovation and high-tech industrialization. More specifically, the programme aims to support the development of high-tech products that are of high technological standards and good economic return, to establish high-tech industrial development zones across the country, and to explore innovations in management systems and operation mechanisms suitable for high-tech industrial development. For more details of the programme, see www.chinatorch.gov.cn/english/xhtml/Program.html (accessed 14 April 2011).
3 For more details, see 'Interim Measures for the Administration of Startup Investment Enterprises' at http://tradeinservices.mofcom.gov.cn/en/b/2007-12-25/18694.shtml (accessed 14 April 2011).
4 For more information about the Israeli Yozma model, see Senor and Singer (2009).
5 For the rest of this section, unless stated otherwise, data are from the same 2011 nation-wide survey.
6 Data are from the website of MOST Torch Centre.
7 See a report in Caijing Net on 10 April 2009, '创业投资引导基金热"背后问题隐现' (Emerging concerns behind the fever of venture capital guiding funds), available at www.caijing.com.cn/2009-04-10/110137001.html (accessed 20 April 2011).
8 See a report in *China Jingji Daobao* on 7 January 2012, '政府引导基金"蝴蝶效应 重构地区发展后劲' (The butterfly effect of government guiding funds to reshape the driver of regional development), available at www.ceh.com.cn/ceh/cjxx/2012/1/7/97382.shtml (accessed 4 March 2012).

6 Incentive for sectoral innovation

The energy sector

The heavy smoke hovering around many cities in the winter illustrates the pressing challenge facing China in speeding up a change in the growth model. Meanwhile, the success story of China's renewable energy industries also demonstrates how China's innovation programme has offered promising solutions. In this chapter, we use the energy sector as an example to show how China's programme of incentive for innovation is in action at the sector level.

The energy industry in China's social and economic development

The energy industry has been a pillar of China's rapid economic growth over the past three decades but also a cause of concern about the country's growth sustainability. As early as in 1994, the Chinese government started searching for solutions to the severe energy-related challenges the country was facing, namely depleting resources to feed rapid economic growth, alarming environmental pollution arising from rapid growth of energy use, and mismatch between the emergence of new technologies and the persistence of old production-consumption patterns. The first comprehensive outlines of energy-saving technology policy were published jointly by the then National Planning Commission, National Economic and Trade Commission, and National Science and Technology Commission in 1996 after three years' planning. The document, with targets and measures to promote use of technologies for improvement of energy efficiency, served as guidelines for policy development at central and local government levels in attempts to shift from resource-intensity to resource-efficiency in the growth mode. Progress was apparently made but was outpaced by the surging energy consumption and was paled by the country's mounting health and environmental concerns. This led to another comprehensive review of the energy industry and the publication of a landmark government white paper, China's Energy Conditions and Policies, by the State Council in January 2007. The policy agenda as stated in this white paper was also reiterated in the 11th Five-Year Plan (2006–2010) which set forth an ambitious target to reduce energy intensity (energy consumption per unit of GDP) by 20 per cent on 2005 levels. The 12th Five-Year Plan (2011–2015) underscored the focus of sustainability and environmental protection with an overall economic growth projection of 7 per cent annually, significantly lower than what was actually achieved in the past. Again, the Plan set out energy and emissions targets, including reduction of energy intensity by 16 per cent and reduction of carbon intensity by 17 per cent, on 2010 levels. At the same time, the Plan placed as priority support of seven strategic emerging industries critical to China's economic development, including electric vehicles, energy efficient products and renewable energy. The Plan also aimed to deliver major increases in non-fossil energy, including a four-fold growth in nuclear power to 40 GW, 63 GW of new hydroelectric capacity, 48 GW of new wind capacity and 5 GW of solar capacity by 2015. In the meantime, China pledged in the Copenhagen Accord a target of 40–45 per cent reduction in carbon intensity by 2020, compared to 2005 levels, and to meet 15 per cent of its primary energy demand from non-fossil sources by 2020. China has buttressed its commitment by firm actions, notably in the development of the country's new renewable energy sectors. As a result of its commitment and actions, China has leapt into the top five in a ranking of G20 countries in restricting greenhouse gas emissions and has been credited with shifting the momentum for action on climate change from west to east.[1]

China's relentless pursuit of innovation and growth sustainability through its energy industry's development policy in general and innovation policy in particular are underpinned by four strong and sensible principles. These can be interpreted as using innovations to achieve sustainability of the energy system, to mitigate the negative effects on health and environment stemming from coal use, to safeguard energy security, and to create economic opportunities for indigenous enterprises (Buijs, 2012; Li, 2010).

Sustainability of the energy system

China's energy system has endured a tremendous pressure from the seemingly insatiable energy demand during the course of two-digit economic growth for nearly three decades. At every one percentage increase in GDP per capita, energy consumption was estimated to grow by 0.48–0.50 per cent (Li *et al.*, 2011). In another measure, the total energy consumption has magnified by approximately 6.1 times from 0.57 billion tons of coal equivalent (Tce) in 1978 to 3.48 billion Tce in 2011.[2] In announcing the 12th Five-Year Plan (2011–2015), the Chinese government has made it clear that the mode of resource-intensive growth is neither sustainable nor desirable any more. Even at the growth rate of 7 per cent annually, however, there is still an acute long-term challenge in achieving a sustainable energy system that can provide sufficient energy to China's enormous population and fuel economic growth.

Negative effects on health and environment

Alarmingly, the current energy system has inflicted widespread health and environmental consequences, as one percentage increase in GDP per capita was estimated to lead to 0.41–0.43 per cent increase in carbon dioxide emissions in China (Li *et al.*, 2011). Emissions of pollutants from coal consumption are the major sources of pollutions, making up 70 per cent of particulates, 90 per cent of SOx, 67 per cent of NOx and 70 per cent of total CO_2 (Fang and Zeng, 2007). The negative effects on health and environment are enormous. The World Health Organization (WHO) estimates that 300,000 premature deaths in China per year can be attributed to urban ambient air pollution (Cohen *et al.*, 2004). The World Bank (2007) put this figure as high as 400,000. The economic cost of mortality and morbidity that results from outdoor air pollution in a typical Chinese city was estimated to be about 10 per cent of that city's GDP in 2000, and, dependent on future technology and policies, this cost is predicted to range from 8 per cent to 16 per cent by 2020 (Wang and Mauzerall, 2006). In a more modest estimate, the economic damage from air pollution caused by the fossil fuels was still at 2–3 per cent of GDP (Zhang *et al.*, 2010). At the 0.858 of carbon dioxide emission coefficient of energy consumption (0.905 for coal consumption), innovation in energy conservation and renewable energy technologies is certainly a necessity of bringing down carbon dioxide emissions.

Energy security

China's surging energy demand has given rise to a serious concern about the country's energy security lately. China was self-sufficient in primary energy supply until the first half of the 1990s. This change was largely because the growth of domestic production of the oil industry at rates of 1–3 per cent per year since the mid-1980s could not match the growth of consumption at annual rates of 5–8 per cent (Andrews-Speed, 2009). China has become a net oil product importer since 1993, net crude oil importer since 1996 and net primary energy importer since 1997 (Ma *et al.*, 2009). The net imported primary energy amount has increased continually from 13 million Tce in 1990, to 557 million Tce in 2010, correspondingly the energy import reliance increased from 1.4 per cent in 1990 to 16.4 per cent in 2010.[3] Since the turn of the twenty-first century, China has used outward foreign direct investment (OFDI) as a means to secure energy supply from abroad, but the concern with the country's energy security is simply mounting.

Economic opportunity

The development of renewable energy sectors can open up economic opportunities. It is noted, for example, that the development of the wind power sector can generate several positive economic spillovers, comprising (1) economic development opportunities by creating new firms in the supply chain, job creation as well as increased local tax base; (2) potential possibility of exporting domestically made turbines to international markets; and (3) cost savings in wind farms project development and thus lower cost of wind electricity (Li, 2010).

Challenges of energy development in China

China, as a large energy producer and consumer, has found its attempt to overhaul the energy system challenging. Policy intervention has to confront the characteristics of the energy system.

Huge coal and hydropower resources and unusually low oil and natural gas endowment

China's energy resources endowment is a mixed blessing – huge coal and hydropower resources but small oil and natural gas reserves. In 2006, coal reserves in China were estimated to be 1,034.5 billion tons, and verified coal reserves accounted for 13 per cent of the global total, ranking third globally behind the USA and Russia. Also, the gross theoretical hydropower resource in China is 689 million KW and economically exploitable resource is 395 million KW, ranking top in the world. In contrast, China's proved oil and natural gas reserves are relatively small. In terms of proved oil reserves, China ranks 13th in the world. The country's proved natural gas reserves are even smaller – ranking only 17th worldwide, and gas reserves amount to a mere 30 per cent of the country's verified crude oil deposits. The low oil and natural gas resources in general, and unusually low natural gas endowment in particular, disadvantage China in a significant way because natural gas is both the most convenient and the cleanest fuel and feedstock for residential and commercial heating and chemical manufacturing (Smil, 2004). Given its extensive coal deposits, China has large unconventional fossil energy reserves such as oil shoal and coal-bed methane, but this kind of natural gas is usually much more expensive and less convenient to recover.

Coal dominance in energy production and consumption

The features of China's energy resource endowment determine that coal is inevitably dominant in the country's primary energy production and consumption. China is currently the world's largest coal producer and consumer. Since 2005, China's coal production maintained roughly 78 per cent of its total energy production, while coal in primary energy consumption made up 68–71 per cent, as compared with an average of 21 per cent in developed countries. In view of the coal-inflicted problems, China has taken measures in recent years to diversify its coal-dominated energy system. As a result, new and renewable energy consumption has grown consistently. The share of coal in primary energy consumption declined from its peak of 76.2 per cent in 1990 to 68.4 per cent in 2011, while the share of renewable energy and nuclear power doubled from 4.0 per cent in 1980 to 8.0 per cent in 2011. In this transition, the success of the wind power sector has caught the international community by surprise. China almost trebled its installed wind power capacity from 25.8 GW in 2009 to 75.3 GW by the end of 2012, maintaining its lead in terms of global cumulative installed wind power capacity (GWEC, 2013).

Rapid growth of energy production but low efficiency of energy use

Thanks to efforts over the last few decades, China's energy production has been growing rapidly. In 2011, the output of primary energy production in China grew five-fold as compared to 1978, to 3.2 billion tons of coal equivalent (Tce), accounting for 23.6 per cent of the global total and ranking second in the world. Specifically, coal production was 3,576 million tonnes (Mt) in 2010, ranking first in the world; crude oil production 203 Mt, ranking fifth in the world; natural gas production 103 Mt, ranking seventh in the world; and hydro production 722 TWh, ranking first in the world.[4] Since the late 1970s, China's energy efficiency, measured as energy consumption of per-unit GDP, has steadily improved as efforts to enhance energy use efficiency and reduce waste of energy bore fruit. Energy consumption of per RMB10,000 of GDP dropped from 3.39 Tce in 1980 to 1.01 Tce in 2011.[5] Adjusted by comparable price index, the annual average rate of energy conservation was 3.22 per cent. However, energy use efficiency in China is still rather low. According to the International Energy Agency (IEA), in 2004, the energy consumption of per-unit GDP in China was 2.66 times the world average, 2.94 times that in Latin America, 5.22 times that in Germany and 8.55 times that in Japan. The integrated efficiency of energy processing, trans-shipment, storage and delivery, and terminal use in China was only 33 per cent, almost 10 percentage points lower than that of the developed countries. The average per-unit energy consumption level of major products in eight industries including electricity, iron and steel, and non-ferrous metal in China was 40 per cent higher than that of the international advanced level. The recycling rate of hydropower resources in China was 50 per cent less than that in developed countries. It is for this reason that energy use efficiency has become a key issue that needs to be resolved in achieving sustainable economic development.

S&T of energy sector in progress and in need of improvement

Since 1949, the energy sector in China has made certain noticeable progress in S&T, with technology development of international excellence in a number of areas. For instance, the home-grown theory and application of continental hydro-carbon generation symbolizes China's advance in basic research in the field of energy and its significant contribution to the discipline of oil and geological science and technology. In the coal industry, China has considerably improved its coal exploration and exploitation technologies and equipment. China now has the capability to design, construct, install and manage opencast coal mines with an annual production capacity of ten million tons and medium and large-scaled coal mines. Modern equipment including mechanical coal-mining equipment has been widely used, and more than 80 per cent of state-owned coal mines have achieved mechanized coal mining. In the petroleum industry, a relatively complete system on exploration and development technologies has been deployed in the oil and gas industry. In particular, technologies of exploration and development in complicated areas and those of improving the recovery rate of oil fields are world leading. In the power industry, high-parameter thermal power generating units with a capacity of 600,000 KW and one million KW have been widely applied. As of end September 2008, a total of ten sets of MKW of ultra-supercritical power generating units were in operation across China. Significant progress of technology development has been made in new and renewable energy. The nuclear power industry has been equipped with the capacity of independent manufacturing of equipment with a capacity of MKW, as well as independent design, construction, operation and management of pressurized water reactors. All the power generating units in the Three Gorges Dam are home-made, indicating that the electric power equipment manufacturing industry has advanced to a new level of R&D and independent innovation. Hydropower station design, construction and equipment manufacturing technologies in China have also reached the level of international excellence, becoming one of the major exporters for small hydropower technologies worldwide. However, technological capability of the energy sector in China is still in need of improvement, as it is confronted with challenges of technological development catching-up, limited application of technologies in terms of energy saving, consumption reduction and pollution control, as well as low level of independent design and manufacturing of some key equipment in energy technologies.

History of energy management system in China

The governance of China's energy management system has undergone significant changes since 1949. In the early 1950s, the Ministry of Fuel Industries (MOFI) was established to act as an umbrella agency charged with overseeing the whole energy sector, namely coal, petroleum, electricity and hydropower construction. In 1955, MOFI was split into three ministries – Ministry of Coal Industry (MOCI), Ministry of Petroleum Industry (MOPI) and Ministry of Electric Power Industry (MOEPI), as an effort to respond to the changing domestic energy requirements. In 1958, the Ministry of Electric Power Industry and Ministry of Water Resources Industry were dissolved and merged into the Ministry of Water Resources and Electric Power. In 1980, after China adopted the policy of reform and opening up, the State Energy Commission was founded, which integrated the administrative functions of the coal, electricity and petroleum sectors. However, the coal-related function was still subject to the administration of MOCI. Two years later, the State Energy Commission was dissolved in part due to the overlapping functions between the State Energy Commission and State Development Planning Commission (SDPC), and in part due to the fact that the power of decision-making on investment and pricing rested with SDPC. In 1988, a new effort to trim government bureaucracy led to the establishment of the Ministry of Energy and the abolition of the Ministry of Coal Industry, Ministry of Petroleum Industry, Ministry of Water Resources and Electric Power, and Ministry of Nuclear Industry, while China National Coal Corporation (CNCC), China National Petroleum Corporation (CNPC) and China National Nuclear Corporation (CNNC) at ministerial level were founded. In 1993, the Ministry of

Energy was dissolved as it was at the same administrative level as CNCC, CNPC and CNNC, and as the power of granting energy-related projects rested with SDPC. In the same year, the Ministry of Electric Power Industry and the Ministry of Coal Industry were re-established. In 1998, the above-mentioned two ministries were dissolved again, while the State Administration of Coal Industry, State Administration of Petroleum Chemical Industry, and the Department of Electric Power were set up under the administration of State Economic and Trade Commission (SETC). In 2001, the State Administration of Coal Industry and State Administration of Petroleum Chemical Industry were dissolved, and relevant agencies under SETC and SDPC were responsible for the energy administration. In 2002, the State Electricity Regulatory Commission (SERC) was established. To enhance the management of the energy sector and remove poor coordination due to overlapping and disjointed management, the State Council decided to form State Energy Administration (SEA) and State Energy Commission, a high-level advisory and coordinating agency, in the institutional reform in 2008. In August of the same year, the State Energy Administration was formally established. Through nearly two years' preparation, the State Energy Commission was founded on 1 January 2010.

In the process of institutional reform aimed at separating government functions from enterprise management, in terms of electricity industry, the State Electric Power Corporation was founded in 1997; in terms of coal industry, the coal mines and coal enterprises that were previously under the jurisdiction of central finance were delegated to local authorities for management in 1998; in terms of oil and gas industry, the state-owned oil and gas companies were restructured. In 2001, the State Administration of Coal Industry and the State Administration of Petroleum Chemical Industry were dissolved, and the State Electric Power Corporation was then split and restructured. As the energy administration agency at national level was scaled down, many general affairs in this regard had to fall back on the relevant state-owned enterprises. This resulted in the functions of energy management distributed among other energy-related ministries and commissions and large-scale state-owned enterprises. Indeed, SEC and energy-related enterprises dominated the process of developing national energy-related policies.

Innovation in the energy sector in China

Innovation in the energy sector in China has dual objectives. The first is to save energy and use energy more efficiently, and the second is to accelerate the development of clean energy and renewable energy technology.

The S&T innovation system of energy sector in China

The innovation system of the energy sector in China has four components: (1) government agencies, such as MOST, NDRC and NSFC, charged with setting up the R&D roadmap and agenda and appropriating financial resources for scientific research; (2) enterprises, including SOEs and private companies, tasked with undertaking technological innovation; (3) universities and research institutions engaged in energy-related scientific research and knowledge production. Such research institutions fall into four categories: public research institutions (e.g. Guangzhou Institute of Energy Conversion, Chinese Academy of Sciences), corporate research institutions (e.g. China Electric Power Research Institute), university research institutions (e.g. Institute of Nuclear and New Energy Technology, Tsinghua University) and other non-profit research institutions; (4) service-based organizations for energy S&T innovation engaged in intermediary services and venture capital investment.

In the development of a sectoral innovation system conducive to innovation in energy-related technologies, China has encouraged research institutions, universities and businesses to establish energy-related innovation platforms, including state key laboratories, CNERC and national certified corporate technological centres.

Key areas of innovation in the energy sector

The Outline of Medium and Long-term National Plan for Science and Technology Development 2006–2020 (MLNP) placed energy technologies as one of the national innovation priorities in order to accelerate energy-related technological progress and support the sustainable development of the energy sector. Progress in innovation in this sector will clearly validate the principles of the country's innovation programme – independent innovation, leapfrogging in key areas, S&T supporting social and economic development, and S&T leading the future, as we explained in Chapter 2, and sets a template for other sectors to follow. More specifically, in the MLNP and the White Paper of China's Energy Conditions and Policies, China has identified five areas as a priority in S&T innovation in the energy sector.

The development of energy-saving technologies

The development of energy-saving technologies emphasized particularly on achieving technological breakthroughs in the high energy consumption areas so as to improve significantly the efficiency of primary energy utilization and final energy consumption. Measures have been taken to focus on: (1) implementing polices as set out in the Outlines of Energy Conservation Technologies issued by the NDRC and MOST in 2006 and guiding private investors to finance the application of energy-saving technologies; (2) supporting key R&D activities in energy-saving technologies and equipment applicable to the manufacturing, transport and building sectors, and the development of applied technologies which helps increase adoption of renewable energy in buildings and in energy-saving building materials; and (3) improving energy measurement, control, supervision and management, and fostering the development of a S&T service system in support of innovation in energy-saving technologies.

Innovation in key technologies

A number of areas have been identified to be of strategic importance for the development of key energy technologies. These key areas include clean coal technologies, advanced technologies of coal gasification, processing and conversion, advanced power generating technologies of integrated gasification combined cycle (IGCC), super (ultra-super) critical power generating units, large-scale circulating fluidized bed (CFB) and gasification-based poly-generation technology. China has also made it a priority of support in acquisition of the third-generation large-scale pressurized water reactor nuclear power technology and breakthroughs of independent innovation in high-temperature gas-cooled reactor (HTGR) industrial experiment technology. In the meantime, China encouraged the development of oil and natural gas exploration and exploitation technologies applicable to complex geological conditions and low-grade oil and gas high-efficiency exploitation technologies. The development of alternative energy technologies was also encouraged, with a priority given to the development of large-scale renewable energy technologies. Consistent support was also given to the development of technologies of ±800 KV direct current transmission and 1,000 KV UHV power transmission, and technologies that enhance the security and reliability of power grid.

Upgrading of equipment manufacturing capability

The equipment manufacturing industry provides the basis for the development of energy-related technologies. China uses national key energy projects to advance the technological progress of the equipment manufacturing industry. With regard to coal technologies, emphasis was placed on the development of integrated mining equipment for coal mines, large-scale, integrated mining, lifting, transport and washing equipment for coal mines, and large-scale mining equipment for open-pit mines. Similarly, support was given to the development of large-scale coal chemical industrial equipment, and the sets of equipment for coal liquefaction and gasification, and coal-to-olefins. In the field of electricity generation, focus was placed on the development of large-scale, highly efficient clean power generating equipment, highly efficient coal-fired power generating units, large-scale hydropower and pumped storage generating units, heavy-duty gas turbines, MKW advanced pressurized water reactor nuclear power generating units, high-power wind power generating units, and UHV power transmission and transformation equipment. In addition, support was given to the development of equipment for oil and gas exploration and drilling, large-scale equipment for off-shore oil projects, 300,000 tons of oil transport ships, transport ships for LNG, high-power diesel engine, and other supporting equipment.

R&D on cutting-edge technologies

Cutting-edge technologies facilitate leapfrogging development of energy technologies in the energy sector. China particularly focused on the development of

technologies in producing hydrogen with fossil, biomass and renewable energies, in hydrogen storage, transmission and distribution in a cost-effective
manner, in manufacturing of basic key parts of fuel cells, in galvanic pile integration, fuel cell power generation and integration of automotive power train
system. Efforts were also made to achieve breakthroughs in the development of
terminal (e.g. micro gas turbine with fossil energy) energy conversion, storage
and CCHP technologies. Measures were taken to speed up the R&D of gas-
cooled fast reactor design and core technologies, and to actively develop technologies of magnetic confinement fusion and natural gas hydrate.

Basic research

Progress in basic research has been seen as a critical source of independent
innovation and will determine the strength of energy development. China has
supported basic science research on the cost-effective, clean use and conversion
of fossil energy, key theories on high-performing thermal power conversion and
highly efficient energy saving and storage, basic technologies on scale-based use
of renewable energy, and basic theories on scale-based use of nuclear and hydrogen power technologies.

R&D in the energy sector in China

Due to data availability, here we only discuss R&D in five energy-related sub-
sectors – coal mining and washing; oil and natural gas extraction; petroleum
processing, coking and nuclear fuel processing; electric and thermal power production and supply; and gas production and supply. Obviously, this only offers
part of the picture for the entire energy sector, leaving out the renewable energy
industries and nuclear energy industry.

Enterprise R&D investment

Enterprise R&D investment in the energy sector has primarily been undertaken
by large industrial enterprises. As shown in Table 6.1, R&D expenses by large
enterprises in five energy industries in 2011 amounted to RMB33.38 billion. Of
which, RMB14.51 billion were spent in innovation in the coal mining and
washing industry, an unmistaken signal of the country's attempt to tackle the
coal energy-related problem through innovation. From 2004 to 2011 enterprise
R&D investment in five energy industries as a share of the total investment of all
industries averaged at 5.9 per cent, with the share fluctuating between the lowest
of 5.3 per cent in 2008 and the highest of 6.8 per cent in 2010.

Innovation in the five energy industries concerned was enterprise-led. This
can be clearly seen from the sources of S&T funding raised. In 2008, for
example, large enterprises raised a total of RMB47.74 billion to fund S&T activities, of which a lion's share of 94.67 per cent came from the private sector with
government funding and bank lending contributing merely 1.27 per cent and 3
per cent respectively (Table 6.2).

Table 6.1 R&D expenditure by large industrial enterprises in the energy sector, 2004–2011 (in RMB million)

Year	The energy industry					Total	% of R&D in all industries
	Coal mining and washing	Oil and natural gas extraction	Petroleum processing, coking and nuclear fuel processing	Electric and thermal power production and supply	Gas production and supply		
2004	2,591	2,186	1,095	1,184	22	7,078	6.4
2005	2,841	2,209	1,041	1,144	10	7,244	5.8
2006	3,690	2,273	1,605	1,543	13	9,123	5.6
2007	4,775	2,718	1,953	1,979	17	11,441	5.4
2008	6,390	3,689	3,014	3,192	34	16,319	5.3
2009	9,379	6,372	3,709	3,249	21	22,730	6.0
2010	10,875	8,811	4,383	3,195	103	27,367	6.8
2011	14,513	8,213	6,254	4,281	123	33,384	5.6

Source: *China Statistical Yearbook on Science and Technology.*

Table 6.2 Fund-raising of science and technology activities of large industrial enterprises in the energy sector in 2008

Item	Funds raised (RMB billion)	Of which (%)		
		Enterprises	Government	Loans
Coal mining and washing	16.90	97.19	1.68	0.46
Oil and natural gas extraction	9.72	97.73	0.53	n/a
Petroleum processing, coking and nuclear fuel processing	7.02	81.31	2.62	14.8
Electric and thermal power production and supply	13.93	96.22	0.56	2.29
Gas production and supply	0.17	94.03	5.67	n/a
Sub-total of the energy sector	47.74	94.67	1.27	3
Total of all sectors	616.05	89.00	3.74	5.82

Source: *China Statistical Yearbook on Science and Technology.*

Energy R&D investment by research institutes

Research institutes are the key source of innovation. Compared with large industrial enterprises, however, spending of research institutes in the energy sector on R&D was much smaller. In 2011, research institutes invested RMB313.87 million in R&D, less than one-tenth of R&D expenditure by large industrial enterprises. In addition, despite an increase in nominal R&D expenditure by research institutes in the energy sector from RMB121.33 million in 2004 to RMB313.87 million in 2011, its share in total R&D expenditure of all sectors in fact decreased to 0.24 per cent in 2011 after a jump to 0.40 per cent in 2008 (Table 6.3). Nevertheless, large industrial enterprises and research institutes displayed a different priority of R&D investment. While the coal-mining and washing industry received the most R&D investment by large industrial enterprises in the energy sector, the electric and thermal power production and supply industry had a lion's share of R&D investment from research institutes.

Investment on R&D in energy sector by higher education institutions

Higher education institutions played a greater role in energy-related R&D than research institutes. In 2011, higher education institutions invested RMB967 million in energy science R&D (Table 6.4), three times as much as compared with research institutes. In the same year, higher education institutions invested RMB53.5 billion in R&D, and energy-related R&D accounted for 1.81 per cent. This was a slight increase from 1.26 per cent in 2004 after a few years' shrinking in share before 2009.

Table 6.3 Internal spending by research institutes on R&D in the energy sector, 2004–2011 (in RMB million)

Year	The energy industry						% of all industries
	Coal mining and washing	Oil and natural gas extraction	Petroleum processing, coking and nuclear fuel processing	Electric and thermal power production and supply	Gas production and supply	Total	
2004	5.23	1.72	0.70	112.88	0.80	121.33	0.28
2005	0.95	0.60	4.06	108.28	0.62	114.51	0.22
2006	2.75	0.71	1.09	110.57	1.11	116.23	0.20
2007	4.24	1.44	4.91	142.52	5.44	158.55	0.23
2008	4.55	–	2.00	313.81	4.78	325.14	0.40
2009	18.53	–	0.83	306.99	2.22	328.57	0.33
2010	8.51	–	0.43	380.80	4.37	394.11	0.33
2011	9.59	–	1.59	289.25	13.44	313.87	0.24

Source: *China Statistical Yearbook on Science and Technology.*

Government support of S&T innovation in the energy sector

Direct support to S&T innovation

At present, direct government support to S&T innovation activities in the energy sector is mainly through MOST's national S&T programmes such as 863 Programme, 973 Programme and National Key Technology R&D Programme. These programmes tended to focus on broad S&T issues and hence there was no independent stream of energy-related S&T programmes in these national level programmes. Instead, energy-related S&T projects were often integrated as the energy component of such comprehensive programmes. Table 6.5 provides an estimate of government spending in the energy component of 973 Programme and the National Key Technology R&D Programme. There was a notable decrease in direct government support to energy-related S&T innovation in both

Table 6.4 Internal expenditure by higher education institutions on R&D in the energy sector, 2004–2011 (in RMB million)

Year	Energy S&T	Total of all the sectors	% of energy sector in all the sectors
2004	186.53	14,773.27	1.26
2005	213.12	19,345.37	1.10
2006	273.89	28,701.80	0.95
2007	278.54	25,823.55	1.08
2008	356.24	32,322.81	1.10
2009	549.03	36,352.98	1.51
2010	726.34	46,699.96	1.56
2011	967.00	53,533.88	1.81

Source: *China Statistical Yearbook on Science and Technology.*

Table 6.5 Funding on energy sector by some national S&T programmes (in RMB million)

Year	973 Programme		National Key Technology R&D Programme	
	Energy-related funds	Per cent	Energy-related funds	Per cent
2001	77.1	13.08	73.8	7.00
2002	68.1	9.73	85.5	6.39
2003	90.0	11.25	84.3	6.27
2004	84.4	9.38	58.6	3.63
2005	94.8	9.48	116.2	7.15
2006	90.2	9.21	184.7	6.16
2007	156.2	12.08	179.1	3.29
2008	168.1	11.18	241.5	4.77
2009	240.4	12.65	158.6	3.17
2010	296.6	10.91	155.3	3.11
2011	320.5	10.36	176.4	3.21

Source: *China Statistical Yearbook on Science and Technology.*

programmes. While energy-related funding as a share of 973 Programme experienced a small reduction from 2001 to 2011, funding of the energy component as a share of the National Key Technology R&D Programme was more than halved over the same period.

Nevertheless, the state has provided strong support to two energy-related Major National S&T Projects under the oversight of MOST: the Major Project of Developing Large-scale Oil and Gas Fields and Coal-bed Methane, and the Major Project of Large-scale Advanced PWR and HTGR Nuclear Power Stations. The first project was aimed at enhancing the capacity of oil and gas equipment technological innovation in China, improving the exploration and production level of oil and gas fields and coal-bed methane, upgrading the oil and gas equipment manufacturing industry and develop coal-bed methane at a large scale, and providing S&T support to maintain the steady growth of oil production and rapid development of natural gas output in China. The second project was designed to promote the development of nuclear power equipment manufacturing in China and further improve the share of nuclear power and the industrial innovation capacity.

Encouraging enterprises to implement upgrading projects with energy-saving technologies

Enterprises are rewarded for the actual amount of energy they have saved after upgrading energy-saving technologies, similar to the practices of the international carbon trading system. While the verification of actual energy saving is conducted by independent organizations, the government mainly assesses and rewards the enterprises which have achieved outstanding results in energy saving. Since 2007, as many as 2,280 projects of energy-saving technological upgrading each with over 10,000 tons of energy saved have been funded, leveraging a total investment of more than RMB120 billion from the business sector. It was estimated that more than 76.60 million tons of standard coal had been saved. Meanwhile, to promote the use of advanced energy-saving technologies, the government has also provided support to enterprises through demonstration projects of new clean production technologies, and those of building energy management centres.

Implementing relevant demonstration projects, accelerating diffusion of energy-saving technologies and products, and facilitating S&T innovation in the energy sector

The Programme of '1,000 New-Energy Vehicles in Ten Cities' has been implemented to conduct demonstration and promotion of vehicles with new energy. Thirteen cities including Beijing have been selected to promote the use of new energy vehicles in public services areas such as bus, taxi and environmental health, and no less than 60,000 units of vehicles were adopted within three years. While the central government mainly provides subsidies in a lump sum for the purchase and use of energy-saving and new energy vehicles to the organizations that took part in the scheme of demonstration and promotion of such vehicles in public service sectors in pilot cities, subsidies provided by the local governments are mainly used to fund the purchase of energy-saving and new energy vehicles, construction of supporting facilities, as well as maintenance of such vehicles. Significant achievements have been made in demonstrating and promoting the policies at the pilot cities, which have expanded the efforts of the enterprises on energy-saving and new energy core technologies R&D, stimulated the consumers' enthusiasm of purchasing and using new energy vehicles, and accelerated the scale-based production process of new energy vehicles.

Similarly, China launched the 'Golden Sun Programme' in 2009, aiming at promoting solar PV technological innovation and market application. Market pull policies such as fiscal subsidy and electricity price discount were used to provide strong support to large industrial, mining and commercial enterprises, public institutions, the remote and underdeveloped areas which cannot access electric power, and areas rich in PV resources in order to demonstrate and promote the application of PV power generating systems.

Demonstration projects on energy efficient buildings were carried out to enhance the application and product development of renewable energy solutions for buildings. A total of 371 demonstration projects in application of integrated renewable energy solutions in buildings have been funded. Demonstration projects on renewable energy buildings in 21 cities and 38 counties have been conducted to accelerate the large-scale application of renewable energy in rural and urban buildings. Moreover, the Solar Power Roof Programme, launched by MOF and MOHURD in March 2009, was implemented to speed up the application of solar PV technologies in urban and rural buildings through subsidized demonstration projects. As of end 2008, the total installed solar PV buildings reached 1.03 billion m^2, and buildings using shallow layer geothermal energy exceeded 100 million m^2.

Utilization of highly efficient energy-saving products is encouraged:

1   The 'Sending home appliances to the countryside' programme has been implemented since 2007. It was to provide fiscal subsidy to farmers in their purchase of home appliances, mainly energy-saving and environment-friendly products. To be eligible for subsidy, for example, refrigerators and freezers must be at minimum level II of energy efficiency and use 20 per cent less power than rival products so as to promote application of products with energy-saving technologies. So far, 32 million of such energy-efficient home appliances have been sold in the countryside with an estimated saving of 6.4 billion kWh of power.

2   A highly efficient lighting products initiative was launched in 2008. A total of 180 million units have since been utilized, saving electric power of 6.8 billion kWh annually. During the life cycle of these products, a total of 34 billion kWh of electric power can be saved, equivalent to the saving of RMB7 billion of electricity costs, reduction of CO_2 emission of 34 million

tons, and creation of RMB2.2 billion of domestic demand. In addition, the programme of 'Promoting 10,000 LED lights in ten cities' has been implemented. Under the Programme, LED technologies will be promoted in public lighting areas in 21 cities across China. It is expected to promote the use of six million units of LED functional and landscape lighting products in three years, helping save 1 billion kWh of electricity annually. By 2015, LED lighting products will be accessible to 30 per cent of the general lighting market, helping save up to 140 billion kWh.

3   In June 2009, the 'Programme of Promoting Energy-efficient Products for the Benefit of the People' was launched to promote highly efficient energy-saving air conditioners and provide fiscal subsidy for manufacturers to promote energy-efficient air conditioners. So far, 2.14 million units of air conditioners have been sold, accounting for over one-third of the total sales volume of air conditioners during the same period. As of end May 2010, more than ten million units of highly energy-efficient air conditioners have been sold, directly stimulating about RMB30 billion of private consumption.

Encouraging R&D and production of first MW wind power generating units and supporting technological innovation in the wind power industry

An approach of 'replacing subsidies with rewards' has been adopted to provide financial support to enterprises in the development of the first 50 units of MW-scale wind power generating units and spare parts, and to support technological progress of wind power generating units and scale-based production of key spare parts. Significant achievements have been made in this regard. As a result of such supports, energy companies in China have acquired an innovation capability to independently develop and produce large-scale MW wind power generating units and key spare parts such as blade, gear box, generator and bearing.

Supporting the development and use of biomass energy

1   *Supporting the development of bio-ethanol.* Over 8.3 million tons of bio-ethanol have been produced. The ethanol gasoline with 10 per cent of ethanol is being promoted in ten provinces and municipalities in China, and the consumption of ethanol gasoline accounts for about 20 per cent of the total consumption of gasoline in China. To date, China has become the third largest bio-ethanol producer and consumer in the world.

2   *Supporting the use of straw-based energy.* China has established 856 sites of providing centralized gas with straw, 102 sites of producing straw densification briquetting fuel (SDBF) and 150 sites of providing centralized biogas with straw. A total capacity of 613 MW is available for the projects of generating power with biomass, which can effectively mitigate the problem of straw burning.

3   *Supporting the development of biogas in rural areas.* As of end 2008, up to 30.50 million households in rural areas in China can access biogas. Projects of treating various types of agricultural waste have been implemented in 39,500 sites. Approximately 12.2 billion m^3 of biogas can be produced annually, benefiting almost 100 million people in rural areas and helping farmers directly increase incomes and save expenditures of RMB15 billion.

Leveraging policy tools of taxation and government procurement to promote S&T innovation

In line with the principle of integrating incentives and regulations, a series of policy measures in terms of income tax, consumption tax and resource tax, etc. have been taken to encourage enterprises to conserve energy and reduce emission with technological means. Tax incentives, such as a lower tax rate, tax reduction or exemption, are offered to production, consumption, and products that can help save energy resources and reduce environmental pollution. For example, a policy of VAT refund is implemented for electric or thermal power generation that uses urban domestic waste, straws, bark and waste residue, sludge, and medical waste for electricity and heating purposes. Enterprises that are engaged in appropriate projects on environmental protection, water and energy conservation can receive corporate income taxes reduction or exemption. On the contrary, punitive measures including higher tax rate have been taken to penalize enterprises that are the culprits of high energy consumption, high pollution and low efficiency of resources use. For instance, a much higher consumption tax rate is levied on passenger cars with large displacement, while export of high energy consumption, high pollution and resource-based commodities such as coal and coke shall be imposed temporary tariffs.

Greater efforts have been made on government procurement of energy-efficient and environment-friendly products to demonstrate the role of government in this regard. China has put in place a system of preferential procurement of energy-efficient and environmental labelling products. It has also developed the Government Procurement List for Environmental Labelling Products. On this basis, it has implemented a mandatory system of procuring energy-efficient and environment-friendly office equipment (e.g. air conditioners and computers), lighting products and water devices in order to promote R&D and application of energy conservation and emission reduction technologies by relevant sectors. So far, 34 categories and 18,000 kinds of products have been included in the energy-efficient products, and the environmental labelling products have increased to 21 categories and over 8,600 kinds.

Enhancing international exchange and cooperation on S&T innovation

China has been actively engaged in a number of international S&T cooperative programmes such as the Joint Implementation Agreement of International

Thermonuclear Experimental Reactor (ITER), FutureGen,[6] the International Partnership for Hydrogen and Fuel Cells in the Economy (IPHE) and Integrated Ocean Drilling Programme (IODP), to name just a few. It has also been involved in the development of many international technical standards regarding resources saving, pollutants discharge control, etc., so as to create a mutually beneficial and win–win situation in which technologies and resources can be shared and integrated.

Innovation in wind power technologies

China's development of wind power has been widely claimed as a success story (GWEC, 2013; Pew Trusts, 2013a). It is a testament to its commitment to the sustainability agenda and its approach to setting clear strategic goals and targets. China first announced its wind power targets for 2020 in the Outline of Medium and Long-term National Plan for Science and Technology Development 2006–2020 (MLNP). It was projected that the country would reach 30GW of wind power capacity when its installed wind power capacity was 1.27GW in 2005, as shown in Table 6.6. The development of wind power has since exceeded all expectations with the 2020 target of wind power capacity met in 2010, ten years earlier than planned. The target for 2020 has later been revised up to 200GW.

China's wind power development had a modest start from 1986 to 1992 through a number of small wind power demonstration projects financially supported partly by international donors. The momentum came in 1993 when the defunct Ministry of Electric Power Industry used its national working conference on wind power to launch an initiative aiming at wind power up-scaling and standardization of wind power grid construction.[7] Policy support, regulations and laws that followed triggered the wave of investment in wind energy across the country since 2005, and the momentum has been maintained to date. Data from Bloomberg New Energy Finance (Pew Trusts, 2013a) show that China attracted US$27.2 billion worth of wind energy investment in 2012, accounting for 37 per cent of G20 wind energy investment. It was also found that China led the world in deployment of clean energy technologies, adding about 16GW of wind generating capacity a year between 2008 and 2012 (GWEC, 2013). In less than a decade, China has emerged from nowhere to become the cornerstone of the global wind industries, making up 20 per cent of the world's total installed wind

Table 6.6 Key wind energy targets for 2020

	2005	Targets for 2020	
	Installed capacity	*MLNP (2006)*	*Latest targets*
Wind power	1.27GW	30GW	200GW

Source: GWEC (2013) and MLNP.

power capacity (Figure 6.1). As China is catching up fast with the old leaders in wind power, the centre of gravity in the wind power world has shifted from the United States and Europe to China. The world was truly amazed that China was able to close the gap in wind power production capability in only ten years and that it has begun to catch up in innovation capability as well (Lema *et al.*, 2013).

In the global clean energy race, China has benefited from its richly endowed wind energy resources. The total wind energy reserves in China's land are 3.226×10^9 kW, among which the developable is 2.53×10^8 kW; developable ocean wind resources are about three times that of the land, i.e. around 7.5×10^8 kW (Zhang *et al.*, 2009). More importantly, the development of wind power technologies illustrates well how policy agenda and actions were underlined by the principles of China's innovation strategy which we have explained early in this chapter. Additionally, the fast expansion of the domestic market in wind power energy under the support of government policies created positive conditions on which new technologies could be developed, trialled and deployed. Equally interesting is the route to innovation domestic firms have taken from international licensing arrangements, co-design to independent innovation.

Market development

The explosive growth of the wind power industry has hugely benefited from two policy supports from the Chinese government for market development. The first was the Wind Power Concession Programme introduced by the NDRC in 2003.[8] The programme was designed to promote the establishment of large-scale wind farms (50 MW and over) to generate electricity for national grids and to attract foreign companies to invest in China's wind energy sector. Under this

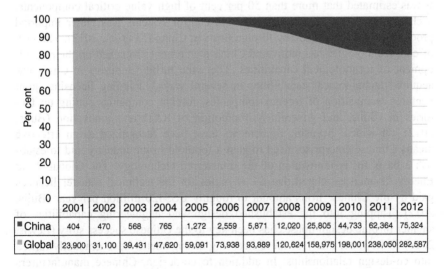

	2001	2002	2003	2004	2005	2006	2007	2008	2009	2010	2011	2012
■ China	404	470	568	765	1,272	2,559	5,871	12,020	25,805	44,733	62,364	75,324
■ Global	23,900	31,100	39,431	47,620	59,091	73,938	93,889	120,624	158,975	198,001	238,050	282,587

Figure 6.1 Cumulative installed wind capacity, 2001–2012 (source: GWEC (2013)).

programme electric utilities enter into long-term power purchase agreements with wind farm developers under the agreement covering the entire forecast operational period of the wind farm, thereby reducing the risk for the developers. End users of electricity receive a tariff increase to cover the increased cost of wind power. The NDRC-sponsored wind farms are forecast eventually to account for most of the wind power produced in China, and therefore represent the principal future market for wind power equipment.[9]

Local governments have also embraced wind energy development with great enthusiasm as projects under 50 MW did not require competitive bidding and so could be granted for development by local authorities.

The Renewable Energy Law in 2005 establishes a purchase system for renewable electricity, but the process of requesting bids for tenders continued for grid-connected wind power projects. In 2007, a target of 15 per cent of China's total energy consumption from renewable energy was set for 2020. The law requires that grid companies purchase the full amount of power generated by wind power projects with the tariff for all projects being set by the winning bid. Domestic clean energy targets for wind power in China have provided ready market pull for indigenous enterprises to rapidly expand their manufacturing capacity, and technology learning and low labour costs allowed Chinese firms to gain a competitive advantage in the global marketplace. The data show that Chinese firms are strong in large-scale manufacturing and high-volume assembly of finished products (Pew Trusts, 2013b).

The development of technological capabilities

International technology transfer has been an important source of technological capacity in wind turbine development in China (Lema *et al.*, 2013; Lewis, 2011). It was estimated that more than 50 per cent of high value critical components, such as converters, spindle bearings and control systems was either imported products or products made by foreign firms in China (Li *et al.*, 2012). The lack of core technologies has motivated Chinese enterprises to speed up their development of technological capabilities. The wind turbine industry in China has acquired technological capabilities in several ways, including licensing, joint ventures, acquisition of foreign companies, foreign companies setting up factories in China, and government promotion of R&D and innovation (Buijs, 2012). Of which, licensing agreements have been recognized as an effective means Chinese enterprises used to gain a foothold in the industry and to establish a basis for re-innovation of the transferred technology. The Global Wind Energy Council estimated that the royalties for the technical transfer licences paid by the Chinese firms amount to roughly US$420 million per year (Buijs, 2012). Tapping into the established design and engineering capabilities of smaller turbine design houses has been key to the Chinese success story (Lewis, 2011). Over time, many of these licensing arrangements have gradually turned into co-design relationships. In addition to co-design, Chinese manufacturers have in some cases used foreign acquisition to enhance their internal technological design capacities. The trajectory of indigenous technological capability development through technology transfer and re-innovation proves just as effective as a technology strategy that prioritizes independent in-house development (Lema *et al.*, 2013). Chinese firms are now working with overseas partners on turbine prototypes that are just as advanced as those being developed by firms in the West.

Leading innovators in the wind sector are large, established Chinese companies. The growth of Sinovel Wind Group is exemplary. Founded in 2006, Sinovel entered the wind power industry and built its technological capability through the import of globally advanced MW-level wind turbine technologies. By 2013, the company became China's first specialized high-tech enterprise engaged in independent development, design, manufacturing and sale of large-scale onshore, offshore and intertidal series of wind turbines. It is also the first in China to have developed independently the globally advanced 5 MW and 6 MW series wind turbines. Sinovel's cumulated installed wind power capacity reached 12,989 MW by the end of 2011, ranking No. 1 in China. Along the way of fast growth, Sinovel has set many milestones in China's wind power industry:

- The first to have successfully completed R&D for and realized the mass production of the global mainstream 3 MW series of onshore, offshore and intertidal wind turbine series with internationally advanced technologies. Sinovel holds independent intellectual property rights.
- The first to have finished the development and production of China's first 5 MW and 6 MW wind turbines with independent intellectual property rights.
- The first to complete China's first demonstration offshore wind farm through the supply of all 34 sets of 3 MW wind turbines for the Shanghai Donghai Bridge Offshore Wind Farm, the first offshore wind farm built outside Europe.[10]

The company regards innovation as its bloodline and consistently spent 3–5 per cent of sales revenue in R&D, which was worth RMB300 million in 2012.[11] In November 2009, the company was granted to set up the National Energy Offshore Wind Power Technology and Equipment R&D Centre, the only enterprise-based, national R&D centre focused on the development of offshore wind power technology and equipment in China. It is one of the 13 national common technology platforms supported by the central government. It is tasked with developing the world's cutting-edge technologies, state-of-the-art equipment, and leading R&D and laboratory capabilities. It is also given the mission of constructing the world pioneering integrated base for the manufacturing, assembly, testing, ocean transportation and ocean installation service for large-size offshore wind turbines. Funding for the creation of the centre was RMB512 million.[12] The centre has developed the leading 3 MW, 5 MW and 6 MW onshore, offshore and intertidal series of wind turbines.[13] Currently, Sinovel has more than 800 engineers working in its R&D centre where efforts address the design and development of wind turbines. As of the end of 2011, the company had filed 166 patent applications and 115 granted patents, of which 40 granted patents were invention patents associated with the company's core technologies.[14] Since its inception, Sinovel has been the beneficiary of the government's tax incentive for innovation. It enjoyed corporate income tax exemption from 2006 to 2008 as a granted high and new technology firm and has paid the corporate tax rate of 15 per cent since 2009.[15]

Such internal innovation efforts are buttressed firmly by state support. For example, research into large-scale wind turbines was funded through the National High-Tech Development Programme, also known as the 863 Programme in the period of the Tenth Five-Year Plan (2001–2005). In 2008, funding was made available through the government Special Fund for the Industrialization of Wind Power Equipment. Under this policy, upon the development and industrialization of a new product sized over 1.5 MW, the first 50 pieces of equipment produced can enjoy a subsidy of RMB600 per KW. A critical step to push wind power research in China was the creation in 2010 of 16 national research centres or national laboratories to undertake basic research. This was followed by the establishment in 2011 of the national key renewable energy laboratory for technology simulation, assessment and certification.

Additionally, China's effort to promote innovation has born fruits as measured by patent filing. In Yan *et al.*'s (2009) research, wind power patent applications in China increased from 71 in 2000 to 625 in 2007 and the rapid increase in patent filing was mainly driven by domestic enterprises (Table 6.7). Of which, a significant proportion was invention patent applications, while applications from foreign companies were not the main driver. From a technology perspective, Chinese companies are clearly catching up with Western firms. Although there might still be quality and reliability issues, major producers such

Table 6.7 Wind power patent applications in China

	Patent applications	Invention patent applications[a]	Patent applications by foreign firms[b]
2000	71	40	6
2001	99	55	18
2002	155	87	34
2003	187	105	41
2004	266	149	31
2005	402	225	30
2006	610	342	43
2007	625	350	22

Source: Yan *et al.* (2009).

Notes

a Estimation based on the assumption that on average 56 per cent of patent applications falls into the invention patent category.

b Applications from six foreign firms, i.e. LM, Gamesa, Nordex, Vestas, Enercon and GE.

as Sinovel, Goldwind and Dongfang Electric are developing large-scale turbines of 3 MW, 5 MW or more (Buijs, 2012). Regarding offshore wind technology, all major Chinese companies are investing heavily in R&D and the development of their capabilities.

China is extremely well-positioned to take a lead in advancing low-carbon technologies. It offers a major growth market and can leverage this in order to gain the technological know-how which it lacks. Furthermore, its push to promote low-carbon industries is very strong, as it is part of broader government policy objectives.

Challenges in S&T innovation in the energy sector

Gaps with international advanced level in energy S&T

Over recent years, the S&T level of energy sector in China has been steadily improved thanks to a relatively stable framework of support for energy STI. However, there still exist some gaps with the advanced countries, and S&T in the energy sector in China is characterized by insufficient innovation capacity, fragmented outcomes, and low level in systematic, industrial and engineering-based development. Specifically, technological and equipment level in the coal industry needs greater improvements as Chinese enterprises are still dependent on import of large technology equipment and their technological capacity falls short in meeting domestic demands. The exploration and development technologies of non-conventional oil and gas including shale gas are yet to achieve significant breakthrough. China suffers from weak structure of power grid, poor power transmission and distribution capacity, and low reliability of power grid operation. In nuclear power, independent R&D capacity is not strong, with a small percentage of key equipment made locally, and the capacity of independently designing and manufacturing MKW of pressurized water reactor nuclear power stations has not been established. In terms of renewable energy, the capacity of independent manufacturing of large high-performing wind power generating units is rather weak in China, and some high technologies including PC cell silicon ingot/pellet are mainly introduced from foreign countries.

Lack of integration and coordination in the management of energy S&T

While the governance system in the energy sector in China has undergone many changes, a uniform and authoritative energy administration authority has not been established for a long time. As such, China suffers from weak macro management at the sector level, which makes it difficult to develop consistent strategies and policies on energy development. Moreover, the management of energy S&T innovation lacks integration and coordination, and no consistent scientific and technological R&D strategy and system has been made available. Projects are scattered, which cannot provide consistent and strong support to enhance the energy S&T innovation capacity. Lack of communication and cooperation among different entities involved in energy S&T innovation makes it hardly possible to establish an innovation system that is closely linked to one another.

Efforts should be made in the following aspects: to establish a coordination mechanism on energy S&T innovation management to strengthen communication and cooperation between departments and units; to conduct overall planning and systematic deployment of energy S&T development strategy to strengthen coordination and connection among S&T development plans, industrial development plans and relevant policies; to integrate and optimize S&T resource allocation and give full play to the advantages and roles of different S&T innovation bodies to together promote energy S&T innovation.

Long-term planning for energy S&T innovation is formulated aiming at the weak points of energy S&T development and future economic and social development needs. At present, the Chinese Academy of Sciences proposes an energy S&T development roadmap; the overall target is to accelerate the building of a sustainable energy system with a step-by-step increase in the share of renewable energy sources and the efficient and clean use of fossil fuels, and to gradually optimize energy structure to meet China's economic and social development needs. Targets in the near future (up to 2020) focus on the development of energy-saving and clean energy technologies to improve energy efficiency; the medium-term target (up to 2030) centres around the promotion of nuclear energy and the development of renewable energy as the main sources of energy; the long-term target (up to 2050) is to build China's sustainable energy system and basically meet the energy needs of China's economic and social development in a gross way. A lot of work can be done on such a basis, such as to formulate energy S&T development plans, to clarify the priority areas of energy R&D and key technologies, and to make a systematic deployment for energy S&T innovation.

Lack of generic technologies innovation platform

At present, the energy sector and its S&T innovation management in China is relatively decentralized, lacking overall planning and deployment of energy-related technological innovation bases and platforms, and lacking coordination among different agencies, systems and organizations. This has, to some extent, resulted in the overlapping of various agencies and sectors' functions in conducting energy-related S&T, and lack of platforms for independent innovation of common purpose technologies, and lack of R&D on industry generic technologies.

This will include: developing energy technology innovation bases; actively promoting the construction of energy technology innovation platforms; increasing supports for technology research bases, such as the state key laboratories in the field of energy, engineering and technology research centres, engineering laboratories etc. Meanwhile, by integrating relatively isolated technology resources in a systematic way, a common technology R&D platform will be formed to support energy S&T development. Furthermore, common purpose technology research should be strengthened so as to promote the overall development of S&T in the energy sector.

Insufficient incentives and capacity in terms of technological innovation for enterprises

Most energy producers and key energy-related equipment manufactures in China are SOEs or state-controlled enterprises. Although many companies have established their own research institutions, they have not paid due attention to R&D innovation and few of them have initiative in independent innovation as the key performance indicator (KPI) system on leaders of large SOEs is profit-oriented and lacks assessment on independent innovation. In terms of the internal environment of enterprises involved in the energy sector, no favourable mechanism on technological innovation has been put in place by enterprises. Technological innovation efforts in most enterprises are decentralized, making it hardly possible to deliver high-quality S&T outcomes.

The innovation capacity of energy-related enterprises in China is far from being satisfied. Compared with major multi-national companies with advanced technologies, domestic equipment manufacturers still have big gaps in terms of design and manufacturing of energy-related products with high technology, capacity and schedule of technological development and innovation, products performance, and management skills. As a consequence, many core energy-related technologies have to be introduced from foreign countries, while more key energy-related equipment and technologies need to be made in China.

Energy S&T projects bear such features as being large scale and fundamental, and their R&D, validation, demonstration projects and supporting projects all require a lot of financial support. The guiding role of government spending for S&T should be brought into full play to establish a pluralistic multi-channel system for energy S&T investment, since it mainly supports public S&T activities, such as fundamental researches, cutting-edge technologies, social benefit studies, significant key generic technology researches, etc. that cannot be done effectively in energy market mechanisms. With an increase in government spending, investment impulse of enterprises will be better stimulated through preferential taxation and financial policies, so as to enhance the status of enterprises as the main S&T investment body. In short, through various efforts made by different parties, investment in R&D in the energy sector will be increased and the capacity of energy S&T innovation will be improved.

By enhancing the role of enterprises as the energy technology innovation subject, enterprises will be guided and encouraged to put more efforts and money in technology innovation. Meanwhile, measures are taken to promote the combination of production, study and research and to highlight the connection and communication among universities, R&D institutions and industries, which will, on one hand, stimulate the innovative vigour of universities and research institutions, and on the other hand, help industries maintain sustainable innovation capacity. With these efforts, different sources of strengths will be effectively integrated, and a mutual cooperation, mutual benefit and win-win situation will be formed. Furthermore, by vigorously strengthening the capacity-building of intermediaries, the gap between technology supply and demand parties will be bridged and information exchange channels will be established, which will provide quality service for technology innovation and application.

Notes

1 See 'China improves low carbon competitiveness', *Financial Times*, 25 March 2013.
2 From online database of *China Statistics Yearbook 2012*, available at www.stats.gov.cn/tjsj/ndsj/2012/html/G0702e.htm (accessed 10 January 2013).
3 Energy import reliance is measured as energy imports as a proportion of total energy available for consumption. Data are obtained from the online database of *China Statistics Yearbook 2012*, available at www.stats.gov.cn/tjsj/ndsj/2012/html/G0703e.htm (accessed 10 January 2013).
4 See International Energy Agency, *2012 Key World Energy Statistics*, available at www.iea.org/publications/freepublications/publication/kwes.pdf (accessed 10 January 2013).
5 From online database of *China Statistics Yearbook 2012*, available at www.stats.gov.cn/tjsj/ndsj/ (accessed 10 January 2013).
6 FutureGen, launched in 2003, is a US government funding scheme to support projects that advance technology to make the United States a world leader in carbon capture and storage.
7 Li *et al.* (2007) provide a good account of the development of wind power in this early period.
8 In 2009, the NDRC replaced the public bidding process and instituted FITs for wind power, scaled according to the available wind resource and construction conditions in the various regions of China.
9 The concession tendering process for wind farm development worked as follows. Prior to arranging for a concession for a wind power project, the NDRC would conduct wind resource assessments for prospective areas and set prices for the electricity generated by these projects. The bidding process would determine the in-grid tariff, with the agreement specifying how much electricity the bidder would provide to the grid. The regional grid power company would enter into a long-term power purchase agreement to buy electricity from the project over the life of the project, with the national government guaranteeing the power purchase.
10 From the company's official website, www.sinovel.com/ (accessed 10 September 2014).
11 See Xinhuanet's interview with Tao Gang, Sinovel's Vice President and Senior Deputy Executive on 9 September 2013, available at http://news.xinhuanet.com/energy/2013-09/09/c_125349579.htm (accessed 10 September 2014).
12 See report on the launch ceremony of the centre by Chinanews, available at www.chinanews.com/cj/news/2009/11-03/1944952.shtml (accessed 10 September 2014).
13 The detail of the company's R&D and business development is available at www.sinovel.com/ (accessed 10 September 2014).
14 From a report 'Wind power industry: development through global positioning' (风电产业：布局全球谋求发展) in IP News on 25 February 2012, available at www.cnipr.com/services/zlxxyysw/wz/201205/t20120525_143679.html (accessed 10 September 2014).
15 Based on the company's 2013 annual report to the stock market, available at http://finance.sina.com.cn/stock/t/20130831/012016622980.shtml (accessed 8 January 2014).

7 Incentive for regional innovation
The Yangtze River Delta

Regions have always been an important layer in China's national development and governance due to the country's super size of territory. The same is true in the country's endeavour to build an innovative economy. Efforts have been made to bring individual regions at the provincial level on board in the formulation and implementation of national innovation strategy. Attention has also been given to encourage coordinated and joined-up actions across regions. Among many initiatives aimed at innovation cross-region level, the development of regional innovation systems in the Yangtze River Delta (YRD) approved by the State Council illustrates how local governments are driving innovation and what challenges they are facing.

YRD is made up of three administrative regions – Jiangsu Province, Zhejiang Province and Shanghai Municipality – and is one of the most developed regions economically and technologically in China. In 2011, the region contributed 21.3 per cent to the country's GDP with 11.7 per cent of the country's population. It has also played a vital role in China's phenomenal economic growth in the reform era. While Shanghai has embarked on reclaiming the honour of the financial centre of the country and beyond, Jiangsu and Zhejiang have developed to the current level of prosperity from two rather different paths. Jiangsu built its success on the historical strength of collective small and medium-sized enterprises (SMEs) in which local governments were a significant stakeholder; in contrast, Zhejiang surged to success on the back of a thriving private sector. Nevertheless, both provinces historically have close economic links with Shanghai. Despite the scale and diversity of the region, Shanghai is undoubtedly the magnet of the YRD, radiating its influence to Jiangsu in the north and Zhejiang in the south.

The recent development of regional innovation system in the YRD can be attributed to two shared interests of all governments concerned. For the central government, a strong and dynamic innovation system in this region is of critical importance for achieving the objectives of the national innovation strategy. For the regional governments, improvements of innovation performance by playing into individual strengths can contribute to the overall competitiveness of each region. Motivation also arose from concerns of local governments that fragmented and duplicative efforts in innovation undertakings would drain public resources and compromise the strengths of all parties in the region. Hence, there was a strong motive in the region to work together in certain capacity at cross-region level to create a win-win situation. In addition, there were pragmatic considerations at the local level too. The re-emergence of Shanghai as a national economic centre has tipped the balance of regional economy in its favour. Jiangsu and Zhejiang Provinces have considered a more integrated regional innovation system to be a countermeasure to prevent their own home-grown, fledgling companies in their regions from re-locating headquarters to Shanghai (Wei and Wu, 2004).

The evolution of the regional innovation system in the Yangtze River Delta

The prelude to regional S&T cooperation in the Yangtze River Delta

The region's effort to cooperate with each other on matters of innovation in recent years can be traced back to as early as the 1980s when the central government took a top-down approach to establish the Shanghai Economic Zone and approved the setting-up of Shanghai Economic Zone Planning Office as its administrative agency in December 1982. The Shanghai Economic Zone at the time was composed of ten cities, namely Shanghai, four cities in Jiangsu Province (Suzhou, Wuxi, Changzhou, Nantong) and five cities in Zhejiang Province (Hangzhou, Jiaxing, Huzhou, Ningbo, Shaoxing). The intention of the central government was to use this initiative to remove barriers to regional collaboration in the long-standing mode of regional governance under the planned economic system and to encourage local governments in the region to cooperate. For this purpose, the central government set forth four principles in the initiative, that is, integrated regional planning, selective development to match with the strengths of each member city, economic collaboration, and cooperation within the existing governance framework in individual cities. It was anticipated that the initiative would bring local governments in the region to work for mutual benefit and a shared sense of achievement. In a broader context, the formation of the Shanghai Economic Zone was designed as an experiment to trial a new institutional set-up in economic system reforms. If successful, the new mode of governance would remove all kinds of local barriers and help the region to fulfil all its potential and achieve greater economic results through stronger internal collaboration. In order to promote intra-regional economic cooperation within the metropolitan area, relevant institutions were established, substantive measures were taken, and some important viewpoints were raised by the government at that time, such as leveraging of economic rules and the establishment of a unified regional market in the Zone. However, all good intentions in the experiment on the economic zone failed to materialize largely due to its heavy dependence on dated government intervention and planning methods which were incompatible with the prevailing goals of reform and opening up. Despite the failed attempt to establish Shanghai Economic Zone by administrative means, needs for economic cooperation in the YRD were widely recognized. This was evidenced by the retention of economic coordination offices within the governments of all cities as an agency to coordinate cross-city collaborations even after the initiative ceased operating.

In 1992, the Directors of Economic Coordination Office of 14 cities in the YRD decided to set up a mechanism for strengthening regional cooperation in the form of Municipal Economic Coordination Meeting.[1] They envisaged a broad agenda of regional cooperation, ranging from commerce, trade to tourism. In its first ever joint meeting attended by the Directors of Economic Coordination Commission/Office of all participating cities, Shanghai played host and was voted as the Acting Chair to coordinate efforts of economic cooperation among cities in the YRD after the meeting. In 1997, after accepting Taizhou City, Jiangsu Province, as a new member, 15 cities agreed unanimously to upgrade the joint meeting from the director's level to the mayor's level, and renamed it as the Yangtze River Delta Municipal Economic Coordination Meeting. It was also agreed that meetings were to be held biannually and hosted by member cities in rotation. This has become what is called today the Mayors' Joint Meeting.

In 2002, regional cooperation in the YRD received a new lease of life. In the second Economic Cooperation and Development Forum, the governments of Shanghai, Jiangsu and Zhejiang agreed to the principles and programmes of regional economic cooperation. The YRD Municipal Mayors Forum at the Vice Executive Governor (Vice Mayor) level was set up as an inter-governmental communication channel with focus on regional planning for transportation system, sharing of electronic information resources and credit system resources, and cooperation on regional tourism, ecological construction and environmental protection.

The development of regional innovation system in the YRD

2003 was an important year for inter-governmental cooperation in the YRD as a series of breakthroughs was achieved. First, an agreement of cooperation was signed by the governments of Shanghai, Jiangsu and Zhejiang, in a consensus that Shanghai should lead the concerted effort to jointly promote economic integration in the YRD whilst Jiangsu and Zhejiang play a supporting role. Three local governments also viewed Shanghai's hosting of the World Expo as an opportunity to accelerate the joint development of the Yangtze River Delta and agreed to set up an acting agency to coordinate YRD-wide activities for the World Expo. Under the same agreement, local governments also agreed to build a regional transportation network, to collaborate on ecological environment protection, to carry out thematic cooperation, and to improve people's living quality. Regional innovation featured more strongly than ever before in regional collaboration. Agreement on the Joint Promotion of Innovation System Construction by Shanghai, Jiangsu and Zhejiang in the Yangtze River Delta was signed, declaring the official start of innovation system building in the YRD. Subsequent actions included the establishment of an innovation-focused joint meeting system represented by the leaders of two provinces and one city, the establishment of the office under the joint meeting, represented by members from Science and Technology Commissions/Departments of Science and Technology of two provinces and one city, as an agency responsible for the organization and coordination of specific tasks on science and technology cooperation in the YRD, and the establishment of special funds to guide and expedite the building of innovative system in the YRD. The developments mark the formation of institutions and working mechanism of regional cooperation in science, technology and innovation (STI) in the YRD in a comprehensive manner.

In 2005, the central government designated YRD as a region for reform pilot in the National 11th Five-Year Plan (2006–2010). In 2007, at the Seminar on Socio-economic Development in YRD Area, Premier Wen Jiabao stressed that "it is of overall significance for the YRD region to be the first to develop in the county". Since then, a new round of regional cooperation in the YRD has been initiated. As of end 2007, 16 municipal governments in Shanghai, Jiangsu and Zhejiang have signed the Taizhou Agreement and Changzhou Agreement, identifying seven issues as priorities of regional cooperation in the year of 2008, namely, port cooperation, installation of standardized tourism signs, installation of a cross-region transport swipe card system, setting up a system of coordination meetings, integrated markets, experience tour of World Expo Shanghai 2010, and environmental protection. In his speech at the Seminar on Regional Coordinated Development of YRD in 2008, Premier Wen inspired the region to be a pioneer of innovation and to adopt a scientific outlook on development, meaning putting people first and aiming at comprehensive, coordinated and sustainable development. Taking all this on board, the S&T departments in Shanghai, Jiangsu and Zhejiang jointly developed the Three-Year (2008–2010) Action Plan on Science & Technology Cooperation in Yangtze River Delta. In the Action Plan, it was proposed that YRD be developed as a national centre of STI, a region of S&T resource sharing, a region for sustainable living and an innovative region for S&T industries.

Since then, the field, scope and intensity of cross-government cooperation in the YRD have been broadened and strengthened, with the adoption of the more pragmatic means to facilitate the development of the regional innovation system. From 2004 to 2008, 16 cities[2] in the YRD signed many protocols and introduced measures to promote regional cooperation and innovation system building. The list of initiatives and actions included the creation of technology service institutions in which Shanghai serves as a bridge and link in S&T cooperation, 'Yangtze River Delta Intermediary Strategic Alliance in Science and Technology', 'Advancement in Technology and Economy Cooperation Platform in the Yangtze River Delta', 'Yangtze River Delta Technology and Information Service Platform', 'Yangtze River Delta Modern Service Industry Cooperation', the promulgation of 'the 11th Five-Year (2006–2010) Cooperation Planning on Informationization of the Yangtze River Delta'; the establishment of a technology alliance, an agreement to set up a common platform for large scientific instrument and facilities, 'the Joint Development of Major Science and Techno-logy Research Projects in the Yangtze River Delta', 'the Joint Establishment of Special Funds for Cooperation in Science and Technology in Yangtze River Delta', more resources sharing, joint S&T research, and technical information exchange, etc. In addition, Shanghai and 19 cities from Jiangsu and Zhejiang Provinces agreed to set up a joint meeting system with a specific focus on talent development in the YRD. Subsequent agreements were signed to promote the mobility of talent, to develop an online platform for the talent market in the YRD, to form a regional alliance on education and research cooperation in the YRD, and to promote S&T cooperation and technology transfer through the establishment of a mutual qualification recognition system in the YRD. At the same time, Shanghai, Jiangsu and Zhejiang have joined up to create a collabora-tive network for product quality and consumer right protection across the region. The quality supervisory departments of local governments have also worked together to set up mechanisms for mutual recognition of market access. In com-pliance with the national policy framework, a cooperation and coordination mechanism in the fields of industry standards, guild regulations and trade dis-putes resolutions was established to address needs for industry-university-research institute cooperation.

Meanwhile, the central government has lent its support to improving and pro-moting policy environment for integrated development of the Yangtze River Delta. In 2007, Premier Wen Jiabao chaired the forum on economic and social development of the Yangtze River Delta, launching the intensive research in the Yangtze River Delta conducted by research teams assembled from more than ten ministries. In 2008, the central government issued 'Guideline on Further Pro-moting the Reform and Opening-up and Economic and Social Development of the Yangtze River Delta'. It was unprecedented that the central government set forth planning requirements for domestic regional development. It was also the first time that the regional integration of the Yangtze River Delta moved up to the national agenda of planning. The key milestones in the development of regional innovation system in the YRD can be seen in Figure 7.1.

The characteristics of the regional innovation system in the YRD

Regional innovation strategy

The development of the regional innovation strategy in the YRD has come a long way and has been part of the broader regional effort to collaborate on all matters of social and economic development. In 2008, the State Council used the issuance of the Guideline for Further Promoting Reform, Opening Up and Socio-Economic Development to envisage the national perspective of regional collaboration and regional development in the YRD.[3] The guidelines spelled out the strategic aims concerning reform, openness and development. Where innovation is concerned, the region was required to significantly strengthen regional innovation capability and

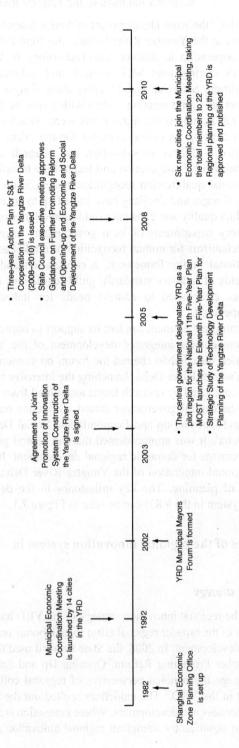

Figure 7.1 The milestones of the development of the regional innovation system in the YRD.

- 1982: Shanghai Economic Zone Planning Office is set up
- 1992: Municipal Economic Coordination Meeting is launched by 14 cities in the YRD
- 2002: YRD Municipal Mayors Forum is formed
- 2003: Agreement on Joint Promotion of Innovation System Construction of the Yangtze River Delta is signed
- 2005:
  - The central government designates YRD as a pilot region for the National 11th Five-Year Plan
  - MOST launches the Eleventh Five-Year Plan for Strategic Study of Technology Development Planning of the Yangtze River Delta
- 2008:
  - Three-year Action Plan for S&T Cooperation in the Yangtze River Delta (2008–2010) is issued
  - State Council executive meeting approves Guidance on Further Promoting Reform and Opening-up and Economic and Social Development of the Yangtze River Delta
- 2010:
  - Six new cities join the Municipal Economic Coordination Meeting, taking the total members to 22
  - Regional planning of the YRD is approved and published

to considerably raise the contribution of technical progress to regional economic development. To this end, the central government set forth four objectives of regional innovation and proposed measures for enhancing independent innovation and speeding up the transformation of an innovative region.

•   To develop an internationally competitive regional innovation system. Proposed policies measures include: (1) encourage the flow of innovation-related resources to enterprises, support prospective firms to set up their own in-house R&D facility and/or overseas R&D centres, and encourage the creation of innovation strategic alliances between enterprises, universities and research institutes; (2) pull together the region's strength of innovation to build a number of first class research universities, research institutes and innovative organizations through intensified efforts in the construction of national key laboratories, engineering technology centres and national key scientific research projects on the one hand, and in the construction of open R&D infrastructure and a shared platform for R&D in general purpose technologies on the other; (3) develop regional innovation networks through the development of R&D service platforms and intermediaries and key science parks to support technology transfer and commercialization; and (4) establish a system of mutual recognition of S&T certification.
•   To achieve innovation breakthroughs in core technologies and in key sectors. More specifically, the region was called upon to concentrate independent innovation on such areas as electronic information, biology, advanced manufacture, new energy, new material, and aeronautics and astronautics. The region was also urged to exploit science parks as a spatial setting of innovation and industrial cluster to push forward innovation of high originality, integrated innovation and re-innovation of imported technologies. The region was asked to support joint application for national key special S&T projects.
•   To create a policy environment conducive to independent innovation. The proposed measures concerned the use of public R&D expenditure to leverage more private investment in all types of innovation, full implementation of innovation incentive policies, improvement in financing of innovation and entrepreneurship, and improvement in IP protection.
•   To increase the pool of innovation talent through regional education efforts and overseas recruitment.

In order to fully implement the Framework Agreement on Regional Cooperation of the Yangtze River Delta, the office under the joint meeting of YRD innovation system construction, with reference to the Agreement of Shanghai, Jiangsu and Zhejiang on Jointly Promoting the Development of Innovation System of Yangtze River Delta, issued the Three-year Action Plan for S&T Cooperation in the Yangtze River Delta (2008–2010) in June 2008.[4] The Action Plan set out the metrics of strategic objectives for the region by the end of 2010:

- R&D expenditure at 2 per cent of regional GDP;
- 800 granted patents per million regional population;
- RMB10 billion of accumulated cross-region technology transaction;
- high-tech exports at 30 per cent or more of regional exports;
- 50 per cent or more of technical progress contribution; and
- nationally leading regional competitiveness.

The Action Plan identified four tasks essential to achieve the regional innovation strategy. These comprised regional joined-up actions on the construction of regional centres of S&T and innovation, regional shared platforms of S&T intelligence, environmentally friendly residential places, and S&T manufacturing centres. The four strategic tasks were further decomposed into five strategic S&T actions: (1) technological leapfrogging action in high- and new-technology industries; (2) upgrading action of traditional industries; (3) technological action on food safety and security; (4) intensive action on resource and environmental technologies; and (5) action on sharing of S&T intelligence.

In May 2010, a new framework of regional planning was agreed by the regional governments. Promotion of independent innovation and building of an innovative region was an integral part of the framework. There were three sections in the framework document concerning independent innovation and regional innovation. In the section on the development of regional innovation system in Chapter 6, the framework identified strengthening of enterprises as the mainstay of innovation and improvements of regional platforms for technological innovation as two key measures. Three targets were set accordingly, namely, enterprise R&D expenditure to make up 85 per cent or more of the region's overall R&D expenditure by 2015, the development of 300 public platforms for S&T services, and equity investment to reach RMB100 billion.[5] In addition, the document identified two areas as the core of the development of regional technological capability. One was to concentrate innovation on core technologies in key industries, and another was to take joined-up action on the development of the innovation value chain of key industries.

Multi-level governance of innovation policy

In support of regional collaboration in innovation, a new governance framework at the regional level was developed. Above the regional level, MOST is the primary central government agency to oversee regional innovation. In 2005, for example, MOST led a strategic research in the preparation of S&T development planning in the Yangtze River Delta for the 11th Five-Year Plan period (2006–2010) and later led the formulation of the S&T development plan of the Yangtze River Delta for the 11th Five-Year Plan period (2006–2010). In 2007, MOST, in conjunction with other government departments, conducted an investigation into regional independent innovation capability and policy research in the YRD. Influencing governance at this level is also the system of ministry-province consultation as described in Chapter 2. Involvement in the regular consultation was mainly MOST with Shanghai, Jiangsu and Zhejiang. There has been another parallel ministry-province consultation which was primarily focused on the implementation of the national IP strategy driven by the State Administration of Intellectual Property. Ministry-province consultations concern actions on major socio-economic policies in which innovation policies are an integral part.

At the regional level, the Mayors' Joint Meeting served as the strategic forum where broader regional issues, including regional innovation, were discussed and agreed at the highest level of the regional administration. Regional programmes, such as the *Regional Planning of the YRD 2010*, set out regional development targets and priorities to which regional innovation was aligned. Nevertheless, for all issues concerning cross-region innovation, the 'Joint Meeting on Building Innovation System in the YRD' was the main platform. This was set up by Shanghai, Jiangsu and Zhejiang in 2003 as a similar model to the Mayors' Joint Meeting. The joint meeting system provides a platform for leaders of two provinces and Shanghai in charge of S&T to meet on a regular basis. Under this governance framework, Jiangsu, Zhejiang and Shanghai work together to conduct policy reviews and formulate plans on S&T cooperation. The 'Joint Meeting on Building Innovation System in the YRD' has an office consisting of the science and technology commission (provincial department of science and technology), responsible for organizing and coordinating tasks on S&T cooperation in the YRD. One of the key roadmaps under implementation was the *Three-Year Action Plan of S&T Cooperation in the YRD*. Key responsibilities of the Office of the Joint Meeting comprised the formulation of an annual action plan and the preparation of an annual call for joint research applications for the region. This multi-level governance of regional innovation policy is illustrated in Figure 7.2.

Innovation policy tools in regions

Financial support to regional joint innovation projects

In order to support joint innovation projects, a major step the region took was to set up a Special Fund for Joint STI Projects in 2004 as one of the key policy

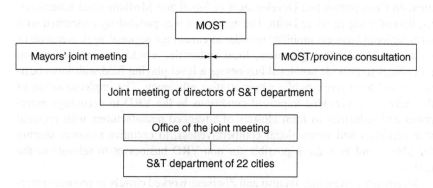

Figure 7.2 Regional governance of innovation policy.

measures. The fund originally had an annual budget of RMB10 million with an equal financial contribution from the governments of Jiangsu, Zhejiang and Shanghai. In its first call for application in 2004, the fund awarded grants worth RMB0.8–1.0 million to nine joint research projects from a total of 117 proposals, with each region receiving three awards of research grants. Grant applicants were required to fulfil such conditions as (1) good experience and facility of collaborative research, and (2) a research team comprising researchers from at least two different regions. Among the nine projects awarded was the project of Yangtze River Delta intercity transport smartcard clearing solutions that aimed at developing a system through which the same smartcard services would cover all cities in the YRD with the capacity of instantly charging and clearing the right fares across cities. The project was successfully completed in September 2005 and the outcomes of the project had an important impact on the planning of the transport system in the YRD (2006–2020). Support of such kind of projects was intended to develop general purpose technologies and increase regional integration.[6] In line with the proposal of the *Three-Year Action Plan of S&T Cooperation in the YRD* issued in 2008, the governments of three regions agreed to increase each one's financial contribution to RMB10 million, bringing the fund's annual budget to RMB30 million.

Furthermore, research institutes in the region were encouraged to apply for national research grants together. In 2009, for example, a research team comprising research organizations in Zhejiang and Shanghai was successful in their bid for National 863 key project funding with a project of 'the major marine red tide disaster real-time monitoring and early warning system'. In addition to a grant of RMB20 million from the National 863 key project fund, the project received a match fund of RMB20 million each from the governments of Zhejiang and Shanghai.[7]

Policies to promote the coordinated development of enterprises within the YRD area

In 2003, the governments of Shanghai, Jiangsu and Zhejiang signed the Agreement on Cooperation and Development of Small and Medium-sized Enterprises (SMEs) of Yangtze River Delta. The agreement was particularly concerned with intra-regional business mobility in order to encourage regional agglomeration of businesses. Under the agreement, local authorities would streamline approval procedures to provide non-local businesses a level playing field with local businesses and to improve public administrative efficiency. The implementation of the Agreement provided improved conditions in the YRD to encourage enterprises and industries to form clusters of advanced manufacturers with regional characteristics and international competitiveness, to optimize resource sharing for SMEs, and to make it possible for non-YRD businesses to relocate to the region.

Meanwhile, Shanghai, Jiangsu and Zhejiang worked closely to promote enterprise cooperation within the YRD. In 2005, 130 private enterprises and over 150 private entrepreneurs were involved in the campaign of 'Private S&T-oriented Enterprises' Journey to Northern Jiangsu'. It was intended to encourage private enterprises and entrepreneurs to exploit business opportunities in the relatively underdeveloped part of the province. Prior to the campaign, three cities in northern Jiangsu had already successfully negotiated and signed more than 130 projects worth RMB7.3 billion with private S&T-oriented enterprises in the YRD. The three-day campaign resulted in another 22 cooperation intentions worth RMB2.47 billion, including nine projects each with an investment of over RMB100 million.

In 2009, to further implement the Guidelines for Promoting Formation of Industry Technological Innovation Strategic Alliance jointly issued by six ministries including MOST and MOF, Zhejiang, Shanghai and Jiangsu, under the guidance of MOST, formed the Technological Innovation Strategic Alliance of Scientific Instruments Industry in Yangtze River Delta. Members of the strategic alliance comprised eleven leading companies in the sector, eight universities, six public institutes and two trade associations in the region. The objectives of the strategic alliance were to prioritize research to meet the needs of national public security and other areas for scientific instruments, to push innovation effectively in key technologies, core parts and major products of scientific instruments, to catalyse technological upgrading and renovation of pillar industries, to increase the contribution of the scientific instrument industry to the growth of GDP, and to promote the leapfrogging development of the scientific instrument industry as a whole.

Policies to promote the sharing of S&T resources and joint tackling of general purpose key technologies

Local governments have jointly designed and implemented projects that aimed at collectively tackling general purpose key S&T problems in socio-economic development in the YRD. For example, in 2003, 19 government agencies charged with administering standardization in Shanghai, Jiangsu and Zhejiang signed the Declaration on Cooperation of Standard Services in the YRD, marking the start of the establishment of a 'technical standardization zone' in the region. In addition, local governments in the YRD established an Intellectual Property Right Protection Alliance in 2003 and used thematic scheme to support general purpose research projects that will have a region-wide impact, such as S&T facilitated capacity-building in the public security sector in 2005, marine eco-safety in 2006, pollution control of Taihu Lake in 2007, and promotion of solar PV and integrated circuit in 2008.

In terms of joint development, sharing of S&T intelligence and joint procurement of large scientific instruments, three provinces (municipality) signed agreements on strategic cooperation among S&T information institutions and the sharing of scientific instruments. A number of public S&T infrastructures have been jointly constructed, such as the Network for Cooperation and Sharing of Large Scientific Instruments, and the Platform of Shared Services of S&T Intelligence. As of

August 2012, 9,206 sets of scientific instruments in more than 504 organizations within the YRD were made available for sharing in the Network, including 2,135 sets each worth over RMB500,000. These instruments were used nearly 23,000 times, an almost four-fold increase as compared with that in 2007.[8]

Additionally, three provinces (municipality) have worked together to undertake international S&T cooperation and exchange, and establish platforms at various levels for international S&T collaboration. Progress has been made since the Innovation System of YRD was formally launched. For instance, the international cooperation divisions under the S&T departments of Jiangsu Province and Zhejiang Province and S&T commission of Shanghai Municipality attended the 2nd Shanghai International Nanotechnology Cooperation Symposium held in Shanghai on 9 December 2004.

Policies to construct information service networks and intermediary platforms

In terms of information cooperation, the governments of Shanghai, Jiangsu and Zhejiang have joined up to build an authoritative information hub for all cities in the YRD, in order to consolidate all the information resources available in these cities and provide policy consulting services for local authorities. For example, Shanghai, Jiangsu and Zhejiang were involved in the project of Constructing High-performance Broadband Information Network under the 863 Programme. Meanwhile, organizations in the information industry in the region signed the Letter of Intent on Enhancing Information Exchange and Cooperation, agreeing to establish a credit collection platform and civil services publishing system for individuals and businesses to promote regional integration. They jointly issued in Shanghai the Declaration on Mutual Recognition of Quality and Technical Supervision Results within YRD. Ten agreements were signed to address issues such as joint cracking down on counterfeit goods, market access, development of a standard system and opening of technical service market, etc. A regular communication system of foreign economic and trade information and analysis, and statistical data have also been put in place. In addition, progress was made on technological cooperation in the YRD, including the establishment of alliances and platforms (i.e. the Strategic Alliance of S&T Intermediaries, the Service Platform to Connect Technologies and Capital, and the Platform for Technological Information Service), holding of trade fairs (e.g. Trade Fair on High- and New-Tech Projects in YRD, and Trade Show on High and New Technologies in YRD), matching of S&T projects and optimization of S&T resources allocation.

In 2003, the industry and commerce administrations of Shanghai, Jiangsu and Zhejiang jointly established a mechanism for case processing and an enterprise credit monitoring system through integrating their discrete systems on investment access, market order and credit information. In 2004, all local authorities in the region signed the Agreement on Jointly Promoting the Development of Regional Innovation System in Yangtze River Delta. The Agreement called upon local governments to develop open key laboratories at national and provincial levels, gradually build information platforms to share S&T resources, jointly tackle key S&T issues, jointly undertake national key S&T projects across different regions, disciplines and organizations, and jointly apply and implement international S&T cooperation projects.

In 2007, the Agreement on Cooperation of Modern Service Sector in Yangtze River Delta was signed. According to the Agreement, the three provinces/municipality would establish a mechanism for public information communication and cooperation in the modern service sector in the region, jointly establish an information sharing and public service platform for the service sector, jointly explore and establish a cooperation and coordination mechanism on industry standards and the settlement of trade disputes, and identify new requirements and opportunities to integrate industry, universities and research institutions. In 2008, by taking advantage of the opportunity of building the supporting platform for business innovation launched by the central government, some key universities, research institutions and leading enterprises in Shanghai, Jiangsu and Zhejiang jointly applied the project of building the national innovation supporting platform of textile industry and the national innovation service platform of integrated circuit in YRD.

Policies to consolidate human capital and improve talent sharing

The YRD region has a long history of cooperation in the development of human capital. The strengthening of collaboration was driven originally by individuals and businesses and later by governments and market forces. In 2003, the Joint Declaration on Integrated Talent Development in Yangtze River Delta was published, and the System of Joint Conference on Integrated Talent Development in YRD was also adopted, paving the way for regional talent cooperation within the YRD. In terms of human resources cooperation, a talents sharing system involving the talent centre of 15 cities within the YRD has been established. The Agreement on Cooperation in Education and Scientific Research in YRD was signed to create a regional alliance of education and scientific research. The System of Mutual Recognition of Qualifications of Technical Brokers in YRD was established to promote the S&T cooperation and technical transfer in YRD. Other efforts include signing of the Agreement on Training Service Centre for Talents in Short Supply in YRD, and the implementation of unified professional qualification certification tests and talents service cooperation in Shanghai and Ningbo.

At present, the local authorities of human resources in Shanghai, Jiangsu and Zhejiang have signed seven cooperation agreements to establish an online platform on talent market in the YRD jointly, covering market access for talent intermediary services, a sharing mechanism for high-level talents, sharing of continuing educational resources for professional technicians, mutual recognition of professional qualifications and exchange of civil servants among the three administrative areas. The education authorities of

Shanghai, Jiangsu and Zhejiang have signed agreements to implement a series of teaching programmes that "mutually recognize the credits, mutually recruit teachers while maintaining their original registered permanent residence". Since 2008 when the global financial crisis broke out, to better implement the requirement of "maintaining economic growth, expanding domestic demands, adjusting the structure, promoting development and benefiting the people's well-being", the S&T service institutions of Shanghai, Jiangsu and Zhejiang, under the guidance of local authorities in charge of S&T, have successfully organized a series of activities, such as Summit on High-level Innovative Entrepreneurs in YRD, the First Competition of YRD on S&T Innovation and Entrepreneurship and Undergraduates' S&T Entrepreneurship, and Workshop on Patents Information Application in YRD. Cultural resources in YRD are also being integrated. The institutions of higher education and scientific research are also working closely based on the identity of 'YRD people' to address the gap of talents flow within YRD.

The challenges in regional innovation system building in the YRD

The development of the regional innovation system in the YRD over the past 20 years has witnessed an expansion of cooperation among local governments. Under the guidance of the three-year action plan and other regional policy frameworks, cities in the YRD have cooperated in cross-region matters concerning transportation, personnel exchanges, tourism and finance, etc. Regional economic integration and regional innovation in the YRD have moved in the right direction. As can be seen in Table 7.1, the region outperformed the nation in key innovation indicators over the 2008-2011 period and appeared to have achieved the main innovation targets as set out in the three-year action plan. However, there were apparent regional differences. For example, in Shanghai, R&D expenditure accounted for 3.11 per cent of regional GDP, the highest among the three regions, yet, business R&D expenditure made up only 66.6 per cent, well below the anticipated level of 85 per cent. On the contrary, in Zhejiang, overall R&D expenditure was 1.85 per cent of regional GDP, but business R&D expenditure made up 88.0 per cent. As far as patenting is concerned, the target in the action plan was to reach 800 granted patents per million population by 2010. All three regions exceeded this target by a big margin. Nevertheless, it is difficult to measure the quality of innovation over the same period in order to judge the extent to which the region's innovation system has become internationally competitive. Compared with the current requirements of China's economic system transition and economic development, the progress of regional economic cooperation in the YRD has appeared to be relatively slow. Among factors that hold back the development of the regional innovation system in the YRD, the most critical is cooperation among local governments. The region still faces many challenges in achieving the aims and objectives of regional innovation.

Table 7.1 Indicators of regional innovation in the YRD, 2008–2011

		R&D as % of GDP	*Domestic patents granted, per million population*	*Exports of high-tech products as % of total exports*	*Business R&D expenditure as % of all sources of fund*
2008	National	1.47	265	29.1	71.7
	Shanghai	2.58	1,296	42.1	67.9
	Jiangsu	1.93	579	n/a	n/a
	Zhejiang	1.61	1,034	n/a	85.7
2009	National	1.70	376	31.4	71.7
	Shanghai	2.87	1,817	44.8	68.1
	Jiangsu	2.08	1,130	n/a	n/a
	Zhejiang	1.73	1,543	n/a	88.8
2010	National	1.76	552	31.2	71.7
	Shanghai	2.81	2,094	46.5	66.7
	Jiangsu	2.10	1,759	n/a	n/a
	Zhejiang	1.78	2,105	n/a	88.1
2011	National	1.84	656	28.9	73.9
	Shanghai	3.11	2,043	44.5	66.6
	Jiangsu	2.17	2,530	n/a	n/a
	Zhejiang	1.85	2,383	n/a	88.0

Source: China S&T Statistics data book, on www.sts.org.cn/sjkl/kjtjdt/index.htm.

Cooperation in the YRD to a certain extent is hampered by administrative division

The YRD is composed of two provinces and one municipality, with each having its own growth targets and vested interest in dealing with regional cooperation in innovation. Furthermore, the existing governance structure in local governments leads to a tendency of local protectionism and market segmentation, causing many obstacles for the free movement of economic and technological resources within the region, even greatly interfering with normal operations of enterprises. For example, in order to safeguard their fiscal revenue and increase disposal resources, some local governments tend to keep tight control over local businesses and are less keen to pave the way for local firms to invest and re-locate in places outside their administration. At the same time, they hold negative attitudes towards enterprises from the outside or even use administrative means to restrict their business operation if they come to compete with local businesses. Such entrenched local protectionism conflicts directly with the need for cross-regional development of enterprises and inter-regional flow of economic resources. Even in the same places, due to management from different supervising departments, normal economic ties between enterprises are from time to time interfered with by administrative power.

The cooperation mechanism of local governments is to be further improved

The regional governance of local government cooperation in the YRD at present is the kind of non-institutional consultative mechanism as a result of the advocate of local governments. It is still in the formative and experimental stage. This mechanism to a great extent is hard to break away from the control of local governments, especially when the administrative power resting in individual governments is so strong. In some aspects, it relies on the political authority of local governments to promote cooperation and coordination. Therefore, the absence of an effective regional cooperation mechanism makes it hard to achieve certain consensus on competition and cooperation and some large-scale trans-regional cooperation projects in the YRD.

Vision and policies for regional coordination mechanism and overall development are still lacking

Complementarity of regional advantage is of vital importance for regional development and regional innovation. However, because the overall planning for economic development and industrial structure for the long-term development of the YRD has not yet been laid out, local governments do not tend to differentiate themselves in strategic priorities but follow the bandwagon effect, leading to identical regional industrial structure in development plans and almost the same development priorities and leading industries. So long as local governments take strategies of different positioning and competition in accordance with their own advantages, disorder or even vicious competition resulting from the lack of a clear targeting and positioning, and a large number of duplicate construction and a waste of resources can be avoided. Consequently, regional economic integration can be promoted smoothly.

The further development of regional innovation system in the YRD

In view of the current status of industrial clusters and industrial value chains in the YRD, the characteristics of local governments, industries, markets and intermediary agencies and their relationships, the regional innovation system of YRD is under transition. Local governments will need to redefine their role to become a facilitator rather than leading actor, while allowing enterprises and markets to play a greater role. The fact that the economic integration in the YRD has been driven by local governments through regional cooperation does not necessarily mean that the role of markets should be substituted by that of governments. Rather, the joint action of local governments in the region and market-oriented institutional innovation should be combined to provide a favourable platform to optimize resource allocation within the region.

The current cooperation of local governments in the YRD shows that institutions are the major impediment to regional innovation. It is for this reason that institutional reform is of crucial importance. For local governments, measures should be taken to create a favourable institutional environment for regional economic cooperation, speeding up of market opening and removal of market barriers. Moreover, under the current institutional framework, special efforts should be made to create a policy and institutional environment conducive to innovation, to reach a consensus on local government cooperation in alignment with the integration of the YRD, and to build a governance structure for local government cooperation. For the central government, it is important to have a clear division of responsibility between the central and local governments, since the core issue of industrial integration and coordinated growth of regional economy in the YRD cannot simply depend on the initiatives of local governments but also requires top-level coordination from the central government.

Local governments should pursue cooperative development based on common industries and technologies

As to local industrial development in the YRD, local governments are required to transform clusters that were originally developed in a disorderly manner into ones that are horizontally and vertically linked and can create added values; to transform clusters that are locally separated each other into ones that are based on regional value chain through accelerating information standardization and exchange, free intra-regional trade and product diffusion. Specifically, local governments should transform their development concepts in the following two aspects.

To envisage regional innovation from the standpoint of an economic region rather than that of an administrative region

Under the original industrial development concept based on administrative region, each city, driven by local economic interests, has the desire to expand and seeks to establish and improve its own industry system based on resources within its own territory. However, due to the immobility of factors and small markets, local enterprises can neither grow stronger, nor they can make breakthroughs. On the contrary, the industrial development concept based on economic region is meant to enhance the overall competitiveness of regional industry, deepen inter-regional economic linkage and establish a regional economic community by adopting a flexible market mechanism, advocating free flow and standard sharing of local resources and factors, reasonable division of labour and complementarity, cooperation and competition of various industries. With this kind of development concept, local governments attract investments that link the upstream and downstream of the industry chain in an orderly manner, coordinate relationships with universities, research institutions and intermediary agencies within and outside the region in an appropriate way, and support and promote the regional consolidation of the S&T intermediary sector in the YRD.

To transform the development concept from the standpoint of industrial zones to that of industrial chains

S&T development in the YRD is aimed at enhancing the independent innovation capacity of the region and jointly promoting the development of the regional innovation system. Regional S&T cooperation and technology transfer is an important approach to achieving this objective. To this end, local governments in the YRD should let the market mechanism play an essential role in resource allocation according to the advantages of each area, build a system on industrial division of labour based on industry chain, and achieve the sharing and free flow of S&T resources within and outside the region. In addition, they are required to mitigate and remove conflicts of different areas in industrial development through administrative means so as to put in place an industrial development pattern in which various factors interact, complement and benefit each other with a reasonable division of labour.

Local governments should define the direction and focus of cooperation through a mechanism of regular dialogue and negotiation

To ensure the positive results of cooperation among different local governments in the YRD, it is necessary to establish a regular mechanism for dialogue and negotiation, and to prepare plans of regional integration which define the direction and spatial distribution of various sectors so as to conduct industry-oriented and space-oriented regulation. Meanwhile, local governments should define the direction and focus for cross-government cooperation at the annual summit, report information on key issues during the course of cooperation, decide major principles and roadmap of tackling these key issues, set up forums to address these issues, negotiate and reach relevant inter-governmental agreements on cooperation, and enhance communication and exchange within the YRD.

In particular, local governments should develop differentiated standards on market access in terms of industrial types, technical contents, land use efficiency and energy consumption according to different conditions and function positioning of different areas. They should also report the actual situations and key issues to the authorities concerned at national level, and to propose recommendations on regional cooperation or institutional development related to the national level in the process of YRD development, so as to ensure the feasibility and effectiveness of regional cooperation.

Local governments should improve the coordination mechanism that promote interests/benefits sharing among different cities

At present, industry distribution, local planning and economic growth in each area of the YRD are seriously lacking coordination, which is one of the root causes that hinder inter-governmental cooperation in the region. To promote inter-governmental cooperation and facilitate regional coordinated development, it is crucial to establish a sound mechanism for mutual benefit, adjustment and compensation. This system of mutual benefit for inter-governmental cooperation should be based on the principle of 'co-pitition', meaning every member government should remove market barriers and enable free flow of production factors in accordance with the principle of reasonable division of labour under the market mechanism, so as to compete without it being at the expense of neighbouring regions.

Local governments should strike a balance between intervention and engagement. In case of conflict of interest, they should appropriately balance relationships between overall regional interest and local interests, and between long-term and short-term interests. In addition, the central government should establish a standard financial transfer system to achieve benefit transfer between/among the central and local governments and the reasonable allocation of benefits among different regions. Through policy coordination at the central level, a new relationship on regional benefit sharing can be established to help enhance the overall economic strength of the YRD.

Central government should enhance macro-control over the regional innovative cooperation of the YRD

With the deepening of the market economy in China, the awareness of local governments in the YRD that the market is the main body of the economy has been increasingly enhanced, while the relationship between/among the central and local governments has tended to become more complex. Therefore, the central government should strengthen macro-control on innovative cooperation in the YRD, remove institutional barriers in inter-governmental cooperation, and improve the performance assessment system of local governments, so as to create a favourable institutional environment for cooperation among local governments.

Mechanism for regulating local government cooperation should be further standardized

Due to immature internal and external environments for local governments, some non-standard actions inevitably occur in the process of cooperation. For this reason, it is of vital importance to develop a mechanism that controls cooperation and standardizes cooperation activities. The central government should provide guidance on actions of local governments based on the consensus and cooperation rules on overall development in the YRD.

Appendix 7.1 Milestones in the development of the regional innovation system in the YRD, 2002 to date

Date	Policies
May 2002	Zhejiang, Jiangsu and Shanghai reach a consensus for regional government cooperation in the YRD through adopting the principles and plan of regional economic cooperation in the Second Symposium Economic Cooperation and Development.
October 2002	The Mayors' Forum in the YRD is adopted as a governance system of regional government cooperation at the International Symposium on the development of the YRD.
April 2003	The personnel departments of Zhejiang, Jiangsu and Shanghai sign the Joint Declaration on Integrated Talent Development in the Yangtze River Delta to promote personnel exchanges in the YRD.
August 2003	16 cities in the YRD sign the Suggestions on Hosting World Expo as an Opportunity to Accelerate the Joint Development of Cities in the Yangtze River Delta.
September 2003	Zhejiang, Jiangsu and Shanghai sign the Agreement of SME Cooperation and Development to attract high growth enterprises and industries to the region, to build advanced manufacturing bases with regional characteristics and strong international competitiveness, to optimize resource sharing system for SMEs, and to offer easy access for non-local enterprises to the YRD. The agreement prioritizes measures on simplifying business approval procedures, improving business service efficiency, reducing business burdens, and providing a level playing field to non-local enterprises.
November 2003	Shanghai, Jiangsu and Zhejiang sign the Agreement of Joint Promotion of Innovation System Construction in the Yangtze River Delta and establish a joint meeting system for coordination of the innovation system construction in the region. Special funds are set up to guide and expedite the building of the innovative system of the YRD.
Year of 2004	16 cities in the YRD sign the Agreement of Building Common Platform for Large Scientific Instrument and Facilities, Yangtze River Delta Intermediary Strategic Alliance in Science and Technology, Service Platform for the Joint of Technology and Capital in the Yangtze River Delta, Advancement in Technology and Economy Cooperation Platform in the Yangtze River Delta, and Yangtze River Delta Technology and Information Service Platform.
May 2004	16 cities in the YRD sign the Declaration of Jointly Building Credit System in the Yangtze River Delta to establish a credit incentive and constraint mechanism for citizens, enterprises and governmental units, to establish and improve regional laws and regulations on credit, and to form a unified social credit system.
June 2004	19 cities in the YRD establish a joint meeting system for integrated talent development in the YRD, and sign agreements to promote the mobility of talents and to build a regional education and scientific research alliance.

continued

Appendix 7.1 Continued

Date	Policies
September 2004	Shanghai, Jiangsu and Zhejiang jointly set up a collaborative network to deal with cross-regional issues in quality assurance and consumer right protection.
November 2004	Shanghai S&T Commission and Zhejiang Provincial S&T Department, Jiangsu Provincial S&T Department jointly issue the Notice on Joint Effort to Tackling Key Problems through Major Scientific and Technological Projects, and jointly establish special funds for cooperation in science and technology in the YRD.
December 2004	Shanghai, Suzhou City and Jiaxing City sign Letter of Intent on Strengthening Technology Cooperation in Shanghai, Suzhou and Jiaxing and Promoting the Construction of Regional Technology Innovation System to build a cross-administration cooperation and exchange system.
Year of 2005	Ministry of Science and Technology launches Strategic Review and Planning of Technology Development in the Yangtze River Delta in its compilation of the 11th Five-Year Plan for Technology Development Planning of the Yangtze River Delta.
March 2005	16 cities in the YRD form the Technology Alliance to advance technology innovation in the region.
November 2005	Shanghai, Jiangsu and Zhejiang signed the Agreement of Joint Promotion of Regional Innovation System Construction in the Yangtze River Delta, and set up a public service platform for regional scientific R&D equipments and facilities and to encourage enterprises to make innovations and start entrepreneurship on this platform.
March 2006	Shanghai, Jiangsu and Zhejiang agree to build an online talent market platform for the YRD.
November 2006	Shanghai Informationization Commission, Jiangsu Provincial Information Industry Department, and Zhejiang Provincial Information Industry Department jointly issue the 11th Five-Year (2006–2010) Cooperation Planning on Informationization of the Yangtze River Delta to promote regional cooperation in informationization and information industry in the YRD.
November 2007	Shanghai, Jiangsu and Zhejiang jointly sign the Framework Agreement on Promoting Coordinated Financial Development of Yangtze River Delta to Support Regional Economic Integration and establish the Yangtze River Delta Finance Forum to promote the coordinated development of regional finance.
December 2007	Shanghai, Jiangsu and Zhejiang sign the Agreement of Cooperation of Modern Service Sector in Yangtze River Delta to establish a mechanism of public information communication and cooperation for modern service sector in the region, an information sharing and public service platform for the service sector, a cooperation and coordination mechanism on industry standards and the settlement of trade disputes.

April 2008	Shanghai, Jiangsu and Zhejiang and People's Bank of China hold the First Joint Conference on Promoting the Financial Coordinated Development of the Yangtze River Delta, and sign a Memorandum of Understanding (MOU) on Jointly Establishing Credit Yangtze River Delta.
June 2008	The office under the joint meeting of YRD innovation system construction issues Three-Year Action Plan for S&T Cooperation in the Yangtze River Delta (2008–2010).
August 2008	Premier Wen Jiabao chairs a State Council executive meeting to discuss and approve the Guidance on Further Promoting the Reform and Opening-up and Economic and Social Development of the Yangtze River Delta. It is the first time the State Council holds a special meeting to discuss domestic regional development and regional integration of the region.
December 2008	The YRD holds a joint meeting on innovation and entrepreneurship for returnees to put forward the construction of a comprehensive service platform for innovation and entrepreneurship for those studying abroad in the YRD.
Year of 2009	Led by the National Development and Reform Commission, the YRD sets up the Planning and Coordination Committee made up of the leading governors of Jiangsu, Zhejiang and Shanghai. The committee is responsible for the formulation, revision and implementation of regional planning; played a role in the organization, coordination and arbitration; coordinated the major issues in planning implementation concerning the interests of all parties involved in the YRD, and made the proposal to amend the planning.
March 2009	Jiangsu, Zhejiang and Shanghai release Outline on Road Transport Integration Plan in the Yangtze River Delta to create a seamless transportation network.
April 2009	Zhejiang, Jiangsu and Shanghai sign a MOU on Jointly Addressing Financial Risks with People's Bank of China in the Second Joint Conference on Promoting the Financial Coordinated Development of the Yangtze River Delta. City commercial banks in the YRD sign an Agreement of Strategic Cooperation of City Commercial Banks within the Yangtze River Delta, a MOU on Jointly Addressing Financial Risks, and a MOU on Cooperation in Credit Yangtze River Delta in the Second Finance Forum of the Yangtze River Delta.
April 2009	The intellectual property management departments of Zhejiang, Jiangsu and Shanghai hold a joint press conference in 2008 for the first time on Intellectual Property Development and Protection Status in the Yangtze River Delta, and the three Intellectual Property Offices sign a Framework Agreement of Intellectual Property Cooperation.
April 2009	Zhejiang, Jiangsu and Shanghai convene a Seminar on Interacted Development of Education in the Yangtze River Delta, and sign an agreement on the establishment of consultation mechanism for education coordination development in the YRD, which signifies the formal establishment of consultation mechanism for education coordination development in the region.

continued

Appendix 7.1 Continued

Date	Policies
June 2009	Shanghai Surveying and Mapping Management Office, Jiangsu Provincial Surveying and Mapping Bureau, and Zhejiang Provincial Surveying and Mapping Bureau hold a joint meeting on Making Joint Efforts to Build and Share Geographic Information Resources in the Yangtze River Delta.
August 2009	The YRD holds the First Joint Meeting of Regional Cooperation and Development and agrees the working system of the joint meeting and the working system of key thematic topics. For the first time, Anhui Province participates in four cooperation topics, namely energy, transportation, technology and finance.
November 2009	Zhejiang, Jiangsu and Shanghai set up a Technological Innovation Strategic Alliance of Scientific Instruments Industry in Yangtze River Delta.
March 2010	Zhejiang, Jiangsu and Shanghai with People's Bank of China hold the Third Joint Conference on Promoting Financial Coordinated Development in Yangtze River Delta, and sign a Cooperative MOU on Jointly Promoting Integration of Financial Services in YRD.
March 2010	The YRD holds the Tenth Mayors' Joint Meeting of Urban Economic Coordination Meeting and signs an (Jiaxing) Agreement of City Cooperation in Yangtze River Delta.
April 2010	The YRD holds the Second Seminar on Interacted Development of Education. The three parties identify 21 units and schools as the training base for primary and secondary school teachers and principals in the YRD and jointly organize the training for teachers.

Notes

1 These 14 cities were: Shanghai, seven cities in Jiangsu Province (Nanjing, Suzhou, Wuxi, Yangzhou, Changzhou, Nantong, Zhenjiang) and six cities in Zhejiang Province (Hangzhou, Jiaxing, Huzhou, Ningbo, Shaoxing, Zhoushan). Economic Coordination Offices were a government agency with the remit to facilitate and support inter-regional economic cooperation and collaboration.

2 Taizhou in Zhejiang Province was accepted as the 16th member of the YRD in August 2003.

3 See 2008_国务院关于进一步推进长江三角洲地区改革开放和经济社会发展的指导意见 (The State Council's Guidance on Further Promoting Reform and Opening up and Economic and Social Development in the Yangtze River Delta Region), available at www.gov.cn/zwgk/2008-09/16/content_1096217.htm (accessed 24 October 2011).

4 See '长三角科技合作三年行动计划' (Three Year Action Plan of S&T Cooperation in YRD), available at www.zj.gov.cn/art/2008/10/8/art_1005_25525.html (accessed 24 October 2011).

5 See '长江三角洲地区区域规划' (Regional Planning of YRD), available at www.sdpc. gov.cn/zcfb/zcfbtz/2010tz/W020100622527425024197.pdf (accessed 24 October 2011).

6 '长三角重大科技联合攻关项目启动 获1000万支持' (YRD launched key S&T joint research projects with the funding of 10 million), available at http://news.xinhuanet. com/newscenter/2004-11/16/content_2223492.htm (accessed 24 October 2011).

7 '上海重大海洋赤潮灾害实时监测与预警系统今年启动' (Shanghai launched the major marine red tide disaster real-time monitoring and early warning system project this year), available at www.chinamapping.com.cn/infomation/hyzx/hydt/page01. php?info_id=9470 (accessed 24 October 2011).

8 '部省会商不断提升安徽自主创新能力' (Consultation between the ministry and province has helped raise Anhui's independent innovation capability), available at www. most.gov.cn/dfkj/ah/zxdt/201212/t20121221_98623.htm (accessed 13 April 2013).

8 Performance of national innovation system

From the launch of the 'Four Modernizations programme'[1] in 1978 that marked the start of China's long march in economic reform to the release of the Outline of Medium and Long-term National Plan for Science and Technology Development 2006–2020 (MLNP) in 2005 that manifested China's heightened ambition of turning the country into an innovative economy by 2020, innovation has been inherently part of China's aspiration. As we have shown in the previous chapters, significant resources have been dedicated to meeting the goals of the national innovation strategy, alongside the overhaul and re-design of the country's system of incentives for science, technology and innovation (STI). As such, China has become one of the few bright spots in the world's innovation landscape where investment in STI is in significant rise against a backdrop of government spending cuts in many other countries in the aftermath of the financial crisis in 2009. How has China performed in STI? What is China's outlook of becoming an innovative economy by 2020? Answers to these questions to a great extent will reveal whether or not the country's structure of fiscal and financial incentives is functioning as it is anticipated.

In his masterpiece, *Science and Civilisation in China*, Joseph Needham (1954) firmly put back on the map China's inventiveness and its justified position in the development of world civilization. Yet, China's road to innovation has been bumpy even in the contemporary period. To answer the question as to whether or not China is well on its way to building an innovative economy, it is important to evaluate how the performance of China's national innovation system has evolved, where it stands now, and how its performance is up against its international counterparts.

Despite the improved availability of STI statistics in China and growing empirical evidence from the literature of Chinese innovation, a comprehensive assessment of the effectiveness of China's STI-focused incentive structure is still beyond us simply because critical data remain unavailable. In this chapter, we will try to piece together information to present a broad picture of the performance of China's national innovation system in respect of knowledge production, diffusion and application. The objective of the assessment is to provide a critical context from which China's prospect of achieving the goals of the MLNP can be better understood. We evaluate innovation performance at national level with a particular focus on innovation output performance, using data from a variety of sources, including National Bureau of Statistics of China, the World Economic Forum, Economist Intelligent Unit and INSEAD. Where possible, we benchmark China's innovation performance against its international counterparts so that measures of performance can be put into perspective.

We start in this chapter with an overview of China's overall innovation performance and its characteristics. We then look more closely at performance of three highly interdependent components within an innovation system: knowledge production (the origination of new knowledge and ideas), knowledge diffusion (the absorption of applied knowledge and its adaptation in use) and knowledge application (the deployment of knowledge and ideas in the real world). We conclude the chapter with our cautious projection of China's trajectory of innovation in years to come.

Overall performance of the national innovation system

In the MLNP, China set forth five critical targets as metrics of the building of an innovative economy by 2020. With policy learning and subsequent modification in policy focus, the 11th and 12th Five-Year Plans have respectively presented a new set of metrics, adding new targets while dropping those no longer relevant. Regardless of all the changes, the target of R&D expenditures as 2.5 per cent of GDP has been consistently a critical metric of an innovation economy by 2020. In 2011, China spent RMB868.7 billion on R&D (US$139.4 billion[2]), equivalent to 1.84 per cent of GDP. This compared to the R&D spending of RMB30.6 billion (US$4.9 billion), or 0.64 per cent of GDP, in 1994. Internationally, as displayed in Figure 8.1, China's investment in R&D as a share of GDP was ahead of some of the developed countries, such as the UK, Canada, Ireland, Norway, Portugal, New Zealand and Italy. China was also leading other emerging economies, such as Hungary, Russia, Turkey, Poland, India, Greece and Mexico. However, compared with those leading innovative economies, such as South Korea, Finland, etc., China's R&D investment in relative terms was still modest.

What is the outlook of China's key metric of innovation in 2020? A simple time-series regression of the data over the period 1995–2011 suggests a clear linear upward trend of this metric (Figure 8.2). Particularly for the years of 2009–2011, spending in R&D as a proportion of GDP consistently increased above the long-term trend. Providing the trend continues, the model projects that R&D expenditures as a share of GDP in China would reach 2.546 per cent by 2020, just hitting the pre-set target. Overall, the projection provides tentative evidence to show that China's use of fiscal and financial incentives to facilitate more investment in STI from all non-governmental sources appears to be working.

Yet, the assessment of other innovation performance indicators as of 2010 (the end of the 11th Five-Year Plan) suggests a mixed picture in progress of innovative economy building (Table 8.1). China performed well in such metrics

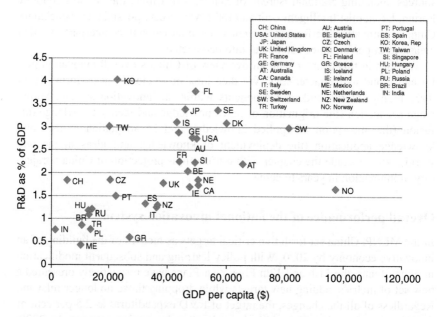

Figure 8.1 International comparison of R&D expenditure as a share of GDP, 2011.

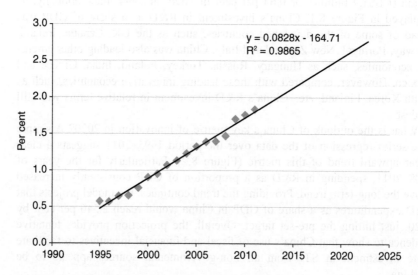

Figure 8.2 R&D expenditures as a share of GDP in China.

Table 8.1 Medium and Long-term National Plan targets and progress

	Achievement as of 2005	11th Five-Year Plan Target for 2010	11th Five-Year Plan Achievement as of 2010	12th Five-Year Plan Target for 2015	MLNP Target for 2020
R&D expenditures as % of GDP	1.32	2.0	1.75	2.2	2.5
Contribution of progress in S&T to economic growth (%)	43.2*	>45	50.9**		>60
Dependence on foreign technology (%)		<40			<30
International ranking for per capita patents granted to Chinese nationals					5th
International ranking for number of citations of scientific papers by Chinese scientists		10th	8th	5th	5th
R&D personnel in 10,000 working population (person-year)		14	34	43	
Number of patents granted in 10,000 residents	1.3		1.7	3.3	
Patent application of R&D workforce (per hundred person-year)			10	12	
Technology market transaction nationwide (RMB billion)	155		390	800	
High-tech value-added as % of manufacturing as a whole		18	13	18	
Citizens with basic science qualification (%)		3.27	3.27	5	
International ranking for patents granted to Chinese nationals		15th			
Human resources in S&T (million)		50			
Personnel engaged in S&T activities (million)		7			
R&D workforce, full-time equivalent (million person-year)	1.2	1.3			

Notes
* For the period 2000–2005.
** For the period 2005–2010.

as contribution of progress in S&T to economic growth, R&D personnel in 10,000 working population (person-year) and international ranking for number of citations of scientific papers by Chinese scientists. Nevertheless, China did not reach the target in two important metrics, i.e. R&D expenditures as per cent of GDP and high-tech value-added as per cent of manufacturing as a whole.

To get a fuller picture of China's innovation performance, we can look beyond a few indicators by assessing evidence from international studies. Admittedly, measuring innovation performance is not a straightforward task. The first challenge has to do with the widely acknowledged difficulty in evaluating innovation performance itself. Years of innovation research in the academic community have unfortunately come up with no consensus on how innovation performance should be measured. Nevertheless, a number of innovation evaluation frameworks have been proposed, and innovation indices and innovation rankings have been compiled. They usually measure innovation performance on the basis of innovation input and/or innovation output, which have noted strengths and weaknesses in their respective methodologies.[3] While these studies have generated rich data available in the public domain, the richness of the data, however, poses another challenge in the sense that no two innovation rankings are compatible and comparable due to their differences in methodology and geographical coverage of countries. Nevertheless, global innovation indices and rankings produced by major international organizations are still credited for their relative clarity of methods, primary data collection and comprehensiveness in international coverage. Bearing in mind the challenges we mentioned earlier, we assess the current state of innovation performance in China, mainly using data from the global innovation rankings compiled by the World Economic Forum (WEF) and INSEAD (a French business school) as our main frame of reference with supplementary indices where appropriate.

WEF started collecting data for compilation of the Global Competitiveness Index (GCI) in 2005 and has since published the Global Competitive Report and Global Competitiveness Index annually. While the GCI is primarily aimed at measuring "the microeconomic and macroeconomic foundations of national competitiveness" (World Economic Forum, 2011: 4), it places innovation performance (the 12th pillar in its framework) as an integral part of national competitiveness. WEF uses eight indicators to measure innovation input and output performance, consisting of capacity for innovation, quality of scientific institutions, company spending on R&D, university-industry collaboration in R&D, government procurement of advanced technology products, availability of scientists and engineers, utility patents, and intellectual property protection. In the GCI 2011, innovation performance evaluation covered 142 economies that were grouped into five categories: factor-driven at stage 1 of development (37 economies), transition from stage 1 to stage 2 (24 economies), efficiency-driven at stage 2 of development (28 economies), transition from stage 2 to stage 3 (18 economies) and innovation-driven at stage 3 of development (35 economies).

INSEAD first published its Global Innovation Index (GII) in 2007, and, like WEF, it has since published its annual report and index. Unlike the WEF's GCI, however, GII is exclusively focused on measuring global innovation perform-ance and is aimed at identifying "the conditions and qualities that allow innova-tion to thrive" (INSEAD, 2011: v). The GII produces its global innovation index on account of five enabler pillars: institutions, human capital and research, infra-structure, market sophistication and business sophistication. Enabler pillars define aspects of the environment conducive to innovation within an economy.[4] Due to its differences in analytical framework and sources of data, GII is not entirely comparable with GCI, as far as the overall ranking and its constituents are concerned.

An analysis of global innovation indices leads us to draw a few observa-tions. First of all, China has been recognized as a top innovation performing economy in the world. This is supported by another recent UK research report (Bound *et al.*, 2013). China has consistently outperformed other economies in the same country group or at the same stage of development in innovation. China was ranked 29th out of 142 economies in the GCI's innovation ranking in 2011. As can be seen in Table 8.2, at an average score of 3.92, China is only second to Malaysia (4.32) among 28 economies that are at the second stage of development characterized with being efficiency-driven, and its overall innovation score even exceeds the average score of 18 economies under the category of transition from stage 2 to stage 3. China was similarly ranked 29th out of 129 countries in GII's overall ranking. China tops the GII rankings among lower-middle-income countries on all three main indices (GII, Input and Output), as indicated in Figure 8.3, and is the only country from this income group in the top 30. At an average score of 46.43, China's overall per-formance is very close to the average score of high-income economies (48.08) in the GII rankings and exceeds that of both lower-middle-income economies (30.42) and upper-middle-income economies (33.36).

Table 8.2 Economies at each stage of development and innovation score

Stage	WEF average score
Stage 1 Factor-driven (37 economies)	2.79
Transition from stage 1 to stage 2 (24 economies)	2.96
Stage 2 Efficiency-driven (28 economies)	3.03
Of which, China	3.92
Transition from stage 2 to stage 3 (18 economies)	3.26
Stage 3 Innovation-driven (35 economies)	4.53
Income group	*GII average score*
High income	48.08
Upper-middle income	33.36
Lower-middle income	30.42
Of which: China	46.43
Low income	25.91

Source: calculation based on The Global Competitiveness Report 2011–2012, p. 11 and The Global Innovation Index 2011, INSEAD.

China's impressive performance has helped it close the innovation perform-ance gap with the developed economies, as suggested in the global innovation indices of WEF and INSEAD. This observation is confirmed in another report, 'Innovation Union Scoreboard 2010', published by the European Commission in February 2011 (EU, 2011). While the European Commission's report was prim-arily concerned with assessing the state of innovation performance among its 27 member states, it did so by comparing the innovation performance of EU27 with other major non-EU countries, including China. Similar to the global innovation reports published by the WEF and INSEAD, the EU report concludes that although the EU27 still has a clear lead in innovation performance over China in most indicators, this lead is shrinking, as China's innovation performance has advanced at a faster rate than that of the EU27. In 2006–2010, for example, China's estimated innovation performance as measured with its score in the innovation index grew at 3.78 per cent annually as opposed to 0.85 per cent for the EU27 as a whole. The report finds that China has been reducing the perform-ance gap in as many as eight indicators (tertiary education, international co-publications, business R&D expenditure, public-private co-publications, PCT patents, PCT patents in societal challenges, knowledge-intensive services exports, and licence and patent revenues) and has been increasing its lead in exports of medium-high and high-tech products. Similar conclusion can also be drawn from the Economist Intelligence Unit's global Innovation Index 2009. It was estimated that China moved from 59th place in 2002–2006 to 54th in 2004–2008, achieving in two years what had been forecast for five years (Eco-nomist Intelligence Unit, 2009). The Economist Intelligence Unit's report reckons that China's prospects are even stronger in the medium term, suggesting that the country will leap eight rungs to 46th place in 2009–2013, the biggest improvement among the 82 countries rated.

China's innovation performance is primarily underscored by the strengths of its innovation system with particular regard to scientific outputs and government procurement of advanced technology. In both respects, Chins outscores the high income group in the GII and the innovation-driven economies in the GCI, as can be seen in Figure 8.3 and Figure 8.4. In addition, with regard to innovation input indicators in the GII's report, China ranks among the top 30 in Market (26th) defined as the availability of credit, investment funds and access to international markets, Business sophistication (29th) defined as the employment of knowledge workers, innovation linkages and knowledge absorption. Comparatively, the Chinese innovation system exhibits apparent weaknesses in its institutional framework as opposed to the high income group with respect to political environment, regulatory environment and business environment as shown in Figure 8.3. The GII report also shows that China scores weakly in indicators of human capital and research as opposed to the high income group. Com-plementary to the GII, the WEF report, as illustrated in Figure 8.4, highlights patenting, quality of scientific research and university-industry collaboration as other weak links in the innovation system when compared with the innovation-driven economies.

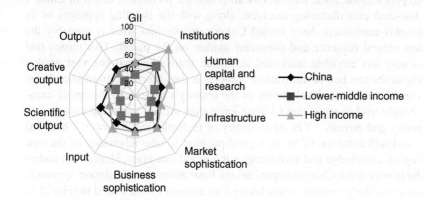

Figure 8.3 GII: average scores by income group and by pillar (0–100) (source: calculation based on The Global Innovation Index 2011).

China's innovation performance confirms that China is transforming itself from a low-cost manufacturer to a global innovation player. It seems fair to say that innovation is becoming one of the driving forces behind the country's phenomenal growth as the country's innovators are moving up the innovation ladder from duplicative innovation to imitative innovation and original innovation. In view of the dynamics of the country's innovation system, two factors are obviously in China's favour. One is the size effect of the country, measured as the supersized low-cost, skilful workforce and supersized wealth. As Ted C. Fishman

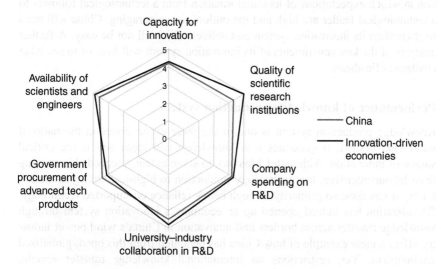

Figure 8.4 GCI: average scores by types of economic group and by pillar (0–10) (source: calculation based on The Global Competitiveness Report 2011–2012).

(2006) puts it, what these numbers mean is that the productive might of China's vast low-cost manufacturing machine, along with the swelling appetites of its billion-plus consumers, have turned China's people into what is arguably the greatest natural resource and consumer market on the planet. This means that China now has enviable resources to pursue innovation and the vast market serving as the test bed of innovation. Another is the accumulation of knowledge that contributes to the development of the country's necessary absorptive capacity. People tend to argue that Chinese innovators are not venturing enough into originality and novelty.[5] Yet, as a country of technological follower, China has been, and will continue to be, in a good position to take advantage of the vast backlog of knowledge and technologies the world can offer. Hence it is understandable why most Chinese organizations have adopted an imitation approach. This is particularly sensible when taking into account China's need to rebuild its innovation system since the 1970s after all those destructive years of the Cultural Revolution. Imitation is not only an affordable and profitable approach to innovation but is also a feasible step in building the country's innovation capability. However, there is no denying that China should step up its effort in original innovation. Breznitz and Murphree (2011) argue that China does not need to operate at the frontiers of global innovation in order to grow its position in innovation-based sectors and markets. They cited the sheer size and scale of the domestic markets as one of the reasons why the country positioning itself as a fast follower can be justified. China's recent experiences suggest that this is not an option. We argue throughout this book that it is exactly because of the size and scale of Chinese domestic markets that China should and would proceed to original innovation. The analysis of China's innovation system performance appears to suggest that China stands in the threshold of another phase of innovation in which expectations of its transformation from a technological follower to a technological leader are high and the outlook is encouraging. China will need to strengthen its innovation system and deliver. This will not be easy. A further analysis of the key constituents of its innovation system will help us to see what challenges lie ahead.

Performance of knowledge production system

Knowledge production system is one of the three cornerstones in the national innovation system. It generates new knowledge and ideas and is the critical source of innovation. Although China has, to some extent, succeeded in moving from labour-intensive, low-technology production to high-technology manufacturing, it has done so primarily through heavy reliance on imported technology. Globalization has indeed opened up an economy's innovation system through knowledge transfer across borders and innovation in China's wind power industry offers a clear example of how China has benefited from this open, globalized environment. Yet, restrictions on international knowledge transfer remain, notably Western governments' restrictions on exportation of advanced technology to China, hence indigenous innovation aspirations are still very much dependent on the country's ability to produce critical new knowledge and ideas from within its own innovation system. Globally, China is currently still a borrower, not a creator of new technology. To achieve China's stated goal of 'building an innovative economy', China needs to build a national innovation system capable of producing new knowledge in both quantity and quality. Here, we assess the performance of the knowledge production system in China using two widely used indicators of scientific paper publications and patenting. We also review emerging evidence on the performance of the Chinese Academy of Sciences and research-intensive universities as a result of the Knowledge Innovation Programme (KIP) and the 985 Project.

Scientific paper publications

Scientific research is concerned with discovery of new knowledge that expands our understanding of the world surrounding us. Scientific research feeds new, original knowledge into the innovation funnel for application and development. A country's strength of scientific research is, to some extent, measured by its scientific paper publications included in the Science Citation Index (SCI) and the Engineering Index (EI).

Judging by its share of the world's scientific publications, China can claim to have become a leading nation in science. Over the past two decades there was an exponential growth in the volume of Chinese scientific paper publications as shown in Figure 8.5. China published 30,499 and 13,163 papers included in the SCI and EI in 2000, and the number of publications in both indices rose to 165,818 and 127,420 respectively in 2011, equivalent to a respective five-fold

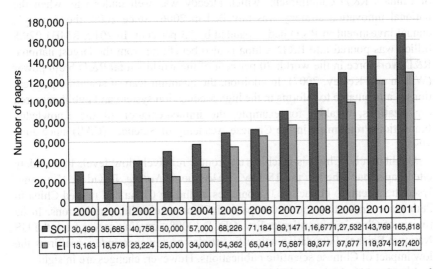

	2000	2001	2002	2003	2004	2005	2006	2007	2008	2009	2010	2011
■ SCI	30,499	35,685	40,758	50,000	57,000	68,226	71,184	89,147	1,16,677	1,27,532	143,769	165,818
□ EI	13,163	18,578	23,224	25,000	34,000	54,362	65,041	75,587	89,377	97,877	119,374	127,420

Figure 8.5 Chinese scientific paper publications, 2000–2010 (source: *China Statistical Yearbook of Science and Technology* (2013)).

and nine-fold growth over the period 2000–2011. Zhou and Leydesdorff (2006) compare China's scientific publications in the SCI against the USA, EU-25, Japan and South Korea and find that over the period 1993–2004 China was the only country that showed exponential growth in the world share of publications. People may suspect that the exponential growth might be attributable to the increase in the number of SCI-indexed Chinese journals from the beginning of the 1990s. For example, over the period 1991–2003, Jin and Rousseau (2005) reckon the number of SCI-indexed Chinese journals rose from 12 journal titles to 71 which predominantly published in English. They, however, find that the explosive increase in China's world share of scientific publications was driven primarily by publications of papers in non-Chinese SCI-indexed journals, as only 26 per cent of SCI-indexed Chinese papers appeared in Chinese journals over the period 1991–2003. In a more updated study, Gupta *et al.* (2009), using the same 'Web of Science' database, confirm the continued growth of China's scientific publications between 2003 and 2007. As opposed to the world's annual publication growth rate of 3.18 per cent between 1997 and 2002 and 5.64 per cent between 2003 and 2007, China achieved a growth rate of 15.37 per cent and 26.54 per cent respectively in these two periods (Gupta *et al.*, 2009). Their research concludes that the growth performance puts China in a league of its own.

In parallel with the quantitative expansion, China's contribution to the world's scientific output has also risen sharply, as measured by China's rankings in both SCI and EI. In 1995 China ranked 15th in the SCI and 7th in the EI. By 2011, China's position moved to 2nd in the SCI ranking and 1st in the EI ranking (MOST online database).

The fast quantitative expansion of scientific publications occurred as a result of China's R&D commitment, which already was well under way when the national innovation strategy was unveiled in 2006. Since 2000, the country's annual investment in R&D had expanded by 23 per cent. In 2012, RMB1,029.8 billion was poured into R&D. China is also benefiting from the largest national R&D workforce in the world: 20 per cent of the world's total R&D brain power (Wilson and Keeley, 2007). In addition, the quantum leap of scientific publications is attributable to reforms in the higher education system and public research organizations, notably, for example, the implementation of the Knowledge Innovation Programme in the Chinese Academy of Sciences (CAS) since June 1998.

Qualitatively, China is catching up from a relatively low level. In a widely cited paper published in the 15 July 2004 issue of *Nature*, David A. King analysed the scientific impact of 31 countries including China and ranked China in 28th place, indicating the low impact of Chinese scientific publications. In its review of China's innovation policy, OECD (2008), quoting scores from the US National Science Foundation scientific articles prominence index, reaffirms the low impact of Chinese scientific publications. However, changes are in sight.

First, global citations of Chinese scientific publications are on the rise. Citations are normally used to measure the quality of publications. In their study of citations of Chinese scientific publications, Zhou and Leydesdorff (2006), while admitting low citations overall, find that from 1994 to 2003 citations to Chinese papers increased at an exponential rate.[6] Second, China's world share of highly cited papers is also on the increase. The top 1 per cent of the most highly cited papers is widely considered the most important measure of a country's influence in science (King, 2004). In this respect, Zhou and Leydesdorff's (2006) research finds that China's percentage change of highly cited papers (the top 1 per cent of the most highly cited papers) increased from 0.22 over the period 1993–1997 to 0.33 for 1997–2001, although the absolute numbers are still low. A more recent analysis of Thomson Reuters' Web of Knowledge database as published in the *Nature Publishing Index 2011 China* shows that China has increased its share of the top 1 per cent of highly cited scientific articles from 1.85 per cent in 2001 to 11.3 per cent in 2011 and that China now ranks fourth globally for highly cited papers.[7] Similarly, Jin and Rousseau (2005) find that the number of Chinese articles reaching the 10 per cent baseline also increased exponentially for the period 1991–2003. They reckon that it takes China 2.35 years to double its share of articles in the most-cited 10 per cent group, in acknowledgement of China's relatively small fraction of articles belonging to the most-cited 10 per cent group. In terms of the number of articles covered in the top 10 per cent international journals, China ranked fourth in 2007–2009, up from 19th place in 1987–1989 (Wilson and Keeley, 2007). The *Nature Publishing Index 2012 China* also shows that Chinese authors featured in 8.5 per cent of papers published in 2012 in 18 *Nature*-branded journals, compared with 5.3 per cent in 2010.[8] The editor of *Nature China* predicted that China could surpass the UK and Germany – currently second and third respectively – as soon as 2014.[9]

As shown in Zhou and Leydesdorff's research (2006), inclusion of Chinese journals in the SCI is not a sufficient condition for raising citations to Chinese papers and integrating Chinese sciences into the world system of scientific publications. The language barrier is a critical factor. Another noted factor is that there is a lag of 10–15 years between research investment and full citation outcomes.[10]

China's scientific production reflects the country's innovation priorities. China has identified engineering, physics, materials science, medicine and chemistry as the high priority areas. The top five subjects of China's international publications are, in descending order, chemistry, physics, material science, electronic, communication and automation, and biology (OECD, 2008). According to a research conducted by Gupta *et al.* (2009), China's most productive subject areas as far as the global publication share in 2007 is concerned were engineering (22.57 per cent), materials sciences (21.42 per cent), energy (20.34 per cent), physics (16.16 per cent), chemistry (14.55 per cent), chemical engineering (19.20 per cent), computer science (18.29 per cent), mathematics (16.29 per cent) and earth and planetary science (16.21 per cent). China has shown strong performance in some specific disciplines. In Kostoff *et al.*'s (2006) analysis of nanoscience publication, China now ranks second globally, behind only the USA. Similarly, the *Nature* publication index 2012 indicated that China, traditionally strong in physical sciences, is making gains in high-quality life sciences research.[11]

As described in Chapter 2, China launched two flagship programmes – the Knowledge Innovation Programme and 985 Project, aiming at transforming the knowledge production capability of the Chinese Academy of Sciences and the most research-intensive universities in China. Governments have made direct investment at an unprecedented scale in these two programmes together with the offering of other incentives for enhancing innovation in the CAS and universities involved. Using a balanced panel of 59 research institutes in CAS from 1997 to 2005, Zhang *et al.* (2011) find that there was 12.5 per cent productivity improvement, measured as a comparison of input and output between the base period (1997) and the subsequent period (2005). The input and output variables in their research include FTE staff (man-year), support expenditure, value of equipment, international papers, citations, and PhD and Masters students. They also find that productivity improvement contributed 8.8 per cent to technology progress and 3.3 per cent to efficiency change in CAS. The significant improvement in performance from this research suggests that government direct investment in KIP had boosted R&D activities in CAS.

The 985 Project is a centrepiece of innovation programme aiming at developing 'world-class' universities in China. The project was jointly funded by the Ministry of Education (MOE), relevant ministerial departments, and provincial and municipal governments. Government investment in the project was massive. In an assessment of the performance of the project, Zhang *et al.* (2013) found that the rate of growth of publications for universities as a whole increased more quickly after the implementation of the 985 Project. It was also found that the rate of growth in publications in foreign journals by lower tier universities exceeded that of China's two most highly regarded universities after controlling for university R&D funding, university personnel size and provincial per capita income.

Patenting

Patenting, despite an imperfect measurement of knowledge production, is commonly used as an indicator because of data availability. Analysing the filings of domestic patent applications in the State Intellectual Property Office (SIPO) in China, we can clearly see a rapid quantitative expansion in the volume of applications. The latest figure in 2010, as in Table 8.3, shows that domestic patent applications reached a little over one million, representing a 16-fold growth over 1995. As can be seen in Table 8.4, firms have emerged to become a dominant player in invention patent applications. In 2008, Huawei Technologies, a leading Chinese ICT company based in Shenzhen, made headlines for topping the world's patent application when it made 1,904 patent applications, according to World Intellectual Property Organization (WIPO).[12]

In a recent analysis of patent statistics published by the WIPO, Li (2012) finds that the number of residential patent applications per million population in China

Table 8.3 Filings of domestic patent applications in SIPO

Year	Total	Domestic application			Percentage		
		Invention	Utility model	Design	Invention	Utility model	Design
1995	68,880	10,018	43,429	15,433	14.5	63.1	22.4
1996	82,207	11,471	49,341	21,395	14.0	60.0	26.0
1997	90,071	12,713	49,902	27,456	14.1	55.4	30.5
1998	96,233	13,726	51,220	31,287	14.3	53.2	32.5
1999	109,958	15,596	57,214	37,148	14.2	52.0	33.8
2000	140,339	25,346	68,461	46532	18.1	48.8	33.2
2001	165,773	30,038	79,275	56,460	18.1	47.8	34.1
2002	205,544	39,806	92,166	73,572	19.4	44.8	35.8
2003	251,238	56769	107,842	86,627	22.6	42.9	34.5
2004	278,943	65,786	111,578	101579	23.6	40.0	36.4
2005	383,157	93,485	138,085	151,587	24.4	36.0	39.6
2006	470,342	122,318	159,997	188,027	26.0	34.0	40.0
2007	586,498	153,060	179,999	253,439	26.1	30.7	43.2
2008	717,144	194,579	223,945	298,620	27.1	31.2	41.6
2009	877,611	229,096	308,861	339,654	26.1	35.2	38.7
2010	1,109,428	293,066	407,238	409,124	26.4	36.7	36.9

Source: MOST online database.

grew almost 13-fold from 1995 to 2007 and that by the end of 2007 China had surpassed Korea in the number of resident domestic patent filings and now ranks third in the world, only trailing Japan and the United States. Godinho and Ferreira's (2012) similar analysis has confirmed China's remarkable performance in patenting. With regard to trademark use, Godinho and Ferreira (2012) also observe similar rapid growth trends in China. They conclude that China is catching up quickly with the so-called triad (the USA, Japan and EU countries) in the world rankings of patents and trademarks. The point was reaffirmed by WIPO's analysis of patent filings in 2013. It was found in the study that the total number of patent filings under WIPO's Patent and Cooperation Treaty (PCT) applications filed in 2013 increased by 5.1 per cent compared with 2012, with China accounting for 29 per cent of the total PCT growth, second only after the United States.[13]

China's impressive quantitative expansion in patent applications domestically and abroad has constantly met with a great deal of suspicion about patent quality. A large proportion of patents filed in China, 36.9 per cent in 2010 for example, are for a new design appearance or new models, which do not require great technical innovation. Utility model patents, making up 36.7 per cent of all domestic patent applications in 2010, are particularly popular with domestic applicants because they are easier and faster to prepare, do not undergo substantive examinations before being granted, and cost less. For these reasons, design and utility model patents may intrinsically be of substandard quality. On the contrary, invention patent applications accounted for just about one-quarter of total

Table 8.4 Patent applications filed and patents granted by SIPO

Year	Invention						Utility model						Design					
	Total	University and college	R&D institutes	Firms	Other public organs	Individuals	Total	University and college	R&D institutes	Firms	Other public organs	Individuals	Total	University and college	R&D institutes	Firms	Other public organs	Individuals
1995	100.0	5.7	8.6	10.8	4.7	70.1	100.0	1.8	3.2	10.9	4.2	79.9	100.0	0.1	0.7	39.1	13.2	46.9
1996	100.0						100.0						100.0					
1997	100.0	5.0	9.9	17.6	0.9	66.6	100.0	1.3	2.8	16.9	0.6	78.4	100.0	0.0	0.6	53.9	0.0	45.4
1998	100.0	5.8	9.1	18.1	0.7	66.4	100.0	1.2	2.8	17.6	0.5	78.0	100.0	0.1	0.6	50.2	0.2	49.0
1999	100.0	6.3	9.1	22.4	0.8	61.5	100.0	1.3	2.6	20.1	0.6	75.4	100.0	0.1	0.5	47.5	0.2	51.8
2000	100.0	7.7	8.8	32.8	0.5	50.3	100.0	1.4	2.4	21.8	0.4	74.0	100.0	0.0	0.6	48.6	0.1	50.6
2001	100.0	8.8	8.9	31.2	0.5	50.7	100.0	1.4	2.0	23.6	0.6	72.5	100.0	0.0	0.3	41.2	0.1	58.4
2002	100.0	10.8	8.6	36.8	0.8	43.1	100.0	1.8	1.8	25.8	0.6	70.0	100.0	0.1	0.4	41.5	0.2	57.9
2003	100.0	13.6	8.3	38.5	0.8	38.8	100.0	2.2	2.0	26.9	0.5	68.4	100.0	0.2	0.2	38.4	0.1	61.1
2004	100.0	14.7	6.9	41.1	0.8	36.5	100.0	2.5	1.7	26.8	0.5	68.4	100.0	0.5	0.3	32.7	0.4	66.2
2005	100.0	15.7	7.2	43.0	0.8	33.4	100.0	2.8	1.9	28.7	0.5	66.1	100.0	0.9	0.2	31.4	0.3	67.2
2006	100.0	14.2	5.6	46.2	0.7	33.4	100.0	2.7	1.7	31.5	0.8	63.3	100.0	0.7	0.2	31.9	0.9	66.3
2007	100.0	15.0	6.4	48.3	0.7	29.7	100.0	3.5	2.0	35.2	0.8	58.5	100.0	1.3	0.3	34.0	1.4	63.0
2008	100.0	15.8	6.4	49.1	0.8	27.8	100.0	4.2	2.1	40.8	0.7	52.2	100.0	1.7	0.5	36.3	0.6	60.9
2009	100.0	16.6	6.3	51.6	0.7	24.8	100.0	4.5	1.9	47.8	0.7	45.1	100.0	2.9	0.3	37.8	0.7	58.4
2010	100.0	16.5	6.2	52.7	0.9	23.7	100.0	4.5	1.8	52.1	1.2	40.5	100.0	3.1	0.3	42.4	1.2	53.0
2011	100.0	15.2	6.1	55.7	1.1	22.0	100.0	5.6	1.8	57.9	1.4	33.3	100.0	2.9	0.4	45.6	0.5	50.6

Source: *China Statistical Yearbook of Science and Technology* (2006); MOST online database.

domestic patent applications, reaffirming the relatively low quality of patenting in China. However, we have also seen an unmistaken sign of improvement in patent quality. Over the period 1995–2010, patent filing growth was primarily driven by invention patent filings. In this period, invention patent applications grew 41-fold, as opposed to nine-fold growth in utility model patent applications and 27-fold growth in design patent applications. WIPO's analysis of China's patent filings under PCT from 2012 to 2013 also concludes that a rapidly growing proportion of Chinese patents are now up to world standards.[14] Equally important is the fact that enterprises are now taking the central role in invention patenting. As displayed in Table 8.4, in 1995 when patent statistics in China were first available, invention patent applications by individuals made up an overwhelming 70.1 per cent of all applications, yet their share shrank significantly to 23.7 per cent by 2010. In contrast, invention patent applications filed by enterprises rose steadily from 10.8 per cent in 1995 to 52.7 per cent in 2010, indicating a fast improvement in patenting quality as well as innovation capability in the business sector.

In sum, the sign of change in China's capability of producing original knowledge is clear and promising. The knowledge production system is still not perfect, but no system across the world is perfect. It has taken China two decades to turn itself into the world's manufacturing hub and there is no reason why the same cannot be repeated in STI. No wonder John Howkins, the UK's eminent thinker of the creative economy, has recently asked people in the West to take Chinese creativity seriously or lose out.[15]

Performance of knowledge diffusion system

Knowledge diffusion is an important bridging mechanism within an innovation system that links together the knowledge production system and knowledge application system through facilitating knowledge transfer, knowledge learning, and absorption of applied knowledge and its adaptation in use. We measure the vitality of the knowledge diffusion system in four respects, i.e. volumes and value of domestic technology transfer in the technology market, industry-university collaboration, absorption of foreign technology, and the development of the STI service sector.

Domestic technology transfer

China's first technology market was set up in Wuhan in 1984, capital city of Hubei Province in the Central Region of China. By the end of 2012, there were 200 technology markets across the country, employing 500,000 people.[16] The development of China's technology markets has been driven by a growing quest for innovation in the business sector, a change from supply-led to demand-led technology markets, the government's development strategy in the STI service sector, and government tax incentives. A technology market is a physical entity set up to facilitate transactions of technology and technological services. More specifically, a technology market in China facilitates various forms of technological trading activities, comprising the transfer of new technologies, technical consultancy, technical training, technical services, technical contracts, joint technical operations, and partnership research-production associations or corporations. A measure of transactions of such technology markets is the volumes and value of technology contract deals.

An analysis of the technology market data reveals two interesting facts as can be seen in Table 8.5. First, the volumes of technology contracts over the period 1997–2012 fluctuated from 282,000 deals in the peak year of 1998 to 206,000 deals in 2006. Technology transactions started picking up again after 2007 and reached 282,242 in 2012. Second, the ups and downs in the growth of volume of transactions conceal a fast increase in the average value of contract deals. An average value of transactions was RMB0.14 million in 1997 and rose to RMB2.28 million in 2012, representing a 16-fold increase in value of contract deals over the same period. These trends suggest that the quality of knowledge diffusion has improved and that market-oriented technology transactions have played an important role in the transfer of technologies in China.[17]

Industry-university collaboration

China's current industry-university linkages are built through three broad mechanisms. The first is through technology transfer by means of licensing, consulting, contract R&D and technical services, the second is through university spin-offs of which the university can be the sole and partial owner, and the third and the most recent is through the government-facilitated formation of innovation-oriented strategic alliances in industries. Statistics are not available to measure directly the frequency, intensity and added value of industry-university collaboration. Hence, assessment in this respect normally relies on survey data at the firm level.

In the innovation survey of 1,399 firms in 42 cities conducted jointly by the National Statistical Bureau of China and Tsinghua University in 2008, all

Table 8.5 Contract deals and value in domestic technical markets

Year	Contract deals (10,000)	Value of contract deals (billion)	Year	Contract deals (10,000)	Value of contract deals (billion)
1995	n/a	n/a	2004	26.5	133.4
1996	n/a	n/a	2005	26.5	155.1
1997	25.0	35.1	2006	20.6	181.8
1998	28.2	43.6	2007	22.1	222.7
1999	26.4	52.3	2008	22.6	266.5
2000	24.1	65.1	2009	21.4	303.9
2001	23.0	78.3	2010	23.0	390.7
2002	23.7	88.4	2011	25.6	476.4
2003	26.8	108.5	2012	28.2	643.7

Source: *China Statistical Yearbook of Science and Technology* (2006); MOST online database.

firms reported in-house R&D as their main source of product and process innovation (Centre for Technological Innovation of Tsinghua University, 2009). With regard to product innovation, 36.4 per cent of firms identified their collaboration with universities as the second most important source of innovation, as opposed to 75.2 per cent saying in-house R&D is the first source of innovation. Similar patterns are found with reference to process innovation: 80.7 per cent of firms indicated in-house R&D as the most important source of innovation and 35.3 per cent suggested industry-university collaboration as the second important source of innovation. However, the China Innovation Survey conducted by the Economist Intelligence Unit in 2006 finds that external partners as a source of new ideas are much less important in China, pointing to a less collaborative approach to innovation in China (Economist Intelligence Unit, 2009).

How businesses fund research at higher education institutions is also another measure to assess industry and university collaboration. Statistics in respect of funds for STI at higher education institutions and their source were first published in 1998. In terms of contribution of firms to the total S&T funding, figures in 1998 and 1999 were unusually high at 43.3 per cent and 51.7 per cent (Table 8.6). The figure dipped to 33.2 per cent in 2000 and has since shown a steady increase. The latest data available show that enterprises contributed RMB20.83 billion to expenditure on R&D worth RMB60.73 billion at HIEs in 2012, or 34.3 per cent of the spending.[18]

Industry-led technology innovation strategic alliances

To improve industry-university-public research institute collaboration, MOST launched a pilot scheme in 2007 to facilitate collaboration through the formation of industry-led technology innovation strategic alliances. The scheme approved the formation of 56 strategic alliances in 2007 and another 39 alliances in 2012. As of August 2013, 95 strategic alliances were in action with more than one-third operating in the material and equipment manufacturing sector (Table 8.7).

Table 8.6 S&T funding at higher education institutions

Year	Funds for S&T (RMB billion)	Of which	
		Enterprise fund	%
1998	8.50	3.68	43.3
1999	10.29	5.32	51.7
2000	16.68	5.55	33.2
2001	20.00	7.25	36.2
2002	24.77	8.96	36.2
2003	30.78	11.26	36.6
2004	39.16	14.86	38.0

Source: *China Statistical Yearbook of Science and Technology* (2006).

Table 8.7 Industry-led technology innovation strategic alliances by sector

Sector	Number
New generation of IT, remote sensing and global positioning system (GPS)	14
Primary industry	21
Energy-saving, environmental protection and biology	26
Material and equipment manufacturing	34
Total	95

Source: Association of Industry Technology Innovation Strategic Alliances (CITISA), www.citisa. org/tongzhigonggao/1392.html (accessed 21 January 2014).

In Zhongguanchun Science Park, the formation of industry technology innovation strategic alliances appears to have revitalized the high-tech cluster. As of 2012, the Science Park had formed 76 technology innovation strategic alliances, of which 24 alliances were in MOST's national pilot scheme. In each strategic alliance, the number of strategic partners was 70 in 2012 as opposed to 23 in 2002. By April 2013, strategic alliances in the Science Park had been granted 16,511 invention patents and had contributed to the development of 23 international technology standards and 54 domestic technology standards.[19]

Absorption of foreign technology

China has been heavily reliant on technology transfer from import of technology and FDI from foreign companies. As far as imports of technology are concerned, Chinese expenditure shows a cyclical pattern attributable to changes in macroeconomic environment but a general upward trend when the economy is growing strongly. From an expenditure of RMB9 billion in 1991, Chinese companies spent RMB38.6 billion in 2010. Nevertheless, spillover of technological know-how to Chinese partners or manufacturers depends, to a great extent, on absorptive capacity of Chinese companies. One way to measure this capacity is expenditure in technology absorption defined as the investment of recipients in installation, utilization, modification and improvement of the imported technology. Statistics show a weak record of Chinese efforts to assimilate foreign technology. For a long period from 1991 to 2003, Chinese companies spent no more than 9 per cent of their technology import budget in technology absorption. Deficient investment in the assimilation of imported technology seemed to be a serious problem in the knowledge diffusion system at the time. However, a turning point can be seen in 2004 when the expenditure on technology absorption as a percentage of expenditure on imports of technology was more than doubled (Table 8.8). Remarkably, the percentage rose steadily and reached 42.8 per cent in 2010. This can be seen as a healthy improvement on the part of Chinese firms and should have a far-reaching impact on the innovation capability of firms.

Table 8.8 Expenditure on import of technology and absorption

Year	Expenditure on import of technology (100 million)	Expenditure on technology absorption (%)	Year	Expenditure on import of technology (100 million)	Expenditure on technology absorption (%)
1991	90.2	4.5	2001	285.9	6.9
1992	n/a	n/a	2002	372.5	6.9
1993	159.2	3.9	2003	405.4	6.7
1994	n/a	n/a	2004	367.9	14.7
1995	360.9	3.6	2005	296.8	23.4
1996	322.1	4.2	2006	320.4	25.6
1997	236.5	5.8	2007	452.5	23.6
1998	214.8	6.8	2008	440.4	24.2
1999	207.5	8.7	2009	394.6	41.5
2000	245.4	7.4	2010	386.1	42.8

Source: *China Statistical Yearbook of Science and Technology* (2006); MOST online database.

The development of the STI service sector

China recognized the importance of the STI service sector in the national innovation system early on and has taken measures to support the development of the sector. In particular, in 2002, MOST used the release of the Opinions on the Accelerating Development of S&T Intermediaries to set out the objectives and measures of S&T intermediary development. In order to raise the profile of the new policy agenda, MOST also announced 2003 to be the year of S&T intermediary building. Attempts have since been made to develop a coherent system of the S&T intermediary sector. In the national innovation system, the STI service sector now comprises the following components:

1 Productivity promotion centres
2 S&T business incubators
3 S&T consulting and evaluation agencies
4 Technology transaction agencies
5 Venture investment services
6 Agricultural technology extension services.

As can be seen in Table 8.9, these STI-oriented agencies have significantly improved their capability to provide professional services in technology transfers, commercialization of research output, technology evaluation, venture investment advice, innovation strategy and management consultancy.

Table 8.9 The development of key STI intermediaries, 2004 and 2012

	2004	2012
Productivity promotion centres:		
• Number of centres	1,218	2,281
• Government spending (RMB billion)	1.09	2.25
S&T business incubators:		
• Number of incubators	464	1,239
• Space of incubators (million m²)	15.2	43.7
• Number of incubated firms	33,213	70,000
National level university-based science parks:		
• Number of science parks	42	94
• Incubation space (million m²)	4.85	9.19
• Incubation fund (RMB million)	500	808
• Number of incubated firms	5,037	7,369
National technology transfer centres:		
• Number of centres	8	275
• Number of technology transfer facilitated	2,000	73,107
• Amount of contracted technology transfer (RMB billion)	0.8	141.8

Sources: China Science and Technology Development Report 2005 and 2012.

Performance of knowledge application system

Knowledge application refers to the deployment of knowledge and ideas in the real world and is where the national innovation system delivers value in knowledge production. We measure performance of knowledge application in the innovation system in three respects, i.e. enterprise R&D expenditure as a share of sales revenue, high-tech exports as a share of total exports, and innovativeness of new and established firms.

Business R&D investment

For China to move up the technological ladder and to produce high-value goods and services, home-grown innovation could be vital. Statistics of business R&D investment as in Table 8.10 show that business R&D investment increased considerably, from RMB53.7 billion in 2000 to RMB784.2 billion in 2012. The business sector has become a dominant R&D player in the national innovation system, now performing 76 per cent of R&D, compared to only 27 per cent in 1990. By international comparison, the percentage of R&D expenditure by the business sector was above all OECD countries except Japan (75.8 per cent) and Korea (75.4 per cent). Globally, examples of Chinese excellence in innovation have been recognized in information and telecommunications technology (ICT), auto assembly and components, PVCs, biopharmaceuticals, nanotechnology, stem cell therapeutics, high density power batteries, high-speed trains, wind turbines, single aisle passenger aircraft, booster rockets, space satellites, supercomputers, shipping containers, internet services and electric power turbines.[20] It can be argued that programmes of incentive for innovation in China have produced positive impact.

Table 8.10 Businesses' R&D investment

Year	Expenditure for R&D (billion)	Basic research	Applied research	Experimental development
2000	53.7	n/a	n/a	n/a
2001	63.0	n/a	n/a	n/a
2002	78.8	n/a	n/a	n/a
2003	96.0	n/a	n/a	n/a
2004	131.4	n/a	n/a	n/a
2005	167.4	n/a	n/a	n/a
2006	213.5	n/a	n/a	n/a
2007	268.2	n/a	n/a	n/a
2008	338.2	0.2	2.2	97.6
2009	424.9	0.1	2.0	97.9
2010	518.6	0.1	2.4	97.5
2011	657.9	0.1	2.9	97.0
2012	784.2	0.1	3.0	96.9

Source: *China Statistical Yearbook of Science and Technology* (2006); MOST online database.

However, the jury is still out on the full scale of impact. First, data in Table 8.10 also reveal that an overwhelming majority of business R&D investment, nearly 97 per cent, was in experimental development which is considered to be a less risky, more incremental type of innovation. OECD's (2008) review of innovation in China also finds that Chinese companies spend far more on technology renovation than on R&D. This has led to the suspicion in some quarters of China's genuine innovation capability, particularly as China is lacking globally recognizable brands in consumer goods. Nevertheless, it has been noted that these 'incremental' efforts to adopt and adapt the latest technologies have been an important driver of China's industrial development and that this is a particularly valuable specialism to capture the value of innovations as the global value chain in R&D become more fragmented (Bound *et al.*, 2013).

Second, large and medium-sized enterprises (LMEs) are mainly responsible for business R&D investment.[21] Innovation investment by the small business sector is still weak. In 2005, LMEs spent RMB125 billion in R&D, accounting for three-quarters of R&D investment of the business sector as a whole. However, measuring R&D investment as a share of turnover, innovation intensity in LMEs is still very low. As shown in Table 8.11, over the period 2000–2010, LMEs roughly spent 0.71–0.96 per cent of their sales revenues in R&D. In comparison, average business R&D as percentage of turnover in the USA in 2006 was 4.4 per cent, 4.1 per cent in Germany, 3.9 per cent in South Korea and 3.8 per cent in Japan (European Communities, 2006).

The OECD's (2008) review of China innovation policy also finds that enterprise R&D was highly fragmented, lacked economies of scale, and in most cases was duplicative or focused on minute incremental improvements to improve the salability of products. Few companies appear to devote serious effort to producing real technological innovation and have made a big impact on global markets. This is starting to change. Recently, home-grown enterprises have started to feature in some high-profile global innovative company league tables. In the 2010 *Bloomberg*

Table 8.11 Large and medium-sized company spending on R&D, 1991–2010

Year	R&D expenditure (100 million)	R&D as % of turnover	Year	R&D expenditure (100 million)	R&D as % of turnover
1991	58.6	0.49	2001	442.3	0.76
1992	76.1	0.50	2002	560.2	0.83
1993	95.2	0.50	2003	720.8	0.75
1994	122.0	0.51	2004	954.4	0.71
1995	141.7	0.46	2005	1,250.3	0.76
1996	160.5	0.48	2006	1,630.2	0.77
1997	188.3	0.52	2007	2,112.5	0.81
1998	197.1	0.53	2008	2,681.3	0.84
1999	249.9	0.60	2009	3,210.2	0.96
2000	353.4	0.71	2010	4,015.4	0.93

Source: *China Statistical Yearbook of Science and Technology* (2006); MOST online database.

Businessweek annual rankings of Most Innovative Companies, for example, for the first time China had four companies feature in the top 50 – up from just one (Lenovo) in 2009. Among the four Chinese companies in the top 50 most innovative companies, BYD was ranked a commanding 8th, Haier Electronics 28th, Lenovo 30th and China Mobile 44th. In a separate ranking published by *Newsweek* in 2010, BYD (8th) and Haier (10th) again featured in its top 10 innovative company list. Worldwide, Huawei Technologies is regarded as one of the few large Chinese firms to have demonstrated real innovative capacity (Kroeber, 2007). Huawei, for example, has established 20 research institutes around the world from Stockholm to Moscow to Bangalore; around 46 per cent of Huawei's employees are engaged in R&D; in 2010 it invested RMB16.55 billion (US$2.6 billion) in R&D.[22]

While innovation investment by the business sector as a whole is still low, Chinese companies are found to have developed ways to beat their global rivals through innovating simple, low-cost solutions that give them an edge on price or through more personalized products (Economist Intelligence Unit, 2009). Chinese companies' ability in frugal innovation prompts the Economist Intelligence Unit (2009) to argue that the 'China price' may not have to be laid by the wayside even as China grows richer: re-engineering products to cut costs and finding novel ways to manage their supply chain may do a great deal to offset higher staffing costs and capital expenditure; working out how to make mobile phones and computers inexpensively enough for the huge number of poor in the world may be as lucrative as producing for the few who are well-to-do.[23]

'High-tech' exports

China's post-reform phenomenal growth has been export-led. One of the surprising changes in this export-oriented model is that the country's biggest exports are now high-tech products. Statistics from MOST over the period 1991–2010 chart the trajectory of change. China's exports of high-tech products started from a moderate value of US$2.9 billion in 1991 and rose exponentially to US$601.2 billion in 2012, representing 207-fold growth in that period (Table 8.12). By 2012, exports of high-tech products accounted for nearly one-third of China's total exports, up from a negligible level in the early 1990s. Undoubtedly, the spectacular rise in high-tech exports is one of the driving forces behind China's ascent to the world's economic superpower.

Yet, it is widely noted that the bulk of China's 'high-tech' exports are actually low-margin commodity products such as personal computers and DVD players, assembled from imported components that account for most of their value (OECD, 2008). In contrast to the home-grown IT industries of Japan and South Korea, two-thirds or more of those exports are from partly or wholly foreign-owned plants.[24]

The information technology sector exemplifies the strengths and weaknesses of China's high-tech exports. In a short span of a decade, China has built a strong manufacturing capability and has become the location of choice for final assembly of IT products whose core technologies are designed in North America,

Table 8.12 National exports of high-tech products, 1991–2012

Year	Exports of high-tech products (US$100 million)	Share in total exports (%)	Year	Exports of high-tech products (US$100 million)	Share in total exports (%)
1991	28.8	4.0	2002	678.6	20.8
1992	40.0	4.7	2003	1,103.2	25.2
1993	46.8	5.1	2004	1,653.6	27.9
1994	63.4	5.2	2005	2,182.5	28.6
1995	100.9	6.8	2006	2,814.5	29.0
1996	126.6	8.4	2007	3,478.0	28.6
1997	163.1	8.9	2008	4,156.1	29.0
1998	202.5	11.0	2009	3,769.3	31.4
1999	247.0	12.7	2010	4,923.8	31.2
2000	370.4	14.9	2011	5,488.3	28.9
2001	464.5	17.5	2012	6,011.7	29.3

Source: MOST online database.

Europe and Japan. China's position as last-stage, low-value assembly in the global value chain means that its estimated value share is generally at 10–15 per cent (Kroeber, 2007). Most of the value of an IT product assembled in China is captured by core technology designers and specialized component makers. In Ali-Yrkkö *et al.*'s (2011) investigation into the geography of the value added for a Nokia N95 smartphone circa 2007, they found that China, as the final assembler of the final product, only commanded 2 per cent of the overall value added.

China has taken measures to redress this problem by pushing forward indigenous innovation and poising to replicate many of the same successful strategies that Japanese and South Korean governments used to establish a technological lead in electronics and automobiles. The strategy, for example in clean technology, includes paving ways for fledgling companies to access loans, funding industry-wide R&D, and supporting enterprises to buy advanced clean technologies. Some signs of China's potential future dominance of clean technology markets are already evident. The country is the world's biggest exporter of solar power components and has one of the biggest wind turbine manufacturing industries. In 2009, China exported the first wind turbines for use in a US wind farm, for a project valued at US$1.5 billion.[25]

Innovativeness of new and established businesses

Performance of knowledge application in the business sector can also be measured by the innovativeness of firms in terms of the newness of their product or service. Newness is usually classified as new to the firm, new to the local market and new to the world. The continuum of newness reflects the type of innovation firms undertake and thus the potential impacts on firms' competitive position. The Global Entrepreneurship Monitor (GEM) China project[26] surveys entrepreneurs and business owners about how they evaluate the newness of their product or service, the competition they face, and the novelty of their technology. The survey data in China in 2007 compare the newness of products and services among newly created businesses of less than 3.5 years old and established businesses that have been trading for more than 3.5 years. The survey results (Gao *et al.*, 2008) show that only 17 per cent of new businesses and 16.6 per cent of established businesses claimed that what they offered is new to all customers and that another 15.8 per cent of new businesses and 17.6 per cent of established businesses admitted that there is nothing new in what they offered to their customers.

Another important indicator of the innovativeness of a business concerns the technologies and production processes it uses. Usually, new technologies and processes are associated with a better utilization of resources, higher quality of routine tasks, and higher productivity. Companies that use innovative technologies and processes can often offer qualitatively superior and/or cheaper products, thereby enjoying higher growth potential. The GEM China survey data again show a low adoption of new technologies in both groups of new and established businesses. About 36 per cent of early-stage entrepreneurs and 14 per cent of established business owners claimed to be using the latest or newer technologies, as opposed to nearly two-thirds of new businesses and almost 86 per cent of established businesses claiming use of process technologies that are at least five years old (Gao *et al.*, 2008). The GEM China survey with regard to product innovation and process innovation portraits an unimpressive profile of innovativeness of Chinese businesses against their international counterparts, confirming that innovation in the business sector as a whole in China is still weak.

In 2005, MOST, State-owned Assets Supervision and Administration Commission (SASAC) and the National Federation of Trade Unions jointly launched a pilot programme, called the innovation-oriented enterprise pilot programme, which was renamed as the National Technological Innovation Project. It aimed at facilitating innovation behaviour in all forms of enterprises (Li and Li, 2014). By the end of 2011, there were 542 enterprises in the pilot programme. In 2011, these pilot enterprises had 6.83 per cent of employees working in the R&D function, compared with 3.37 per cent in all large and medium-sized enterprises (LMEs); they spent 1.83 per cent of operating income in R&D as opposed to 0.93 in LMEs.[27]

Conclusion

China's economic growth success over the past three decades apparently has had positive implications for the country's innovation aspirations. The size effect as measured by the wealth together with innovation policies appears to have significantly improved China's innovation infrastructure and capabilities. This combined effect has placed China in a favourable term in the two leading global innovation rankings. At 29th position in both WEF and INSEAD rankings, China outperforms those economies in the same group or region and its overall performance in innovation is closer to the top group in the rankings. This clearly indicates that China has done a good job in reforming and revitalizing its innovation system and that the pursuit of goals of building an innovation country is transforming China.

Much of the evidence reviewed in this chapter consistently indicates that China has already made impressive strides in innovation in all three aspects of its innovation system with regard to knowledge production, diffusion and application. The advancements appear to be in line with China's clearly stated goal to make China 'an innovation-oriented economy' by 2020. Crookes (2012) argues that China is certainly a challenger in technology innovation, but does not yet appear to have become a leader. We agree that if leadership is meant by world-class level of innovation in the country as a whole, China is not there just yet. Nevertheless, gaps are getting smaller and the world has witnessed China's emerging leadership in a growing number of sectors. We are confident that the day will surely come.

Another clear message from our review of evidence is that China's knowledge production, a backbone of China's independent innovation aspiration, is in a clear trajectory of 'quantitative expansion' while in the meantime gradually moving into a 'rising quality' phase. Despite obvious problems and shortcomings, the quality of the Chinese innovation system as a whole is improving very quickly.

While China has emerged to become a world-leading nation in science and patenting, it still has a long way to go in connecting the knowledge production system with the knowledge diffusion and knowledge application systems. For the latter in particular, China's innovation strategy has made it the centre of attention. The incentive system has been structured in a way that firms are placed at the centre of the innovation system and that firms' effort to move up the innovation ladder from duplicative innovation to imitative innovation and creative innovation are properly awarded.

As described in Chapter 3 and in this chapter, since the implementation of the MLNP (2006–2020), China has seen a rapid increase in government funding of S&T and a steady improvement in the management of research projects and research grants which have resulted in a significant support to the development of S&T. The Chinese government is also acutely aware of problems in the innovation support system in respect of dispersal and duplication of S&T projects, lack of transparency in S&T management, and low efficiency in fund use. Actions have been taken in order to rectify the problems. This is epitomized by the release of new policy measures by the State Council in March 2014 in its 'Several Opinions of the State Council on Improving and Strengthening the Management of Scientific Research Projects and Funds Financed by the Central Financial Budget'. This latest development in shoring up low efficiency of R&D expenditure aims to establish a scientific research project and fund management mechanism that is "clear in responsibilities, scientific in regulation, open and transparent, and strong in supervision".[28] The document specifies measures in seven broad areas: (1) strengthening research project and funding allocation and coordination; (2) differentiating S&T management in accordance with the nature of projects into which they fall into four categories – basic and frontier science research, social welfare research, market-oriented research, and key and major research; (3) improving research project management process in respect of preparation and publication of call for research grant application, application approval, research grant monitoring and research project evaluation; (4) improving research project funding management; (5) strengthening research project funding monitoring and auditing; (6) improving S&T systems, including information access system, national S&T reporting system, S&T expert selection system, and incentive system; and (7) clarifying responsibilities of all parties involved in S&T projects.

Notes

1 They are referred to as the modernization of agriculture, industry, science and technology, and the military.
2 Exchange rate at May 2014.
3 For an excellent discussion on measuring innovation, see Keith Smith (2005).
4 For more details about the methodology of GII, please see INSEAD (2011).
5 A typical argument can be found in Nandani Lynton's viewpoint, entitled 'China's innovation barriers', *BusinessWeek*, 15 December 2006.
6 It is suggested that citations could also be explained by recognized trends for European and US researchers to cite each other rather than look further afield in their specialization (Crookes, 2012).

7 See News in brief 'China: the land of the cited', *Times Higher Education*, 31 May 2011, p. 12.
8 See News in brief 'Research in China: Red stars rise on Nature's horizon', *Times Higher Education*, 6 June 2013, p. 13.
9 See News in brief 'China: the land of the cited', *Times Higher Education*, 31 May 2011, p. 12.
10 Simon Marginson, 'Tigers burning bright', *Times Higher Education*, 17 June 2010, p. 36.
11 Also see News in brief 'Research in China: Red stars rise on Nature's horizon', *Times Higher Education*, 6 June 2013, p. 13.
12 See article 'Huawei on the high seas' in *Beijing review online*, 17 October 2011, available at www.bjreview.com/print/txt/2011-10/17/content_398426.htm (accessed 26 August 2012).
13 See WIPO's report 'US and China Drive International Patent Filing Growth in Record-Setting Year', available at www.wipo.int/pressroom/en/articles/2014/article_0002.html (accessed 25 May 2014).
14 Ibid.
15 See his article in the *Financial Times* on 12 December 2013.
16 See MOST (2013), *China Science and Technology Development Report 2012* (p. 22).
17 The value of technology transactions in technology markets totalled RMB640 billion, an increase of 34 per cent over the previous year, according to Wang Gang, Minister of MOST in his press conference on 11 October 2013, available at www.gov.cn/wszb/zhibo579/wzsl.htm (accessed 9 November 2013).
18 See China Science and Technology Statistics databook 2013, available at www.most.gov.cn/kjtj/ (accessed 15 May 2014).
19 See report 产业技术联盟激活中关村集群创新 (Industry technology innovation alliances revitalizing innovation in Zhongguanchun cluster), *Sina Finance and Economy*, 7 January 2014, available at http://finance.sina.com.cn/leadership/mroll/20140107/173317872795.shtml (accessed 21 January 2014).
20 The World Bank (2010) 'China's growth through technological convergence and innovation', Supporting Report 2 to China 2030, Washington DC: World Bank.
21 According to the National Bureau of Statistics of China, LMEs are defined as those industrial enterprises with 300 and more employees and sales revenue above RMB20 million.
22 'Huawei on the high sea – the Chinese telecom tech supplier continues to expand abroad', *Beijing Review*, 20 October 2011.
23 *The Economist* weekly publication credits Lenovo as a frugal innovator for its success in the global market for personal computers and more lately smartphones. See 'The rise of the frugal innovator', *The Economist*, 24 May 2014.
24 Guy de Jonquières, 'The China high-tech myth', *FT.com*, 24 January 2005.
25 'Asia set to overtake US in green technology race', *FT.com*, 19 November 2009.
26 The Global Entrepreneurship Monitor (GEM) project is a global research consortium led by the Babson College in the USA and conducts surveys in 60 countries, including China.
27 See 《中国创新型企业发展报告2012》发布 (The release of Report of the Development of Innovative Enterprises in China 2012), *Chinese Social Sciences Net*, 11 November 2013, available at www.cssn.cn/hy/hy_zyhy/201311/t20131111_829110.shtml (accessed 21 January 2014).
28 The full original document is available on MOST's website www.most.gov.cn/kjbgz/201403/t20140312_112280.htm (accessed 15 March 2014).

9 Incentives for innovation
Chinese experiences

China has come a long way to put in place a suite of policies to support independent innovation. Many of these policies are similar to international good practices and some others are new, novel and experimental. Due to the lack of hard data, work is yet to be done to assess the effectiveness and efficiency of these incentive policies for innovation, namely whether the objectives of these policies have been met and whether the outcomes these policies have used resources to deliver are value for money. The tentative assessment of the performance of the national innovation system we have done in the previous chapter leads us to contemplate the outlook of innovation in China in an optimistic mood. It has become clear that there appears to be a consensus about the quantitative change in China's STI output these policies have facilitated to achieve. Results in this regard seem to indicate positive changes in line with the pre-set objectives within the proposed timeframe. Apparently, a great deal of debate has now centred on the extent to which qualitative change of independent innovation has occurred. Some China observers tend to use China's lack of game-changing consumer products and world-beating innovative companies as evidence to suggest that qualitative change remains elusive. However, the business-to-consumer visibility gap, as identified by Orr and Roth (2012), does not conceal the fact that China is innovating and that the country has already become a force to be reckoned with in a growing number of product categories, particularly in the segment of business to business (B2B). The Chinese government is fully aware of both the imperfections in the national innovation system and the policy tools in use and has taken measures to redress them.

Like China's rise to become the world's manufacturing powerhouse, China's push to transform the country into an innovative economy is another great experiment being openly conducted in front of the world. Policy-makers in many countries, particularly emerging economies, are observing the unfolding of the new drama with great interest. Where incentive for innovation is concerned, what have been China's experiences so far? Are there any lessons other emerging economies can draw from the Chinese experiment? Answers to these questions are not straightforward. First, the development of an innovative economy is still in a fast-pacing, fluid state and time will tell if policies deliver. Second, it depends on how people judge China's accomplishment of the national innovation strategy up to now. Third, even for those optimists like us who believe the day of success will come, some of the practices in China may admittedly be idiosyncratic and context-specific and therefore may not be transferable to different contexts to which innovation policies with Chinese character are applied. Nevertheless, from our own reflection of China's progress in transition to an innovative economy, we argue that eight lessons arising from the country's experiences of encouraging innovation through public intervention offer a lot of food for thought.

Playing with both the 'visible hand' and the 'invisible hand'

When it started the engine of economic vehicle and set off on the path of economic reforms, China was deeply entrenched in the mentality, governance and administration of the closed, economic planning regime. Governments at all levels were bound to overuse the 'visible hand' – regulations and public intervention – to impact on all spectrums of economic life. Economic reforms were deemed to curtail the influence of a big government and to let markets – the 'invisible hand' – to function properly for resource allocation. Unlike reforms in many former socialist countries in Eastern Europe, China has adopted a pragmatic approach to reforming the governing apparatus of the planning regime rather than discarding it at all costs. As a result, the new system, called the market system with Chinese characteristics, is underpinned by two complementary mechanisms, functions and roles of the 'two visible and invisible hands'. As Hu (2013) explains in his elaboration of the hybrid mechanisms, the hand of the market aims to promote economic prosperity and the hand of the plan to promote a harmonious society; the hand of the market is engaged in providing private goods and the hand of the plan in providing public goods. If playing it right, the 'two hands' are complementary and mutually reinforcing: the role of government is to supplement and mitigate the market instead of to exclude it or replace it; it is also to facilitate a market-friendly environment and to guide actors in the market with foresight and road-mapping.

We can see many examples in the previous chapters that China has used the hybrid mechanisms to facilitate innovation. For example, governments at central and local levels have used public venture capital initiatives to leverage private risk capital to invest in new- and high-tech ventures. Policy implementation has shifted from the approach of more direct investment-oriented in the early stage to one that uses fund-of-funds to allow the market to play a leading role. Governments have also played a facilitating role in the development of new ST-oriented financial products in support of technology enterprises. Furthermore, the role of the government is critically important in a country like China where institutions and innovation infrastructure are significantly underdeveloped. To boost capacity-building in a short span of time, China needs to increase its intensity of learning to be supported by resources. In the fragmented and underdeveloped markets, for example, a lack of development of the STI service sector in China, the 'invisible hand' may not be effective enough to bridge demand and supply of resource when this 'hand' remains largely missing. Under these circumstances, Chinese experiences suggest that both hands have their respective roles to play.

China's painful memory of the drawbacks inherent in the old planning regime has also served as a reminder of the danger of overplaying the 'visible hand'. Gradually, Chinese governments have defined their role in the economy as a facilitator of innovation rather than an undertaker of innovation. Policy design in respect of incentives for innovation over the last few years has emphasized incentivizing innovators through the market mechanisms and retreating governments from direct investment in commercialization projects. More specifically, China has seen the distinction between the 'visible hand' and the 'invisible hand' as such that the 'visible hand' should play a facilitating role in the development of key S&T infrastructure, basic research, and the development of an innovative environment, while the 'invisible hand' should play a leading role in the development of innovation capability in key industries and social innovations. Of course, finding the right balance between the 'visible hand' and the 'invisible hand' is rather challenging. With resources under its control, governments at the local level particularly may become too entrepreneurial and step over the line at the expense of the market. It is fair to say that the process of economic reforms in China has been the process of the government wrestling the 'visible hand' with the 'invisible hand'.

In addressing the annual ceremony held to honour distinguished scientists and research achievements in Beijing on 10 January 2014, Premier Li Keqiang stated that the government should free innovative scientific activities from administrative intervention and "let the market speak" in terms of research orientation, resource allocation and use of funds. He also emphasized that the government should also aim to create an environment that promotes fair play and encourages creativity and initiative among scientists and researchers.[1] This clearly marks the government's determination to reform itself once again as the market capacity has become more sophisticated.

Planning strategically and building a consensus

The importance of strategic planning in STI has never been doubted by policy-makers around the world. Strategic planning aims to align the objectives of the national innovation system with the long-term national economic objectives. In their account of the OECD model of policy-making in science policy, Henriques and Larédo (2013) point out planning as an integral part of the model. They also state that OECD preferred flexible approaches to planning over determining approaches and favoured bottom-up initiatives. China differs from the OECD model in that it is government-led with many top-down initiatives which are supplemented by bottom-up ones.

China has a long history of economic development planning. This is manifested in its five-year plan cycle starting in 1953. The five-year planning as a macroeconomic management tool has been retained and refined throughout the economic reform period when China has increasingly embraced the market system. Nevertheless, as Heilmann and Melton (2013) point out in their examination of the tool, the development plan in China has changed fundamentally in its function and content, performing an important role in strategic policy coordination, resource mobilization and macroeconomic control. Hu (2013) echoes this viewpoint by highlighting three fundamental changes in today's planning mechanism as opposed to one in the pre-reform era, namely a shift from an economic plan to a public affairs governance plan, from a mechanic system to a more democratic, scientific and institutionalized one, and from the paradox of 'tightening' and 'loosening' to the 'initiatives of two parties' (central and local governments). We argue that the current revamped planning system has displayed four strengths. First, it benefits from an involvement of wide stakeholders in the planning process. In his analysis of China's industrial policy-making process, Ahrens (2013) identified ten actors who play their roles in the policy process. These actors are (1) the National People's Congress (NPC), (2) the State Council, (3) State Council Leading Small Groups (LSGs), (4) the State Council Legislative Affairs Office (SCLAO), (5) ministries, bureaus, agencies and commissions, (6) governmental and non-governmental research institutions, (7) business and industry associations (governmental and non-governmental), (8) domestic companies, business managers and individuals, (9) foreign associations, companies and governments and (10) the Chinese Communist Party. The process for the MLNP took nearly three years to complete from the initiation of a proposal to its final approval by the State Council and involved almost all actors identified above. Over time, China has opened up this policy decision-making process to the business sector and the general public.

Second, the planning system has become a vehicle to embed cross-party consensus in long-term innovation programmes and short-term action plans. It is now recognized that the outcomes of strategic planning, such as the MLNP, have exemplified a consensus across party that is to serve as the guidelines for ministry-specific and lower-level implementation (Ahrens, 2013). This cross-party consensus is primarily referred to as the general agreement on the overarching objectives of national development in general and innovation in particular within the communist party. This is particularly manifested in the communist party's conference in 2006 where a number of landmark decisions were made. Underpinning this cross-party consensus system through development planning is a consultation mechanism in which the aims and objectives of major policies are elaborated through several rounds of consultation within and outside the party.

Third, deliberation in development planning delivers the clarity of strategic focus and predictability of policy objectives and implementation. This in turn enhances the creditability and the confidence that investors and industries must have to engage in the implementation of policies.

Finally, the planning system as foresight activities contributes to innovation policy dialogue. The exercises of long-term planning have broadly positive effects on innovation policy design and implementation through creating awareness and increasing consensus.

The drafting of the Outline of Medium and Long-term National Plan for Science and Technology Development 2006–2020 (MLNP) exemplifies this process. The planning started with the formation of the State Council MLNP steering group chaired by then Premier Wen Jiabo. The steering group was to provide the oversight of the planning and was made up of 24 ministers as steering group members. It set up an office at the MOST as a platform of coordination. The steering group's first meeting on 13 June 2003 marked the start of the planning process. The drafting of the MLNP took 24 months to complete, involving over 2,000 experts from a wide range of institutions and sectors. The process as a whole was divided into three stages, namely research on strategic issues, outline drafting, and review and approval. The first stage lasted for one year. Strategic issues were grouped into three streams, i.e. macro strategic issues of S&T development, major tasks of S&T development, and input and policy environment for S&T development. These strategic issues were further decomposed into 20 research themes. The background research on all research themes involved over 2,000 experts from the communities of S&T, social science, management and business. Reports of background research were then disseminated for consultation in the Chinese Academy of Sciences (CAS), Chinese Academy of Social Sciences (CASS) and Chinese Academy of Engineering (CAE). In addition, the consultation process involved various ways, ranging from general public survey, collection of online feedback, focus group meetings and interviews with experts. For example, the steering group office consultation involved many focus group meetings in a number of cities and distributed 3,000 questionnaires. The steering group office also set up a planning-specific website as an interface with the general public for consultation purpose. In 12 months the website published ten million words of content concerning the strategic issues of MLNP and attracted 410,000 visitors who submitted through the website nearly 1,000 proposals. The steering group office also invited representatives of the private sector to participate in focus meetings.[2]

In the planning process, all options were considered and major differences were ironed out. The cross-party consensus in the end leads to a blueprint for more specific policy development. The political stability over the last three decades for the benefits of policy continuity should not be underestimated. Business investment in innovation to a great extent is for the future of undertaking. Similarly, transforming China into an innovative nation is a long-term endeavour. Policy stability clearly offers a much-needed assurance to all involved in their actions.

The process of strategic planning with involvement of key actors or stakeholders in China lends the innovation strategy the critical legitimacy for being able to address issues in the public interest and having platforms for consultation. The elaboration and refinement in the policy process also allow the different strands of innovation policy and associated policy instruments to mould and fit together, hence leading to the more coherent policy. Moreover, the connection between the national innovation strategy and the five-year planning cycle provides China with sufficiently stable framework conditions, institutions and policies. Stability and predictability in this sense remove uncertainty for innovators in their undertaking of risky activities with a long time horizon such as R&D. The connection has also allowed policy-makers to reassess the evolving innovation environment and adapt policies and governance arrangements to developments in innovation systems and the emerging challenges they face. We can argue that the process of strategic planning in China thus displays traits of good quality governance such as legitimacy, coherence, stability and adaptability, which OECD (2010) claims are the essential ingredients of high-quality governance and policy-making. In a comparative analysis of China, the UK and the USA in mission-oriented research development and demonstration (RD&D) institutions in energy between 2000 and 2010, Anadón (2012) argues that, contrary to those of the UK and the USA, the government of China has the ability to implement its policies without securing consensus from a broad range of stakeholders outside the communist party. The policy decision-making process we have described above suggests that this observation would no longer be the truth.

Building institutions through experimentation

Incentive for innovation to a great extent was a new concept to China in the early days of economic reforms when the legacy of the old planning regime still loomed large. The country needed to be, and has been, a quick learner in overhauling its entire economic system under reforms. Facing no template to follow, China has developed a mentality of experimentation, particularly at the local level, and institutional innovations were achieved largely through learning by doing and learning by experimenting.

China's large size and emerging scope of domestic market give the Chinese government an additional element of leverage in the formulation of innovation policy. As Naughton and Segal (2003) note, the big size and regional diversity give China an option of maintaining two or more separate, competing, and not necessarily integrated approaches toward technology acquisition and development. Local governments may run competing S&T development programmes, or try to exploit opportunities implicit in national policies in ways that are not necessarily consistent with the spirit of national policy. Policies first promoted and experimented at the local level may be recognized as good practices and eventually be elevated to central government policy. The combination of decentralized experimentation with central coordination results in selective integration of local experiences into national policy-making. Heilmann (2008) argues that China's experience strongly points to the potency of tapping local knowledge, mobilizing bottom-up initiatives, and embracing decentralized policy generation. In their analysis of China's technology policy over three decades (from 1978 to the new millennium), Naughton and Segal (2003) conclude that regional decentralization aids policy innovation.

The way of institution-building through experimentation as described above has proved to be constructive, even though the process could be messy and chaotic at the time. This may be inevitable. As we have shown in previous chapters, China has created a new system of incentive for innovation almost from scratch. Inevitably, the system is imperfect while reforms are still ongoing.

Governments in China are acutely aware of the weaknesses in the system and are open to new ideas and good practices from its international counterparts. We argue that assessment of the current system of incentive for innovation in China should be placed in the context of institution-building. As we described in Chapter 2, the pre-reform system was not up to the purpose as far as innovation is concerned. Designing a new system to encourage innovation is not a stand-alone action. Rather, it is just one piece of the jigsaw in the building of an entirely new economic system catering to the need for developing a market economy. This is a tall order and mistakes are bound to be made. Clearly, institution-building through experimentation has developed a feedback loop as a self-correction mechanism. Indeed, developments of incentive structure to support innovation are obviously a learning process for governments in China. It is understandable that the incentive policies in the early periods of reform had traces of mentality and policy tools from the planned economic system. The process of learning new ways of managing and unlearning dated methods is clearly path dependent. Nevertheless, over time there is a clear sign that China has gradually opted for market-based instruments for intervention. Greater efforts were made to use markets to incentivize the business sector to innovate in compliance with the protocols of the World Trade Organization (WTO). Examples illustrating this significant change include greater use of universal taxation policy, fund-of-funds in public venture capital, and financial innovation.

Resolving differences and conflict of interest through consultation

The decentralized system in China means that it has created a scope for flexibility, autonomy and adaptation at the local level. This is needed. On the one hand, the size of the country suggests that policies risk the danger of becoming irrelevant if policy-makers believe that one size can fit all. On the other, a scope for local experimentation will give local government the incentive to find solutions best fit to their local circumstances. Overall, the body of knowledge on the local entrepreneurial state seems to converge upon the view that decentralization and the corresponding local empowerment was crucial to the unique brand of contemporary Chinese innovation and entrepreneurship. Thus, Gibb and Li (2003: 418) argue that decentralization "means allowing freedom for local actors within resource constraints, and under pressure, to build real coalitions forcing synergy between political, social, and economic goals". It has become well-known with Deng Xiaoping's remarks that it does not matter whether the cat is black or white, as long as it catches mice. Mao Zedong's 'walking on two legs' is equally influential. Under this pragmatic philosophy, while the aims and objectives of policies are defined and agreed, implementation will allow for local experimentation in accordance with regional characteristics. Major policies will never have been rolled out without extensive periods of local pilot. Good practices are identified and policies are fine-tuned in the process. Breznitz and Murphree (2011) refer to this autonomy in experimentation as "structured uncertainty", which they define as an agreement to disagree about the proper objectives and methods of public policy or business practices. They argue that structured uncertainty can lead to short-termism in the goals that businesses and policy-makers pursue as it is impossible to know *ex ante* what behaviours will be encouraged or sanctioned. In her analysis of China's decentralization, Wong (1987) highlighted the detrimental effects inherent in the allocative powers of local governments: (1) the fragmentation of control tended to obstruct resource flows, and opposition could have slowed or even curtailed the development of local capital markets; (2) resource allocation was not necessarily following 'market regulations', as local governments were making the bulk of investment decisions; and (3) local governments reduced competition by shielding enterprises from market pressures and by intervening in interregional trade.

To reconcile the long-term goals of the national innovation programme and short-termism behaviours and to resolve differences and conflict of interest, China has come up with an institutional innovation in the form of inter-governmental consultation. Inter-governmental consultations comprise two main forms, namely the ministry-province consultation (部省会商) and multiple governmental joint meeting (联席会议).

MOST started piloting the ministry-province consultation as a coordination mechanism in 2002 as a tool of policy implementation in an attempt to develop national key laboratories in selected provinces. The consultation system with Anhui, Shanghai and Tianjin was formalized in 2005. In 2007, MOST issued the Interim Regulation on Ministry-Province Consultation to provide a working template for the practice. The consultation system serves to fulfil three objectives: to agree upon a joined-up action plan on agreed S&T projects, to find coordinated solutions to emerging problems during the course of project implementation, and to share information for the oversight of the action plan. It is underpinned by four principles: (1) the local government take the lead to facilitate the consultation process between the ministry and province; (2) consultation is to focus on overall planning and joined-up action; (3) the process aims to identify priorities of action and to pool resources together; and (4) execution is to emphasize task achievability and is conducted through institutional innovation. The consultation usually sets forth four main agendas, namely (1) overall S&T planning and proposals of S&T development, (2) critical needs and development priorities of the province, (3) S&T plan implementation and support for prioritized projects, and (4) complementary policy measures, institutional innovation, and regulation and administration. The Interim Regulation originally set three criteria upon which the eligibility of a province to enter a consultation arrangement is assessed but they were relaxed later on as by 2011 MOST had set up a consultation mechanism with all provinces. The consultation system is often formalized in an agreement signed by MOST and the participating provincial government. The agreement will lay out the focus of consultation, working mechanism, and duration of the agreement.

The agreement signed by MOST and Shanxi Province in September 2010 exemplifies this system. First, both parties agreed to engage in consultation on the pressing issues of green development, clean development, and safety and development which are of priority in the MLNP and are of relevance to the coal resource rich province. Five specific themes were identified as of mutual interest: (1) coal and coal-related technological innovation; (2) S&T capability to support the improvement of the eco-environment; (3) agricultural S&T innovation; (4) the development of strategic industries that fit the regional conditions; and (5) institutional innovation. Second, the agreement spelled out the working mechanism for the consultation system. This included the setting-up of a 'ministry-province cooperation committee' (MPCC). MPCC was co-chaired by the minister of MOST and the governor of Shanxi Province, and whose members were made up by heads of departments from both MOST and the province. It was also specified that a consultation meeting would be held once a year and that the S&T department of provincial government and the development and planning department of MOST would take responsibility for drafting the agenda. Finally, it was specified that the consultation agreement would be valid for five years from 2010 to 2015. By 2011, MOST had signed such an agreement with all 31 municipalities and provinces.

As an extension of the consultation system, Henan provincial government signed a similar agreement with 18 cities for the implementation of its action plan agreed upon with MOST. Similarly, the State Administration of Intellectual Property has used the ministry-province consultation as a vertical coordination mechanism in the implementation of the National Patent Development Strategy (2011–2020).

The consultation system bridges the central and local governments who are differently motivated. For local governments, they are motivated to compete with other regions for a bigger piece of cake from the central government expenditure on S&T by inviting more national key STI projects to locate in their regions. Equally importantly, these massive projects may also become the catalyst for the development of new industries and industrial clusters. Local governments have also courted the central government because of its power to authorize national status on local STI projects and to select regions for new pilot projects such as pilot provinces for national technological innovation and pilot national innovation cities. For central government, the consultation system can be used to steer local development to the direction of the national strategy and to facilitate additional local expenditure on STI. MOST estimated that projects in national major S&T programmes could magnify local government expenditure by 1 to 10 and that projects in policy guidance programmes had a multiplier effect of 17 on additional local government expenditure.[3]

There is no denying that China's campaign of building an innovative economy is government-led. However, as we have shown throughout the book, the governance structure of the national innovation system is complicated as it involves multiple ties of policy-makers. The central government will have to coordinate conflict of interest across ministerial departments and work with over

30 provincial governments. To bring all players in this multi-agent system to sing in the same tune is a real challenge. In this regard, China's consultation system between MOST and provincial governments is a refreshing organizational innovation. It helps bring relentless local innovations under the desirable national framework of regional division of labour to serve coherent national aims; it also allows the central government to tailor its incentive policies to meet local needs. Naughton and Segal (2003) point out that a degree of decentralization in interaction with a continued central government role creates one of the most crucial dynamics of the system.

Encouraging complementary forms of innovation to achieve the ultimate aim of independent innovation

China has been clearly the beneficiary of technology import and imitation since it opened up to the outside world in the late 1970s but has also felt deep down very unsatisfied with its unabated reliance on the Western countries for core technologies. The campaign of independent innovation embodied in the MLNP displays an unmistaken intent to address this concern. From the beginning of the campaign, nevertheless, the Chinese government has made it clear that the emphasis on independent innovation referred to as the process of creating value of new products through developing home-grown core technologies independently should not exclude the absorption of existing S&T achievements from outside the country. China has thus encouraged organizations to innovate in an open rather than self-contained environment and has supported different forms of innovation to thrive in order to achieve the ultimate aim of building China into an innovative economy. To this end, China defined independent innovation in a broad term in 2006, embracing the forms of original innovation, integrated innovation and re-innovation. Since 2011, a fourth form of innovation, i.e. collaborative innovation, has been included in the campaign. These four forms of innovation are considered to be complementary not substitution.

First of all, China has attached enormous importance to original innovation in hope that it will generate more home-grown technologies in the frontier of technological innovation. Original innovation is referred to as innovations resulting from new major scientific discoveries, novel technological inventions and new disciplines creating technological breakthroughs. It is a major technological innovation that transcends accepted scientific doctrines or challenges existing technological theories. It represents achievements of unique discoveries or inventions of research and development especially in basic research and high-technology research. China's strategies of original innovation appear to have achieved desirable results. In 2013, China ranked fifth in the world in terms of the number of international citations of scientific papers and third in the world in terms of the number of annual granted patents. Meanwhile, there have been a growing number of intellectual property rights created by China in such fields as information, materials, new energy and biology that have long been dominated by the United States and the European Union.

Nevertheless, innovation can come from an effective fusion of technologies from all existing sources in the development of competitive products and industries. This is what China has referred to as integrated innovation in its campaign of independent innovation. China's distinct answer to integrated innovation is to establish 16 national major special S&T programmes, covering multiple areas including information technology, high-end manufacturing, genetic modification, new drug development and nuclear power. The scale and scope of integrated innovation in China have been unprecedented. Judging by the results of the 16 programmes over the past eight years, China has not only made breakthroughs in some major areas but has also become a pioneer in many areas such as high-speed train technology and mobile telecommunication standards that have already become international standards. In the meantime, Chinese enterprises are also increasingly competing in the fields of international frontier of technological innovations.

China has also highly valued re-innovation as an effective form of independent innovation. Re-innovation refers to imported technology absorption-based innovation as a result of learning, assimilating and absorbing in the development of proprietary intellectual property rights. This is built on the understanding that S&T knowledge is the common asset of humanity and that S&T activities are relays of global innovation. The strategy of re-innovation based on import and absorption aims to match innovation with local knowledge, resources and competence for good innovation performance and quick technological catching-up. An illustrative example of re-innovation is the development of 700,000 kWh hydraulic power generation technology. Initially reliant on the import of design and manufacturing of the 700,000 kWh hydraulic power generation units in the construction of the Three Gorges Dam, China soon absorbed and assimilated the technology through re-innovation and quickly acquired the complete local manufacturing capability. Soon afterwards, China became an exporter of all such equipment. Today, China has not only become a contributor to international scientific advance and technological innovation but also a sharer of risks of global technological innovation and, more importantly, a strong player in the relays of global innovation. In parallel with numerous multinational firms setting up their R&D centres in China, many Chinese companies have also established overseas R&D institutions. Re-innovation has become an important avenue for China to integrate into the rest of the world and for other countries to reach into China.

While identifying the above-mentioned three forms of innovation as an integral part of independent innovation in the MLNP, China has also acknowledged that all efforts can be thwarted and resources wasted if innovation players are not working together. In recognition of such a problem, China has started championing collaborative innovation as a new form of independent innovation since 2011. Collaborative innovation refers to the effective pooling of innovation resources and capabilities to achieve closer cooperation by breaking down barriers to collaboration among innovation entities and fully releasing the dynamism of such innovation factors as talent, capital, information and technology.

Support for collaborative innovation is particularly necessary because there is a significant difference between national innovation systems in China and in developed countries, i.e. universities and national research institutes remain the most important forces of R&D activities in China. Specifically in technological innovation, the capacity of individual enterprises remains relatively limited. Such an unbalanced distribution of innovation capability in organizations has given rise to an urgent need for removing barriers to innovation collaborations between industry, HEIs and PRIs. Therefore, since 2011, collaborative innovation has become an important component of the strategy of independent innovation. After over three years of implementation, cooperation among manufacturers, universities and research institutions, and various types of alliances is becoming an effective means to magnify the effect of technological innovation and remove various barriers.

Reforming the S&T system through evolutionary institutional innovations

China has recognized that a country's environment of technological innovation has a decisive influence on its innovation capacity and that the quality of innovation environment is determined by the appropriateness of institutional set-up. Efforts have been made to reform the country's S&T system. Our observation on the 35 years' history of changes from 1978 to 2013 suggests that China's institutional innovations of the S&T system have displayed a trajectory of evolution characterized by the cycle of reform, stabilization, further reform and re-stabilization. In other words, China's institutional innovation is neither a process of sweeping transformative changes nor a resistance to change. Rather, it has been a gradual process of change in numerous moderate steps. In retrospect, the effect of evolutionary institutional innovation of the S&T system over the span of 35 years can be seen more clearly. With reforms of the S&T system evolving from regional pilots to national implementation, from passive reaction to proactive action, and from being unsure of one's actions to unswerving devotion, such evolutionary institutional innovations have largely shaped up the layout, strength, capacity and efficacy of S&T in China today. It is such a process of institutional innovation that has contributed to China's stability and rapid progress.

There are five cycles in the institutional innovations. The period between 1978 and 1985 marks the first evolutionary cycle of institutional innovations in China. Two events in 1978 served as a watershed in this first cycle: the Third Plenum of the 11th CPC Congress with far-reaching impact was held and the basic principle of focusing on economic development as the key priority was adopted. The National S&T Conference with delegations representing broad communities was convened, in which Deng Xiaoping remarked that the key of modernization is the modernization of S&T. For the first time, China aligned modernization with S&T in its development programme, signalling a remarkable new chapter of progress in S&T in the contemporary history of China.

If the period between 1978 and 1985 can be regarded as a transition from the planned economy to the market-based economy, this period may also be seen as the period of a comprehensive recovery of S&T activities in China. Hence, the focus of institutional innovations for S&T during this period was to clear up any misconception inherited from the ten-year Cultural Revolution of the importance of S&T in the country's economic life and to prioritize S&T funding in the national budget. Due to the considerable changes in policies, for a successive six years from 1980 to 1985, China's fiscal allocation of S&T accounted for more than 5 per cent of national total fiscal spending. By 1985, China's national fiscal allocation on S&T amounted to RMB10.259 billion, or 5.1 per cent of China's total fiscal spending. Also, from 1982 onwards, China set up special funds to support the newly established key S&T programmes in the implementation of the five-year national economic plan.

The period between 1986 and 1993 is the second cycle of China's institutional innovations. After the recovery and development, China's S&T community has increased its interactions and exchanges with the outside world. As a result, Chinese scientists have seen widening gaps between the country's S&T research and that of international excellence. In order to reduce these gaps, the Chinese leadership accepted suggestions on institutional innovations from the S&T community, i.e. adopting an S&T follower and imitation strategy and developing a supporting mechanism through reforming the S&T management system, increasing S&T funding level, and restructuring S&T governance for innovation. As measures to implement this strategy, China once again adjusted its fiscal policy on S&T.

Specifically, important institutional innovations of S&T in this period included: (1) the establishment of the principle of aligning S&T with economic development, thus making S&T policies an integral part of national economic policy; (2) the development of a tentative fiscal policy system targeted at the unique needs of different S&T activities, with various national S&T programmes replacing individual institutions as major recipients of the national fiscal budget on S&T; (3) issuance of fiscal policy on the industrialization of S&T, which laid down the institutional foundation for the development of China's high-technology industries; and (4) gradual inclusion of national institutional innovation of S&T under the rule of law, thereby creating a policy environment conducive to the long-term and stable development of S&T. The promulgation of *the Law of the People's Republic of China on the Progress of S&T* in 1993 has provided the legal underpinnings for the promotion of progress in S&T, priority-setting for the development of S&T, and aligning S&T with economic development.

The period between 1994 and 1999 is the third cycle of institutional innovation. The year 1994 marked the inception of China's socialist market economy under which markets become the fundamental and core mechanism in the organization of economic activities. Against this backdrop, the Second S&T Conference was held in 1995 and the basic principle for developing S&T was endorsed. The principle states that all parties should adhere to the philosophy that S&T is the primary productivity, that economic development must rely on S&T, that efforts of S&T must be oriented towards economic development, and that all should strive to advance S&T to a new level. Under this guiding principle, China initiated the strategy of 'S&T-driven nation building'.

The period between 2000 and 2005 is the fourth cycle of institutional innovation. This period witnessed the rapid growth of China's high-technology industries and also coincided with ever-closer integration of S&T with the economy and the trend of economic globalization. China's national institutional innovation of S&T in this period can be characterized as S&T industrialization and internationalization. Correspondingly, notable changes can be observed. First, fiscal reform further improved the mechanism of S&T investment with a greater emphasis on the effective use of government funding. Second, in order to speed up industrialization of S&T, national fiscal policy on S&T provided targeted support to the further reform of different types of research institutions. Third, in order to maintain the momentum of national scientific research, China further increased its spending on basic research. Fourth, high-tech incubators were used as a focal point of policy support for commercialization and industrialization of results of S&T research. Fifth, most national S&T programmes adopted a project funding system consistent with international practices.

The period from 2006 onwards is the fifth cycle of institutional innovation. The promulgation of the Outline of the National Programme for Medium and Long-Term Science and Technology Development (2006–2020) (MLNP) ushered in a stage of relative stability for the institutional innovation of S&T in China. The MLNP highlights the objective of turning China into an innovative economy and demonstrates China's determination to embark on independent innovation. During this cycle, the invisible hand of market and the visible hand of government have delineated a clearer boundary. Very significantly, markets have been elevated into a decisive role from a previously defined fundamental role in determining resource allocation of the society, while the decisive role of governments is gradually transformed into a comprehensive role of planning, guidance, supervision and services. The Chinese experiences in the five cycles of institutional innovations suggest that institutional changes will maximize their impact if they correspond to the unique societal context of a specific period and address the distinct needs of that period.

Giving space to spontaneity within the scope of innovation strategic planning

While the government-led innovation programme in China has been characterized with national strategic planning, China's innovation trajectory cannot be described as linear and many success stories of innovation have come from outside of the strategic planning. Observed from an industrial perspective, a number of China's innovation developments and breakthroughs are unplanned.

First, the transfer of tacit knowledge has been recognized as a major source of rapid development of innovation in China. Prior to becoming the world's workshop in the 1970s and 1980s, China's manufacturing sector was dominated by state-owned enterprises (SOEs), whose technological development remained stagnating for a long period of time. When market forces were initially released, a large number of engineers and managers left SOEs to work in the private sector or to set up their own businesses, bringing with them tacit technology knowledge that enabled the takeoff of new private enterprises. Later, with the expansion of foreign-invested enterprises in China, another group of engineers and managers have emerged and their tacit knowledge has once again become the source of innovation in new enterprises. Eventually, the rise of indigenous private technology enterprises provides a new or greater source of tacit knowledge. Such an unplanned pattern of knowledge transfer and diffusion may have certain features of copycat but has indeed upgraded the society's capacity to rapidly increase industrial scale and business competitiveness.

Second, major breakthroughs in the area of industrial technology mainly emerge from non-government planning. Government-led national S&T programmes are not able to address non-consensual research projects, nor are they able to provide effective financial support to those projects. Hence, some major technological breakthroughs are made by private enterprises. Such examples include Huawei's world-class telecommunication technologies, Tencent's ground-breaking inventions of web-based software and communication devices, Xiaomi's frugal innovation in smartphones, and Alibaba's disruptive innovation in Internet finance – none of them is the result of government planning. Of course, these innovations took place thanks to changes in China's innovation environment that enable innovators, individuals or institutions, to access venture capital to make their dreams come true.

Third, at a regional level, the results of China's non-linear, unplanned innovation are equally astonishing. Since the establishment of the first Zhongguancun National High-Tech Industrial Zone by the Chinese governments in the 1990s, a total of 119 national high-tech zones have been created so far. In addition, there are a large number of provincial and municipal-level high-tech zones. Initially, these high-tech zones either lacked resources or had very few enterprises. But after 20 years of development, almost all of them have become centres of local high-tech industries, magnets of innovation resources and cradles of new firms and new industries. This indicates that regional innovation has a tendency of concentration that will not only bring about the agglomeration of innovation resources but will also give rise to the chain reaction of innovation.

Typical examples of technological innovation observed from the spatial perspective also include a large number of industrial clusters in China. In China's Zhejiang and Guangdong Provinces, numerous regional economies and specialized towns featuring one single industry in one locality, or industrial clusters, have emerged spontaneously. These industrial clusters as a form of organization seem to have a loose structure but actually feature close interactions between enterprises and rapid and efficient models of innovation. Any new technology or business model, once acquired by one enterprise in the cluster, is quickly imitated by firms within the cluster. This model of technology development and diffusion based on shared resources has become the source of sustained competitiveness in many local economies in Zhejiang, Guangdong and Jiangsu Provinces.

The intriguing facts of innovations outside strategic planning as described above clearly suggest that national strategic planning ought to give space to spontaneity of creativity and innovation to allow hundreds of flowers to bloom. This will include removing barriers to flow of people, capital and other resources to allow resources to move to where innovations can flourish. This also suggests that there is always a need to reassess the balance between the government and the market in organizing innovation so that strategizing will not overstep its line once circumstances have changed.

Building university innovation capacity and developing innovative talents

Talent is the key to a country's innovation performance and talent development requires greater efforts to strengthen universities and vocational education. China currently has 1,170 colleges and universities in addition to 1,321 senior vocational schools with more than 30 million students enrolled. Nevertheless, Chinese colleges and universities still have a big gap in education, innovation and funding if compared with leading universities of the world. Under resource constraint, the question is: how can the country rapidly improve the quality of education in colleges and universities? The Chinese government has used special national programmes as a countermeasure to concentrate financial resources on selected key universities to develop high-quality colleges, universities and vocational schools and to achieve leapfrogging result within a clearly defined timeframe.

In 1995, for example, the Chinese government implemented the '211 Project', that is, to develop around 100 universities and key disciplines for the twenty-first century. After 20 years of development, remarkable improvement has been witnessed in the education quality in the 112 universities included under the '211 Project'. In 1998, on the basis of implementing the '211 Project', the Chinese government selected 39 universities for the implementation of the '985 Project', that is, to develop a number of world-class research universities, with a particular emphasis on the development of innovative talents and innovation capacity in these universities. In 2011, the Chinese government implemented the '2011 Programme', which aims to enhance the innovation capacity of universities and calls for the integration between universities, between universities and research institutions, and between enterprises and development of collaborative innovation centres in order to achieve the objective of developing internationally first-class capabilities to address urgent national needs. The first cohort of 14 collaborative innovation centres has been established. As a result, some high-quality universities have emerged with remarkable improvement in the development of innovative talents, innovation capacity, institutional development of modern universities and international competitiveness. These universities have become the symbol of high-quality Chinese universities.

Meanwhile, the Chinese government attaches great importance to the development of modern vocational education, putting forth the objective of creating a modern vocational education system with Chinese characteristics and international excellence by 2020. Equal emphasis is laid on the development of high-quality research universities and the developments of senior vocational schools. It is intended to turn some colleges and universities into applied technology-oriented universities and to foster a new model of postgraduate education that orients to vocational needs, employability and the integration of industry, university and research institution. In this way, universities under the new model will provide an alternative support to the enhancement of national innovation capacity.

The above are the eight main experiences in China's effort to build an innovative economy. Admittedly, China still faces some striking challenges in innovation. For instance, the status of enterprises as innovation entities is yet to be established firmly and the alignment between technological innovation and economy is not close enough; results of original scientific and technological research are inadequate and home-grown key technologies are limited; resource allocation for scientific and technological research is highly dominated by the government, and problems such as duplicative, fragmented, closed and inefficient research and development are wide-spreading; industrial application of R&D results is limited, etc. These issues have to be resolved by further reform, system improvements and policy refinement. Meanwhile, valuable experiences and good practices of other countries also need to be learned in order to improve China's scientific and technological innovation.

Notes

1 Premier Li's speech is available on the central government's official website, www. gov.cn/ldhd/2014-01/10/content_2563826.htm (accessed 15 January 2014).
2 Reports on the consultation process are available in '国家中长期科技发展规划程序大变 三院首度会审' (A significant change in the planning procedure of Medium and Long-term National plan for S&T development – first consultation by three academies), available at www.china.com.cn/chinese/2004/Jun/577707.htm (accessed 18 December 2013) and '公众可参与国家中长期科技发展规划制定' (The public are able to participate in the planning of Medium and Long-term National Plan for S&T development), available at www.china.com.cn/chinese/2003/Nov/439954.htm (accessed 18 December 2013).
3 See MOST (2006), *2006 China Science and Technology Development Report 2005*, p. 66.

Bibliography

Ahrens, N. (2013) *China's Industrial Policymaking Process*, Washington, DC: CSIS.

Ali-Yrkkö, J., Rouvinen, P., Seppälä, T. and Ylä-Anttila, P. (2011) Who captures value in global supply chains? Case Nokia N95 Smartphone. *Journal of Industry, Competition and Trade*, 11(3): 263–278.

Altenburg, T., Schmitz, H. and Stamm, A. (2008) Breakthrough? China's and India's transition from production to innovation. *World Development*, 36(2): 325–344.

Anadón, L.D. (2012) Missions-oriented RD&D institutions in energy between 2000 and 2010: a comparative analysis of China, the United Kingdom, and the United States. *Research Policy*, 41(10): 1742–1756.

Andrews-Speed, P. (2009) China's ongoing energy efficiency drive: origins, progress and prospects. *Energy Policy*, 37: 1331–1344.

Atkinson, R.D. (2007) Expanding the R&E tax credit to drive innovation, competitiveness and prosperity. *Journal of Technology Transfer*, 32: 617–628.

Bleda, M. and del Río, P. (2013) The market failure and the systemic failure rationales in technological innovation systems. *Research Policy*, 42(5): 1039–1052.

Bloom, D.E., Canning, D. and Sevilla, J. (2003) *The Demographic Dividend: A New Perspective on the Economic Consequences of Population Change*, Santa Monica, CA: RAND.

Bound, K., Saunders, T., Wildson, J. and Adams, J. (2013) *China's Absorptive State: Research, Innovation and the Prospects for China-UK Collaboration*, London: Nesta.

Breznitz, D. and Murphree, M. (2011) *Run of the Red Queen: Government, Innovation, Globalization and Economic Growth in China*, New Haven, CT: Yale University Press.

Buijs, B. (2012) *China and the Future of New Energy Technologies: Trends in Global Competition and Innovation*, Clingendael International Energy Programme, Netherlands Institute of International Relations.

Cai, F. (2010) Demographic transition, demographic dividend, and Lewis turning point in China. *China Economic Journal*, 3(2): 107–119.

Campbell, R.J. (2010) China and the United States – A Comparison of Green Energy Programs and Policies, CRS Report for Congress, Washington, DC: Congressional Research Service.

Centre for Technological Innovation of Tsinghua University (2009) Technological innovation: a survey of manufacturing firms in 42 cities, 2008. *Management of Innovation and Entrepreneurship*, 5: 90–136.

Chen, G.M. (2008) *An Overview of China Venture Capital Development in 2008*, Hong Kong: China Venture Capital Research Centre.

Chenery, H.B., Robinson, S. and Syrquin, M. (1986) *Industrialization and Growth: A Comparative Study*, London: Oxford University Press.

Clarysse, B., Knocjaert, M. and Wright, M, (2009) *Benchmarking UK Venture Capital to the US and Israel: What Lessons Can Be Learned?* London: BVCA.

Cohen, A.J., Anderson, H.R., Ostro, B., Pandey, K.D., Krzyzanowski, M., Kuenzli, N., Gutschmidt, K., Pope, C.A., Romieu, I., Samet, J.M. and Smith, K.R. (2004) Urban air pollution. In M. Ezzati, A.D. Lopez, A. Rodgers and C.J.L. Murray (eds), *Comparative Quantification of Health Risks: Global and Regional Burden of Disease due to Selected Major Risk Factors*, Geneva: WHO.

Commission of the European Communities (2009) *Financing Innovation and SMEs*, Commission Staff Working Document, Brussels: European Commission.

Crookes, P.I. (2012) China's new development model: analysing Chinese prospects in technology innovation. *China Information*, 26(2): 167–184.

Cumming, D. and MacIntosh, J. (2006) Crowding out private equity: Canadian evidence. *Journal of Business Venturing*, 21: 569–609.

Da Rin, M., Nicodano, G. and Sembenelli, A. (2006) Public policy and creation of active venture capital markets. *Journal of Public Economics*, 90: 1699–1723.

De Meyer, A. and Garg, S. (2005) *Inspire to Innovation: Management and Innovation in Asia*, Basingstoke: Palgrave.

Ding, X.D., Li, J. and Wang, J. (2008) In pursuit of technological innovation. *Journal of Small Business and Enterprises Development*, 15(4): 816–831.

Ding, X.L. (1998) *An Economic Analysis of China's Science and Technology System Reform*, Beijing: The Science Press.

Doran, A. and Bannock, G. (2000) Publicly sponsored regional venture capital: what can the UK learn from the US experience? *Venture Capital*, 2(4): 255–285.

Economist (2005) The OECD on China's economy: a model of reform. 15 September 2005.

Economist Intelligence Unit (2009) *Unlocking Innovation in China*, London: Economist Intelligence Unit.

Edler, J. and Georghiou, L. (2007) Public procurement and innovation – resurrecting the demand side. *Research Policy*, 36(7): 949–963.

Edquist, C. (2005) Systems of innovation: perspectives and challenges. In J. Fagerberg, D.C. Mowery and R.R. Nelson (eds), *The Oxford Handbook of Innovation*, Oxford: Oxford University Press.

European Commission (2011) *Innovation Union Scoreboard 2010: The Innovation Union's Performance Scoreboard for Research and Innovation*, www.proinno-europe. eu/metrics (accessed 28 January 2012).

European Communities (2006) *2006 EU R&D Investment Scoreboard*, Luxembourg: European Communities.

Falk, R. (2007) Measuring the effects of public support schemes on firms' innovation activities: survey evidence from Austria. *Research Policy*, 36: 665–679.

Fan, P. (2006) Catching up through developing innovation capability: evidence from China's telecom-equipment industry. *Technovation*, 26(3): 359–368.

Fang, Y.P. and Zeng, Y. (2007) Balancing energy and environment: the effect and perspective of management instruments in China. *Energy*, 32: 2247–2261.

Fishman, T.C. (2006) *China, Inc. The Relentless Rise of the Next Great Superpower*, London: Pocket Books.

Freeman, C. (1987) *Technology Policy and Economic Performance: Lessons from Japan*, London: Frances Pinter.

Froud, J., Johal, S., Leaver, A. and Williams, K. (2012) Apple Business Model: Financialization across the Pacific, CRESC Working Paper Series, Working Paper No. 111.

Gao, J., Chen, Y., Li, X. and Jian, Y. (2008) *Global Entrepreneurship Monitor (GEM) China 2007: Entrepreneurial Transition and Employment Effect*, Beijing: Tsinghua University Press.

García-Herrero, Alicia, Gavilá, Sergio and Santabárbara, Daniel (2006) China's banking reform: an assessment of its evolution and possible impact. *CESifo Economic Studies*, 52(2): 304–363.

Gibb, A. and Li, J. (2003) Organizing for enterprise in China: what can we learn from the Chinese micro, small, and medium enterprise development experience. *Futures*, 35(4): 403–421.

Godinho, M.M. and Ferreira, V. (2012) Analyzing the evidence of an IPR take-off in China and India. *Research Policy*, 41(3): 499–511.

Gupta, B.M., Gupta, N. and Gupta, R.P. (2009) Status of China in science and technology as reflected in its publications output, 1997–2007. *China Report*, 45(4): 301–341.

GWEC (Global Wind Energy Council) (2013) *Global Wind Report: Annual Market Update 2012*, Brussels: GWEC.

Harding, R. (2000) Venture capital and regional development: towards a venture capital 'system'. *Venture Capital*, 2(4): 287–311.

Harrison, R.T. and Mason, C.M. (2000) Editorial: the role of the public sector in the development of a regional venture capital industry. *Venture Capital*, 2(4): 243–253.

HCCPA (House of Commons Committee of Public Accounts) (2010) *Department for Business, Innovation and Skills: Venture Capital Support to Small Businesses*, Seventeenth Report of Session 2009–10, London: The Stationery Office Limited.

Heilmann, S. (2008) Policy experimentation in China's economic rise. *Studies in Comparative International Development*, 43(1): 1–26.

Heilmann, S. and Melton, O. (2013) The reinvention of development planning in China, 1993–2012, *Modern China*, 39(6): 580–628.

Henriques, L. and Larédo, P. (2013) Policy-making in science policy: the 'OECD model' unveiled. *Research Policy*, 42(3): 801–816.

Hood, N. (2000) Public venture capital and economic development: the Scottish experience. *Venture Capital*, 2(4): 313–341.

Hu, A. (2013) The distinctive transition of China's Five-Year Plans. *Modern China*, 39(6): 629–639.

Hu, M.C. and Mathews, J.A. (2005) National innovative capacity in East Asia. *Research Policy*, 34(9): 1322–1349.

Hullman, A. (2006) Who is winning the global nanorace? *Nature Nanotechnology*, 1: 81–83.

INSEAD (2011) *The Global Innovation Index 2011: Accelerating Growth and Development*, Paris: INSEAD.

Jefferson, G., Hu, A.G.Z., Guan, X.J. and Yu, X.Y. (2003) Ownership, performance and innovation in China's large- and medium-size industrial enterprise sector. *China Economic Review*, 14: 89–113.

Jia, C. (2010) China's venture capital guiding funds: policies and practice. *Journal of Chinese Entrepreneurship*, 2(3): 292–297.

Jin, B. and Rousseau, R. (2005) China's quantitative expansion phase: exponential growth but low impact. *Proceedings of the 10th International Conference on Scientometrics and Informetrics*, Stockholm, July, 2005.

Johnson, W.H.A. and Liu, Q. (2011) Patenting and the role of technology markets in regional innovation in China: an empirical analysis. *Journal of High Technology Management Research*, 22: 14–25.

Kaplinsky, R. and Messner, D. (2008) Introduction: the impact of Asian drivers on the developing world. *World Development*, 36(2): 197–209.

King, D.A. (2004) The scientific impact of nations. *Nature*, 430: 311–316.

Kostoff, R.N., Briggs, M., Rushenberg, R., Bowles, C. and Pecht, M. (2006) The structure and infrastructure of Chinese science and technology, DTIC Technical Report No. ADA443315, Fort Belvoir, VA: Defense Technical Information Center.

Kroeber, A. (2007) China's push to innovate in information technology, in L. Jakobson (ed.), *Innovation with Chinese Characteristics: High-Tech Research in China*, Basingstoke: Palgrave.

Kwong, K.C.L. (2011) China's banking reform: the remaining agenda. *Global Economic Review*, 40(2): 161–178.

Lema, R., Berger, A. and Schmitz, H. (2013) China's impact on the global wind power industry. *Journal of Current Chinese Affairs*, 42(1): 37–69.

Lerner, J. (1999) The government as venture capitalist: the long-run impact of the SBIR program. *Journal of Business*, 72: 285–318.

Lerner, J. (2004) When bureaucrats meet entrepreneurs: the design of effective 'public venture capital' programs. In D. Holtz-Eakin and H.S. Rosen (eds), *Public Policy and the Economics of Entrepreneurship*, Cambridge and London: The MIT Press.

Lerner, J. (2009) *Boulevard of Broken Dreams: Why Public Efforts to Boost Entrepreneurship and Venture Capital Have Failed and What to Do about It*, Princeton, NJ: Princeton University Press.

Leung, Guy C.K. (2010) China's oil use, 1990–2008. *Energy Policy*, 38: 932–944.

Lewis, J.I. (2011) Building a national wind turbine industry: experiences from China, India and South Korea. *International Journal of Technology and Globalisation*, 5(3/4): 281–305.

Li, F., Dong, S., Li, X., Liang, Q. and Yang, W. (2011) Energy consumption-economic growth relationship and carbon dioxide emissions in China. *Energy Policy*, 39: 568–576.

Li, J. (2010) Decarbonising power generation in China – is the answer blowing in the wind? *Renewable and Sustainable Energy Reviews*, 14: 1154–1171.

Li, J.F., Gao, H., Shi, P.F. *et al.* (2007) 中国风电发展报告2007 (China Wind Power Outlook 2007), Beijing: China Environmental Science Press.

Li, J.F., Cai, F.B., Qiao, L.M. *et al.* (2012) 中国风电发展报告2012 (China Wind Power Outlook 2012), Beijing: China Environmental Science Press.

Li, X. (2012) Behind the recent surge of Chinese patenting: an institutional view. *Research Policy*, 41: 236–249.

Li, Z. and Li, J. (2014) State-owned enterprises in China's transition to an innovation-driven economy. In J. Li and L.M. Wang (eds), *China's Economic Dynamics: A Beijing Consensus in the Making?* London and New York: Routledge.

Lin, J.Y. Cai, F. and Li, Z. (1996) The lessons of China's transition to a market economy. *Cato Journal*, 16(2): 201–232.

Ma, H.Y. Oxley, L. and Gibson, J. (2009) China's energy situation in the new millennium. *Renewable and Sustainable Energy Reviews*, 13: 1781–1799.

MOST (2006) *China Science and Technology Development Report 2005*, Beijing: Science and Technical documentation Press.

MOST (2007) *China Science and Technology Development Report 2006*, Beijing: Science and Technical documentation Press.

MOST (2011) *China Science and Technology Development Report 2010*, Beijing: Science and Technical documentation Press.

MOST (2012) *China Science and Technology Development Report 2011*, Beijing: Science and Technical documentation Press.

MOST (2013) *China Science and Technology Development Report 2012*, Beijing: Science and Technical documentation Press.

National Audit Office (NAO) (2009) *The Department for Business, Innovation and Skills: Venture Capital Support to Small Businesses*, December, London.

Naughton, B. (2013) The return of planning in China: comment on Heilmann-Melton and Hu Angang. *Modern China*, 39(6): 640–652.

Naughton, B. and Segal, A. (2003) China in search of a workable model: technology development in the new millennium. In W.W. Keller and R.J. Samuels (eds), *Crisis and Innovation in Asian Technology*, Cambridge: Cambridge University Press.

Needham, J. (1954) *Science and Civilisation in China. Volume I. Introductory Orientations*, Cambridge: Cambridge University Press.

NESTA (2009) *From Funding Gaps to Thin Markets: UK Government Support for Early-Stage Venture Capital*, Research Report, September, London: NESTA.

OECD (2008) *OECD Reviews of Innovation Policy: China*, Paris: OECD.

OECD (2010) *The OECD Innovation Strategy: Getting a Head Start on Tomorrow*, Paris: OECD.

OECD (2011) *The International Experience with R&D Tax Incentives*, Testimony by the OECD at United States Senate Committee on Finance, 20 September 2011.

Orr, G. and Roth, E. (2012) A CEO's guide to innovation in China. *McKinsey Quarterly*, February 2012.

Pew Trusts (2013a) *Who's Winning the Clean Energy Race?* Washington, DC: The Pew Charitable Trusts.

Pew Trusts (2013b) *Advantage America: The U.S.-China Clean Energy Trade Relationship*, Washington, DC: The Pew Charitable Trusts.

Porter, M.E. (1990) *The Competitive Advantage of Nations*. New York: Free Press.

Senor, D. and Singer, S. (2009) *Start-Up Nation: The Story of Israel's Economic Miracle*, New York and Boston: Twelve.

Shang, Qingyan, Poon, Jessie P.H. and Yue, Qingtang (2012) The role of regional knowledge spillovers on China's innovation. *China Economic Review*, 23: 1164–1175.

Shi, Yaobin (2009) China's tax policies for promoting innovation. In Qimiao Fan, Kuoqing Li, Douglas Zhihua Zeng, Yang Dong and Runzhong Peng (eds), *Innovation for Development and the Role of Government: A Perspective from the East Asia and Pacific Region*, Washington, DC: World Bank Publications.

Shi, Yizheng (1998) *Chinese Firms and Technology in the Reform Era*, London and New York: Routledge.

Smil, V. (2004) *China's Past, China's Future: Energy, Food, Environment*, New York and London: RoutledgeCurzon.

Smith, K. (2005) Measuring innovation. In J.F. Fagerberg, D.C. Mowery and R.R. Nelson (eds), *The Oxford Handbook of Innovation*, Oxford: Oxford University Press.

Snee, H.R. (2000) The case for an enterprise development fund for Wales. *Venture Capital*, 2(4): 343–355.

Söderblom, A. and Wiklund, J. (2006) *Factors Determining the Performance of Early Stage High-Technology Venture Capital Funds – A Review of the Academic Literature*, London: DTI Small Business Service.

Stiglitz, J.E. (2008) China: towards a new model of development. *China Economic Journal*, 1(1): 33–52.

Sun, Y., Lu, Y., Wang, T., Ma, H. and He, G. (2008) Pattern of patent-based environmental technology innovation in China. *Technological Forecasting and Social Change*, 75(7): 1032–1042.

United Nations Economic Commission for Europe (2009) *Policy Options and Instruments for Financing Innovation: A Practical Guide to Early-Stage Financing*, New York and Geneva: United Nations.

Wang, X. and Mauzerall, D.L. (2006) Evaluating impacts of air pollution in China on public health: implications for future air pollution and energy policies. *Atmos Environ*, 40: 1706–1721.

Wang, X.B. and Weaver, N. (2013) Surplus labour and Lewis turning points in China. *Journal of Chinese Economic and Business Studies*, 11(1): 1–12.

Wechsler, A. (2011) Intellectual property law in the People's Republic of China: a powerful economic tool for innovation and development. *China-EU Law Journal*, 1(1-2): 3–54.

Wei, Shouhua and Wu, Guisheng (2004) 我国跨行政区科技合作的成因、模式与政策建议 (The cause, model and policy implications of cooperation and communication of science and technology among administrative regions in China). *China Soft Sciences*, 7: 100–105.

Whalley, J. and Zhou, Weimin (2007) Technology Upgrading and China's Growth Strategy to 2020, Working Paper No. 21, Waterloo, Ontario: The Centre for International Governance Innovation, Canada.

Wilson, J. and Keeley, J. (2007) *China: The Next Science Superpower?* London: Demos.

Wong, C.P.W. (1987) Between plan and market: the role of the local sector in post-Mao China. *Journal of Comparative Economics*, 11: 385–398.

Woo, W.T. (2012) China meets the middle-income traps: the large potholes in the road to catching-up. *Journal of Chinese Economic and Business Studies*, 10(4): 313–336.

World Bank (1997) *China 2020: Development Challenges in the New Century*, Washington, DC: World Bank.

World Bank (2007) *Cost of Pollution in China*, Washington, DC: World Bank.

World Economic Forum (2011) *The Global Competitiveness Report 2011–2012*, Geneva: World Economic Forum.

Wu, Guiseng and Liu, Jianxin (2006) Understanding indigenous innovation. *Management of Innovation and Entrepreneurship*, 2: 1–11 (in Chinese).

Wu, W. (2007) Cultivating research universities and industrial linkages in China: the case of Shanghai. *World Development*, 35(6): 1075–1093.

Yan, Y., Xu, Y., Li, J.L., Yu, S.T. and Dai, H.T. (2009) 中国风电专利形势综述 (The Status of Wind Power Patents in China), Baoding Gao Xin Qu Dian Gu New Energy Research Centre and WWF.

Yang, Z.A. and Nie, Y. (2011) 我国企业创新投资财税激励政策的实证研究成果 (On finance and taxation policies encouraging enterprises' innovation capital). *Journal of Liaoning University (Philosophy and Social Science)*, 39(6): 98–102.

Yusuf, S., Wang, S. and Nabeshima (2009) China's fiscal policies for innovation. In Qimiao Fan, Kuoqing Li, Douglas Zhihua Zeng, Yang Dong and Runzhong Peng (eds), *Innovation for Development and the Role of Government: A Perspective from the East Asia and Pacific Region*, Washington, DC: World Bank Publications.

Zero2IPO (2010) *China Venture Capital Annual Report 2010*, Beijing: Zero2IPO.

Zhang, D., Banker, R.D., Li, X. and Liu, W. (2011) Performance impact of research policy at the Chinese Academy of Sciences. *Research Policy*, 40(6): 875–885.

Zhang, H., Patton, D. and Kenney, M. (2013) Building global-class universities: assessing the impact of the 985 Project. *Research Policy*, 42(3): 765–775.

Zhang, P.D., Yang, Y.L, Shi, J., Zheng, Y.H., Wang, L.S. and Li, X.R. (2009) Opportunities and challenges for renewable energy policy in China. *Renewable and Sustainable Energy Reviews*, 13: 439–449.

Zhang, W.W. (2012) *The China Wave: Rise of a Civilizational State*, Hackensack, NJ: WorldCentury.

Zhang, X.L., Wang, R.S., Huo, M.L. and Martinot, E. (2010) A study of the role played by renewable energies in China's sustainable energy supply. *Energy*, 35: 4392–4399.

Zhang, Y.B., Wu, J. and Ai, H.S. (2009) The technology gap and the limit of imitation: an inspection of the strategy of 'exchanging market for technology'. *Journal of Chinese Economic and Business Studies*, 7(4): 447–456.

Zheng, J., Bigsten, A. and Hu, A. (2009) Can China's growth be sustained? A productivity perspective. *World Development*, 37(4): 874–888.

Zhou, P. and Leydesdorff, L. (2006) The emergence of China as a leading nation in science. *Research Policy*, 35(1): 83–104.

Index

For Product Safety Concerns and Information please contact our
EU representative GPSR@taylorandfrancis.com Taylor & Francis
Verlag GmbH, Kaufingerstraße 24, 80331 München, Germany